SERIOUS

ESSAYS ON AUSTRALIAN HUMOUR

FROLIC

SERIOUS
ESSAYS ON AUSTRALIAN HUMOUR
FROLIC

Edited by Fran De Groen and Peter Kirkpatrick

UQP

First published 2009 by University of Queensland Press
PO Box 6042, St Lucia, Queensland 4067 Australia

www.uqp.com.au

Typeset in 11/16 pt Adobe Garamond by Post Pre-press Group, Brisbane
Printed in Australia by McPherson's Printing Group

The editors gratefully acknowledge funding support from the
School of Humanities & Languages, University of Western Sydney,
and the School of Letters, Art & Media, University of Sydney.

Cataloguing-in-Publication Data
National Library of Australia

Serious frolic : essays on Australian humour / editors,
        Fran De Groen, Peter Kirkpatrick.

9780702236884 (pbk.)

Includes index.
Bibliography.

Australian wit and humour.

De Groen, Fran.
Kirkpatrick, Peter John.

808.7

To Ken Stewart

CONTENTS

Humour in Australian fiction

Parody

Performance

Notes on contributors

Bruce Bennett is Emeritus Professor of English in the School of Humanities & Social Sciences at the University of New South Wales at ADFA. He is a Fellow of the Australian Academy of the Humanities and holds an Adjunct Professorship at the Australian National University and an Honorary Professorship at the University of Queensland. He is the author of *Homing in: Essays on Australian literature and selfhood* (2006), *Australian short fiction: A history* (UQP, 2002), and co-editor, with Jennifer Strauss, of *The Oxford literary history of Australia* (Oxford University Press, 1998).

Virginia Blain is Adjunct Professor of English in the Division of Humanities at Macquarie University. Her research interests include nineteenth- and twentieth-century British and Australian literature, feminist theory, literary biography, and gay and lesbian theory. Among her many publications is her edition of *Victorian women poets: A new annotated anthology* (Longman, 2001). She was one of the three editors of the ground-breaking *Feminist companion to literature* (Batsford/Yale University Press/Oxford University Press, 1990) and one of the section editors (nineteenth-century literature) of the *New Oxford dictionary of national biography* (Oxford University Press, 2004).

Philip Butterss teaches Australian literature and Australian film in the School of Humanities at the University of Adelaide. He has edited *Southwords: Essays on South Australian writing* (Wakefield, 1995) and, with Elizabeth

Webby, *The Penguin book of Australian ballads* (Penguin, 1993). He is currently working on a biography of CJ Dennis.

Jessica Milner Davis co-ordinates the Australasian Humour Scholars Network from the University of Sydney as an Honorary Associate in the Faculty of Arts. Her latest book, *Understanding humor in Japan* (Wayne State UP, 2006), won the 2008 AATH book-prize for humour research. She is a member of the editorial boards for leading international humour research journals and book series and served as President of the International Society for Humor Studies in 1997 and 2001.

Fran De Groen is Adjunct Professor in the School of Humanities & Languages at the University of Western Sydney. Author of *Xavier Herbert: A biography* (UQP, 1998) and co-editor of *Xavier Herbert letters* (UQP, 2002), she is currently researching the responses to captivity of Australian prisoners of the Japanese and writing a detailed history of a group of Australian prisoners held by the Japanese in Korea.

Lillian Holt was born on Cherbourg Aboriginal Settlement, Queensland. Her working career in Aboriginal education spans over thirty years including sixteen years (1980–1996) at Tauondi (formerly Aboriginal Community College) in Port Adelaide, the last seven as the first Aboriginal Principal. From there she went to Melbourne University, where she was the Director of the Centre for Indigenous Education (1998–2002), and then a Vice-Chancellor's Fellow (2003–05). She regards her best asset to be her humour and is passionately interested in the healing of race relations in Australia. She currently works part-time with Relationships Australia, Adelaide.

Peter Kirkpatrick teaches Australian Literature in the School of Letters, Art & Media at the University of Sydney. His research interests are in Australian literary and cultural history, and poetry and poetics. He is author of *The sea coast of Bohemia: Literary life in Sydney's roaring twenties* (UQP,

1992), and co-author, with Jill Dimond, of *Literary Sydney: A walking guide* (UQP, 2000).

Susan Lever teaches English in the School of Humanities & Social Sciences at the University of New South Wales at ADFA. Her latest books are *David Foster: The satirist of Australia* (Cambria Press, 2008) and, edited with Anne Pender, *Nick Enright: An actor's playwright* (Rodopi, 2008). She is currently working on a history of Australian television writing, including a series of interviews for the Australian Writers' Guild.

John McCallum teaches in the School of English Media & Performing Arts at the University of New South Wales. He has published widely, since the 1970s, on contemporary and early modern Australian playwrights. He has been a theatre critic, for the *Australian* and for ABC radio, since the 1980s. His new history of Australian drama, *Belonging: Australian playwriting in the 20th century*, will be published by Currency Press in 2008.

John McLaren is Emeritus Professor at Victoria University, where he continues to write and research about Australian literary culture and politics. He was Associate Editor of *Overland* for many years, Editor from 1993 to 1997, and is now Consulting Editor. He was Foundation Editor of the second series of the *Australian book review*, from 1998 to 1986. His publications include guides to Xavier Herbert and Patrick White, an introduction to Australian Literary History, and studies of Australian literary magazines and their editors. His most recent publication is *Not in tranquillity: A memoir* (2006), and he is now working on a critical life of Vincent Buckley.

Anne Pender is Senior Lecturer in English & Theatre Studies at the University of New England. She is currently working on a biographical study of Barry Humphries funded by the Australian Research Council. Anne has published essays on satire and humour and a monograph, *Christina Stead:*

Satirist (ASAL, 2002). Recently she edited a book of essays with Susan Lever, *Nick Enright: An actor's playwright* (Rodopi, 2008).

Peter Pierce has recently retired from his role as Professor of Australian Literature in the Humanities at James Cook University. His research interests are in Australian literature and literary history, and Australian, American and European war literature. He was general editor of *The Oxford literary guide to Australia* (Oxford University Press, 1987) and compiler of *From go to whoa: A compendium to the Australian turf* (Crossbow Publications, 1994). Among his more recent books are *The country of lost children: An Australian anxiety* (Cambridge University Press, 1999) and *Australian melodramas: Thomas Keneally's fiction* (University of Queensland Press, 1995). He is currently editing *The Cambridge History of Australian Literature*.

Michael Sharkey teaches writing, rhetorical analysis and American literature at the University of New England. He edited *The illustrated treasury of Australian humour* (Oxford University Press, 1988), and has also published criticism, literary biographies and reviews. His most recent collection of poems is *The sweeping plain* (Five Islands Press, 2007). He is currently collecting essays and poems for publication.

Ken Stewart, Adjunct Associate Professor in the School of Humanities & Languages at the University of Western Sydney, distinguished scholar of nineteenth- and early twentieth-century Australian literature, and a founding member and honorary life member of the Association for the Study of Australian Literature, is currently writing a history of the literary culture of 'marvellous Melbourne', funded by a large ARC grant. Noted for the grace and humour of his style, he is regarded within ASAL as a delightful parodist and mimic of many larger-than-life characters, including Sandy Stone and Camille Paglia.

Elizabeth Webby has been researching Australian literature for forty-six years and is the author, editor or co-editor of a dozen books. She also edited Australia's oldest literary journal, *Southerly*, for twelve years. She recently stepped down from the Chair of Australian Literature at the University of Sydney. Current projects include scholarly editions of Henry Lawson's stories, Charles Harpur's poems, and Patrick White's notebooks.

Michael Wilding is a distinguished writer and Emeritus Professor in the School of Letters, Art & Media at the University of Sydney. Among his most recent publications are *Wildest dreams* (University of Queensland Press, 1998), *Raising spirits, making gold and swapping wives: The true adventures of Dr John Dee and Sir Edward Kelly* (Shoestring Press/Abbot Bentley, 1999), *Academia nuts* (Wild & Woolley, 2002), *Wild amazement* (Central Queensland University Press/Shoestring Press, 2006) and *National treasure* (Central Queensland University Press, 2007).

Introduction: A saucer of vinegar

Fran De Groen and Peter Kirkpatrick

It's painfully obvious that scholars should be kept at arm's length from any manifestation of humour. (Phillip Adams and Patrice Newell)[1]

This book is a collection of essays on some versions of Australian humour. 'Is it funny?' was the first question from one well-known academic publisher we approached. 'No', we replied. And with that communication ceased.

This is a *serious* frolic. To write seriously about humour sets you up for a pratfall. In the first place, there is the paradox of writing in an unfunny way about funny things. One solution, of course, is mimicry: to write as amusingly as possible about those funny things – which was what that publisher-who-shall-remain-nameless was hoping we might do. Authors interested in Australian humour have tended to write for a popular market, and to have links, on the one hand, with journalism (such as Keith Willey and Phillip Adams) or, on the other, with the folkloric left (Bill Wannan and Ron Edwards). Historically, this has produced impressionistic accounts of Australian humour, full of wry examples, or else anthologies of jokes and comic anecdotes – notably the bush yarn – but relatively little in the way of scholarly analysis.[2] Yet the scholar of humour traditionally faced a further difficulty.

Until not so long ago, academic discussion of popular humour was compromised by the subject's very popularity, which, unless it overlapped with classic drama or fiction, was inclined to render it insufficiently worthy of learned attention. Serious frolic could look like intellectual slumming. Interdisciplinary challenges to older aesthetic hierarchies from cultural studies and, more recently, from dedicated humour studies have made it somewhat – but still only somewhat – more respectable to write in a scholarly way about such a traditionally unscholarly topic.

Even so, the basic problem of striking the right tone remains. Humour often depends on an intimate appreciation of fine shades of verbal and social inflection refracted in surprising or absurd ways. How to analyse the component elements without seeming to mishandle them, losing a sense of what's at stake, and so destroy their comic power? Who breaks a butterfly upon a wheel? In their introduction to *The Penguin book of Australian jokes*, Phillip Adams and Patrice Newell claim that:

> as soon as you start thinking about the construction and purpose of a joke the humour evaporates. It's like confusing sexual intercourse with gynaecology or art with criticism. Because it must be remembered that among the many things that jokes mock is reason itself. Jokes are anathema to logic and, consequently, hostile to analysis.[3]

That doesn't stop them having quite a bit to say about the origins of humour in the fear of death: 'Our sense of humour allows us to blow a raspberry at the fates, to defy the nemesis we cannot escape'.[4]

Then there's the problem of definition. If you consult literary dictionaries, you will find lengthy entries on 'comedy' defined broadly as 'any amusing and entertaining work' and narrowly as 'an amusing and entertaining form of drama' that contrasts with 'tragedy' because it ends happily and focuses on 'the lighter side of life'. Similarly, although there are detailed and informative discussions of the (four) 'humours' (blood, black bile, yellow bile and phlegm, the bodily fluids that in Hippocratic tradition in the medieval era and the renaissance were believed to determine human temperament and behaviour), you will be hard-pressed to find an entry on 'humour' per se.

'Comedy of humours' (à la Ben Jonson) will get a guernsey, but 'humour' rarely appears. Why might this be so? Perhaps because 'humour' in the modern sense of 'the quality of being funny' or 'having the faculty of perceiving what is amusing or comical' (*Macquarie dictionary*) is judged to pertain more to the psychology of laughter than to the fine distinctions of rhetoric. This modern usage of 'humour' is comparatively recent, arising in the eighteenth century as a term contrasted, somewhat pejoratively, with the superior intellectual brilliance of 'wit'. 'Humour' encompassed notions of eccentricity or peculiarity, mood and temper, and, through its etymology (from Latin = 'moisture') and connections with laughter, came to seem more affiliated with the body than the mind.

Clearly there is considerable overlap among the theories of laughter and comedy, indicating *a plurality of determining factors*. There are formal theories that analyse the nature and features of the object producing the laughter (these tend to focus on the drive towards harmony) and psychological theories that analyse the nature and effect of laughter. Contemporary analysts pay particular attention to the sociological dimensions of laughter (its context, audience and target/s), especially the ways jokes operate to include and exclude particular groups, reinforcing social bonds and differentiating the teller of the joke ('ourselves') from its target ('others').

All the essays in this collection address their diverse subject matter under the inclusive and 'fluid' rubric of 'humour' rather than 'comedy', though some, like those by Susan Lever and John McCallum, focus on modes of local 'comedy' in the traditional theatrical/performance sense of the term. Many have a literary focus, exploring the humorous nuances in the work of particular writers or genres of writing. Some are more pointedly interested in the social and/or cultural significance, within a particular historical context, of humorous linguistic practices that involve the characteristically inventive and often mischievous or scurrilous use of Australian English – such as Peter Pierce's bravura reading of racehorse names. To suggest their broader affiliations with one another, the essays are arranged in loose, permeable categories that indicate their focus (be it predominantly rhetorical or cultural) but at the same time seek to delineate particular traditions (and the departures from those traditions) and encourage the reader to make connections across historical periods and genres. Rather than attempting to provide a comprehensive or definitive account, this collection aims to stimulate discussion and offer a variety of approaches to the rich and variegated terrain of Australian humour, especially though not exclusively in its literary manifestations.

The collection begins with what we have called here 'classic' Australian humour – that is, the humour that accompanied the emergence in the 1890s of a self-conscious 'bush-bred' nationalist literary tradition associated with the *Bulletin* magazine. Attempts to define a national sense of humour have generally taken their bearings from the '*Bulletin* school' phenomenon via subsequent discussions of national identity by (generally) left-leaning historians and folklorists.[5] In what is probably the best summary account of Australian humour, in 1988 Dorothy Jones and Barry Andrews wrote:

> To define a national humour is impossible. Jokes, bandied around from country to country through many retellings assume their own local colour, so that distinctions between the humour of one nation and another eventually come to depend on subtle differences of tone, nuance and language.[6]

The point is well made in the light of attempts to construct a unified national type of 'Aussie' humour based on the anti-authoritarian larrikin and his later ocker incarnation. Clearly there is a need to look beyond older, predominantly masculine stereotypes to seek an up-to-date reassessment of the relationships between comedy and cultural identity. The present collection therefore acknowledges the range, variety and complexity of local humour. Chapters cover humorous fiction and poetry, TV sitcoms, stand-up and performance comedy, joking as cultural ritual, multicultural and Indigenous humour, the sardonic humour of prisoners of war, and the special wit required in naming horses. But does that diversity mean that no general conclusions about the distinctness of the Australian humour can be drawn?

After saying that it's impossible to define national humour, Jones and Andrews nevertheless go on to state that 'Australian humour is characterised, not so much by content, as by a special configuration of attitudes. Irony predominates, and individuals manipulated by circumstances, or a destiny they are unable to control, wryly resign themselves to their own powerlessness'.[7] This is one implication of *Waltzing Matilda*, of course, which is a jolly song about self-murder by drowning. The same 'configuration of attitudes' led Henry Lawson to declare that 'Death is about the only cheerful thing in the bush'[8] – a view perfectly illustrated by a story that Mrs Spicer tells Mary and Joe Wilson in 'Water them geraniums':

One of the yarns Mrs Spicer told us was about a squatter she knew who used to go wrong in his head every now and again, and try to commit suicide. Once, when the station-hand, who was watching him, had his eye off him for a minute, he hanged himself to a beam in the stable. The men ran in and found him hanging and kicking. 'They let him hang for a while,' said Mrs Spicer, 'till he went black in the face and stopped kicking. Then they cut him down and threw a bucket of water over him.'

'Why! What on earth did they let the man hang for?' asked Mary.

'To give him a good bellyful of it: they thought it would cure him of tryin' to hang himself again.'

'Well, that's the coolest thing I ever heard of,' said Mary.

'That's jist what the magistrate said, Mrs Wilson,' said Mrs Spicer.[9]

Some forty years later in *Capricornia* (1938), Xavier Herbert cast a similarly sardonic glance at the suicidal possibilities of military service in World War I. In seeking to convince civil servant Oscar Shillingsworth of the benefits of 'going South' to enlist with Oscar's dissolute brother Mark, Chook Henn waxes enthusiastic:

'We're tryin to get away. If we can, we're going to have a crack at the war. Can't, of course, till the debts are paid.'

'Yes you can. The Government will fix that for you.'

'Not less you've passed the doctor and got your papers for goin' down to a recruitin'-station. We tried it long ago. But Mark couldn't pass. That noo quack says he's got a crook heart. Bosh, ain't it? This here quack's too damn strict. You know Sam Stiff? Well he's got miner's complaint he got down in the West so bad he can hardly talk. Course they wouldn't look at him here. So, he went down South and got away right off and got killed. Shows what you can do if you can only get down South.'[10]

Ken Stewart, a humorist in his own right and 'first-foot' in our serious frolic, takes up this theme of the 'cheerfulness of death' (or humour as a coping mechanism) in the opening chapter of this book, where he explores the relationship between 'human gregariousness' and 'the hardness of things', 'two central and inseparable preoccupations' of Lawson's fiction, in that classic bush yarn 'The Loaded Dog'. As Jessica Milner Davis points out in her essay, humour scholars have long demonstrated the value of humour as a 'moderator of stress and trauma' in a variety of contexts: disaster zones, concentration camps, sick-rooms and, arguably, also the harsh Australian outback. But Lawson and his heirs are not alone in their recourse to survival humour. Lillian Holt's multi-vocal conversation about Aboriginal humour in 'A conversational corroboree' reveals its pervasiveness and efficacy in Aboriginal communities. And in 'Risus sardonicus' Fran De Groen examines the role of the sardonic grin as a survival strategy among prisoners of war.

Certainly hardship engenders a special kind of humour. In a parodic essay called 'Henry Lawson: Australian humorist', the *Bulletin*'s first literary editor, AG Stephens, imagined Lawson's characters Steelman and Smith discussing their author while camped 'under a middle-sized tree that might have been a coolibah and then again mightn't'.[11] Steelman describes Lawson's humour as fundamentally English, but 'with a bit of a twist I put down to struggling for a living in Australia. There's a word I don't altogether know the meaning of – S-A-R-D-O-N-I-C. It comes close to what I'm trying to get at'. Smith asks him what he thinks it means: 'It means a saucer of vinegar, as far as I can make out – or a dash of bitters; a hard kind of humour, that has always got a come-back to misery, even when you're laughing. A kind of grin with your teeth shut, which is a kind you get in the Bush often – it belongs to hard living'.[12]

Yet, alongside the sardonic strain, bush humour also encompasses larger-than-life fantastic elements and a certain imaginative exuberance, as in the yarns about Crooked Mick of the mythic Speewah, 'said to be a station somewhere out beyond the black stump, where the pumpkins grow so large that people hollow them out and live in them and where the wool on the sheep grows so high you need a ladder to shear them'.[13] Ian Mudie gleaned several such tall stories, along with literary and historical fragments, for his verse compendium of Australian identity, 'They'll tell you about me', first published in the *Bulletin* in 1952:

Me, I'm the man that dug the Murray for Sturt to sail down,
I am the one that rode beside the man from Snowy River,
and I'm Ned Kelly's surviving brother (or did I marry his sister?
I forget which), and it was my thumbnail that wrote that Clancy
had gone a-droving, and when wood was scarce I set the grass on fire
and ran with it three miles to boil my billy, only to find
I'd left the tea and sugar back with my tucker-bag . . .[14]

The dinkum provenance of such yarns is, however, questionable. Both Bill Wannan and Ron Edwards agreed that Australian tall stories often reworked American originals, Wannan going so far as to suggest their ultimately literary origin in the adventures of Baron Munchausen.[15] This liberating 'European' strain of absurdist and sometimes surrealist fantasy continues in the tragi-comic verbal-visual arabesques of Flacco and Michael Leunig, and the (mostly) silent assaults on behavioural logic of mime artists the Umbilical Brothers.

A deeper blow to national pride is struck (as Jessica Milner Davis points out) by Phillip Adams and Patrice Newell, who wrote that 'sadly it must be reported that there seem to be few genuinely Australian jokes'. 'Show us an Australian joke and we'll show you an English, an American or a German joke that has been on a long journey.' Writing in 1994, they also asserted that 'This is not the collection that would have been gathered twenty or thirty years ago when the idiom had been less subjected to the bombardment of global media'.[16] But is this true? As a former colony, when was Australia not subject to 'global' media? Even Lawson's Drover's Wife on her dismal, isolated selection reads the London-based *Young Ladies' Journal* rather than the *Bulletin*, let alone the *Dawn*.

Furthermore, the media flow can run the other way as well. Stan Cross's famous cartoon 'For gorsake, stop laughing: this is serious!', discussed by John McLaren in '"This is serious": From the backblocks to the city', has been called 'the funniest joke ever produced in Australia'. Yet on its first appearance *Smith's Weekly* modestly dubbed it 'The Funniest Drawing in the World', implying it had a global resonance – a claim backed up by its subsequent popularity. The paper was forced to employ extra staff to fill a worldwide demand for reprints: 'Requests for copies came from such curious places as the Khyber Pass (from British troops stationed there), Tristan da Cunha and Mombasa'.[17]

Despite this wide appeal, it's unlikely that the Japanese, who apparently find Australian and New Zealand humour to be cruelly sarcastic, would enjoy it. Distinguished Japanese interpreter and cross-cultural humour scholar, Masumi Muramatsu, appreciates the way Aussies and Kiwis insult one another 'without critically damaging their relationship' but points out that this kind of humour is lost on his own countrymen and women. To illustrate the point, he recounts an incident that occurred during a visit to Japan by the New Zealand prime minister, the late Robert Muldoon (dubbed 'Piggy' Muldoon by the New Zealand press). When a Japanese reporter asked about the status of a proposed New Zealand–Japan journalist exchange program, Muldoon answered that he had already drawn up a long list of journalists for exchange and, 'after a brief pause, he added "for good"'. The New Zealand reporters covering the visit were 'amused if not pleased', but despite interpreter Muramatsu's 'best efforts to convey [its meaning] by tone as much as words', their 'Japanese colleagues' did not see the joke. Sarcasm, he explains, is 'an art not much enjoyed by the Japanese'.[18]

Clearly, different nations don't laugh at exactly the same things, but what accounts for the culturally specific aspects of Australian humour? Jessica Milner Davis in her chapter '"Aussie" humour and laughter', drawing on a wealth of international laughter scholarship, argues that what distinguishes local humorous practice is not so much *what* it targets or even *how* it does so but rather the fact that it is both compulsory and characteristically offensive – all comers, and new comers to Australia in particular, are obliged to 'take the mickey'. Davis's detailed account of the Irish and cockney origins of this phrase, equivalent to 'taking the piss', has already been published electronically.[19] Her essay in this volume provides a wide-ranging introduction to the subject of Australian humour more generally, challenging previously received ideas (about its alleged anti-authoritarianism, for example), while at the same time suggesting that the *way* in which humour is used in Australia *is* distinctive and serves as an adaptive, unifying experience.

The rise of Kiwi writer-comedian John Clarke to the status of Australian comic icon suggests that, as Muramatsu observed of the shared Australian–New Zealand propensity for mickey-taking, there may in fact be an identifiably 'trans-Tasman' brand of humour which belies the differences that obtain elsewhere between the two nations (in history, geography and ethnic composition, for example). Elsewhere in discussions of the national character, however, landscape is frequently cited as a major factor. Recall that AG Stephens related the sardonic tone of Lawson's humour to 'hard living' and the bush. Similarly, Keith Willey, in his 1984 study of Depression-era humour, *You might as well laugh, mate*, insisted that 'The bush ethos had an indelible influence on our humour as it flourished in the 1930s . . . Many Australians, whether city or country dwellers, found in their national humour of sardonic pessimism an antidote for despair, a substitute for tears'.[20] Yet the rigours of frontier life don't explain the origins of the Australian tall story, which was adapted from the United States, possibly during the Gold Rush period.[21] Did bush tradition necessarily impart the particular quality of Australian irony? Jones and Andrews proposed that the flavour of local humour is a function of attitude rather than content; but a feeling for irony is hardly unique to Australia, as the success of immigrant Kiwi John Clarke demonstrates. After all, the British pride themselves on ironic understatement. And, like the British, Australians are apt to think that American humour entirely lacks irony. Yet this is the culture that produced Washington Irving, Mark Twain, Ambrose Bierce, Dorothy Parker, *The Simpsons*, *Seinfeld* and *South Park*.

Perhaps the real source of sardonic Australian irony lies in social class rather than natural landscape. Of course, given the sheer physical labour needed to subdue the bush, the two are not unrelated. But Australia's beginnings as a convict gulag made the locals especially sensitive to class differences as a product of coercive power relations. In his 'A convict's tour of Hell', Frank the Poet gave it back to the floggers:

> Frank rapped aloud to know his fate
> He louder knocked and louder still
> When the Devil came, pray what's your will?
> Alas cried the Poet I've come to dwell
> With you and share your fate in Hell
> Says Satan that can't be, I'm sure
> For I detest and hate the poor
> And none shall in my kingdom stand
> Except the grandees of the land.[22]

Their convict 'birthstain' tended to make Australians suspicious of social distinction and, later on, dismissive of it. And so the 'typical Australian', in Russel Ward's famous formulation, 'believes that Jack is not only as good as his master but, at least in principle, probably a good deal better, and so he is a great "knocker" of eminent people unless, as in the case of his sporting heroes, they are distinguished by physical prowess'.[23]

The egalitarian, anti-authoritarian character of much Australian humour also accounts for its historically masculine character. The best-known Australian comedians have all been working-class heroes: Roy Rene, George Wallace, Paul Hogan, Kevin Bloody Wilson, Dave Hughes. Mythic versions of the larrikin have ranged from the Bastard from the Bush (widely attributed to Henry Lawson), who, in his violence, sexism and racism, outdoes the Push that takes him in, to CJ Dennis's much milder Sentimental Bloke, who tosses in larrikinism for a settled domestic life with his 'ideel tart' Doreen. The Bastard symbolises the homosocial world of the public bar, where his tale circulated by word of mouth for decades; the Bloke a happy homelife and broader 'vision of social consensus' – as Philip Butterss argues in his chapter, 'Compounded of incompatibles'. Between the misogyny of the one and the uxoriousness of the other lies a host of humorously fractured marriages in Australian fiction, from which one or the other partner – more often the male – seeks release for a greater or lesser period, often at the end of a bottle. Best remembered of these tales of foiled escape is Lennie Lower's classic *Here's luck*, a morality tale about getting what you wish for. In 'We are but dust, add water and we are mud', Peter Kirkpatrick closely examines the poetics of humour in Lower's prose; then Michael Sharkey, in 'Why men leave home', takes a long-angled look across a range of comic novels from the first half of the twentieth century – including *Here's luck* – and finds more to their gender politics than meets the twenty-first-century eye.

The humour of cultural elites has had very little impact in Australia, except where they intersected with the demotic. There is no one in Australia who writes like Gore Vidal, for instance. Patrician self-assurance – the unwavering belief in the superiority of one's own cultivation and civility – is rare in Australia. We do not like tall poppies, especially of the patrician hue. Martin Boyd and Patrick White are each, at different times and in very different ways, humorous writers, but that's not why they were canonised, and, though White can affect a patrician disdain for the middle classes, his visionary celebration of the least valued members of Australian society undermines simplistic 'classist' readings of his oeuvre. While Boyd can be affectionately amused by the antics of his eccentric upper-crust relations, White's darker humour, nourished by a delight in 'vulgar' demotic forms including pantomime, burlesque and cabaret, often targets his own class and those below it who ape its smugness and materialism. Robert Hughes, too, has some claims to the caustic humour we associate with a Waugh or a Vidal, though his larrikinism often competes with a more magisterial tone, even in his art criticism – as when, in *The shock of the new*, he dismissed the failed modernist utopia represented by the city of Brasília as 'miles of jerry-built nowhere, infested with Volkswagens'.[24]

In the Australian context, aspirations to lofty and exclusive wit are more apparent among intellectuals and literary autodidacts who delight in the arcana of the in-joke than in the (admittedly scarce) ranks of the bunyip aristocracy. Joseph Furphy is a case in point. So, too, is Christopher Brennan. In his *Musicopoematographoscope* (1897), Brennan parodied the avant-garde form of 'Un coup de dés' by his master Mallarmé, but it was a jeu d'esprit with an intended audience of one, his close friend Dowell O'Reilly, who had accused him of wilful obscurantism.[25] Compare this with the verse parodies and satires that appeared in nineteenth-century newspapers which, as Liz Webby shows in her chapter, 'To write or not to write', took their cue from poems that were all well-known to the readership. Later, 'serious' poets who wrote satires, such as AD Hope and James McAuley, are now probably not best remembered for them. McAuley was, of course, one half of that hoax figure Ern Malley, who was narrowly intended to sabotage the pretensions of Max Harris and *Angry Penguins*. He ended up making a much bigger splash, though, when his cover was blown by the *Sunday Sun*, which presented his poems to the masses as a joke. Virginia Blain, from whose essay this collection takes its title, traces the laugh-lines that run through the Malley escapade all the way to the United Kingdom.

In 'Writing humour' British-born Australian novelist and critic Michael Wilding reflects on the seminal influences on the deadpan humour of his fiction. In linking the demise of the campus novel with a more general decline in academic culture, Australian and worldwide, however, it also suggests that the local tradition of intellectual humour may be played out. By way of contrast, humour in Australian short fiction is alive and well, as Bruce Bennett's survey, 'Seriously funny', clearly shows. The same might be said of local performance humour, be it stand-up comedy or in other theatrical genres.

From *The Mavis Bramston show* (which grew out of the Phillip Street reviews) to programs like *The Games*, *The dream* and *Summer Heights High*, the most memorable Australian satires have taken on topical rather than 'timeless', common rather than 'cultured', themes. Barry Humphries began as an undergraduate dadaist, and later starred as Estragon in the first Australian production of *Waiting for Godot*; but, as Anne Pender shows in 'The rude rudiments of satire', it was Edna Everage, born out of the Melbourne Olympics of 1956, that propelled him to eventual stardom.

Likewise, Billy Birmingham, who spoofs Australia's sporting heroes and the television commentators who report their contests, drew inspiration for his enormously popular spoken-word comedy albums while watching coverage of the 1978 World Series Cricket fracas with a few mates. After parting company with stand-up comedian Austen Tayshus (for whom he had been writing 'Australiana') he began experimental parodies of the cricket commentariat, most notably Richie Benaud and Tony Greig, which were an instant hit. As he later told sporting journalist Warwick Hadfield, 'there are two great Australian pastimes: watching sport and taking the piss, and I stumbled across the magic combination of putting them together'.[26]

In bringing a range of critical approaches to bear on noteworthy aspects and examples of Australian humour, this book is unlikely to achieve such a magic combination. Humour may well be 'hostile to analysis', as Adams and Newell suggest, but hostility needn't imply complete resistance. In any case, the relationship isn't necessarily one-sided. *Serious frolic* may not be funny, but it is nonetheless frolicsome. It began as – and remains – a festschrift for Ken Stewart, one of the great scholars of Australian literary humour, and it takes something of its tone from his work, work that included memorable conference performances parodying larger-than-life figures such as Sandy Stone (in dressing-gown) and Camille Paglia (in drag). While all the chapters in this book remain, in their different ways, serious, that doesn't make them solemn. We don't pretend to have exhausted the subject of Australian humour – far from it. Think of this, rather, as a conversational gambit, an invitation to further discussion and speculation. Want to hear a joke?

How many academics does it take to change a light bulb?

That depends on what you mean by *light bulb*.

Classic Australian humour

'The Loaded Dog': A celebration

Ken Stewart

The Loaded Dog inhabits the background of millions of Australian minds, where he jostles amiably and vitally among the stiffer corpses and tutored shades of Bell Birds, My Country and Gallant Cook sailing from Albion. There is nothing dutiful, however, about the way the dog lingers in our minds. He is approved. He remains voluntarily, neither as an official and required patriotic cliché of the olden times, like the land of sweeping plains, nor as a drilled and tinkling set piece, like 'Bell Birds', learnt by rote without a meaning. In a central and formative position in Australian popular literary culture, the Loaded Dog grins and slobbers and wags his tail with the inerasable certainty of a figure in a nursery rhyme.

In spite of its popularity, the story has received little attention from commentators. Henry Lawson's critics, I suspect, have assumed that a straightforward legendary yarn written within a recognisable tradition does not require discussion. There is also the possibility that a popular, 'happy' story that lacks characteristic Lawsonian sombreness has been held necessarily to lack seriousness. To put the work aside and unexamined on these grounds is hazardous. The comic simplicity and folk acceptance of popular writing is often inseparable from its accessible human seriousness: the appeal of the story itself courts explanation. I believe that a discussion of its meaning, artistry and cultural significance can help us to appreciate the significance of Lawson's comic celebration of a dream, and that the context

of Lawson's fiction itself best establishes the concepts that give meaning to
the comic world of 'The Loaded Dog'. The two central and inseparable
preoccupations in his stories that are most helpful, and which I will need
to define in my own way, are 'human gregariousness' and 'the hardness of
things', my labels for what are frequently accepted as quintessentially Lawsonian themes.

Lawson's emphasis on gregariousness is obvious and elusive: obvious,
because we attest to it in every story about loneliness, isolation, mateship,
neighbourliness, the masculine bush ethos, love, husband and wife, madness, the bush itself as humans experience it; potentially elusive, because
we may so easily fail to perceive that he alone among authors of recognised
stature writes of little else: this instinct and need within the human species,
its potential and limitations, the forms it may take and the effects of its
repression, are virtually his exclusive subject, determining action and plot,
or passivity and plotlessness, and the complexity of his narrative tone, as
well as defining the area in which his insight into human behaviour and
human nature operates. It is possible for characters to live by themselves in
Furphy's fiction, for example, without becoming mad, or eccentric, or intolerably deprived; and if, like Tom Collins, the loner may be judged as rather
fussy, pedantic and self-deluding – then, such is life. Such *isn't* life for Lawson: the gregarious impulse, in his view of the nature of things, is dominant
and paramount; the loner is to be perceived as a curious individual, like
Mr Smellingscheck, whose mystique and mystery derive from the fact that
he is *not* gregarious. The isolate in Lawson is eccentric; or mad; or sulky,
sullen and selfish; or intolerably deprived. The salvation of the Bush Undertaker and of the swagman 'Rats' is that they create their own gregarious
reality from illusion. The Drover's Wife is an archetypal image of maternal
isolation and loneliness – intolerably deprived. The urgency and extensive-
ness of Lawson's preoccupation with the gregarious impulse is artistically
valid (his art validates it) but it is almost exclusive: nobody climbs Mount
Everest, or experiences an epiphany or invents the wheel, or is 'justified'
through romantic love or religious experience, or occupies himself in any

way satisfactorily, unless it be gregariously; and the author's values and priorities adjust themselves to this perspective on human lives.

Lawson's subject, then, is the instinct of human beings for human company and contact: to huddle, to be and to interact, preferably warmly, with others of the species. His first-person narrators are 'insiders'. They write critically, ambivalently and loyally from inside the group, accommodating themselves to the bullies and big kids, like Barcoo Rot and One-eyed Bogan; the innocuously stupid, like Tom Hall; and the hard cases, like Mitchell. The relationship of the narrator to the group establishes the paradox of conformity as a theme or problematic element within many of the stories (for example, 'Lord Douglas', 'The Union buries its dead', and 'Telling Mrs Baker'), but gregarious solidarity must win, or at least continue. In 'The Union buries its dead' it is not the loner's death that is disturbing; it is Lawson's evocation of the fear that a man, or all men, could be cut off from the human race, unredeemed by the gregarious impulse, locked without recognition within the individual self. His Union is a huddle of schoolboys; the verandah of the Bourke Imperial is like the quadrangle of a segregated boys' secondary school. Although the characters in these settings are 'types', they are realised psychologically only to the extent that social rituals and the breaking of them permit and define. They are real people whom the reader gets to know socially, but not intimately; and their mores and routines, the unwritten rules for gregarious behaviour, are, as Hal Porter would write, 'equally of air and of iron'. From time to time a fight breaks out in the quadrangle; and occasionally, as in 'That pretty girl in the Army', a strange foreign creature called a girl wanders into alien precincts, and you have to patronise her delicately and watch your language. The exclusiveness of Lawson's preoccupation with the lights and shades of human gregariousness provides a context for discussing the Loaded Dog – he is the gregarious impulse incarnate, canonised and canine-ised.

Lawson's second pervasive assumption is 'the hardness of things'. The most universal practice among sane people in his fiction is overt worry, in the manner of Joe Wilson, or the suppression of outward concern, as with

Mitchell. His celebrated 'realism' is flecked with constant emotional regret: external reality is not his subject – the narrator's emotional response, his voice, is the subject. The difference between Lawson's 'Ah, well' and Furphy's 'Such is life', or rather his many 'Such is life's, is that Lawson's expresses a direct emotional avowal, whereas Furphy's characters offer a more cerebral diversity of clinching observations in the face of the variety and enigma of life itself. 'Ah, well' expresses *felt* resignation: it is a kind of sad moan. The contrast with 'Such is life' is illustrated inadvertently by Manning Clark in volume 4 of *A history of Australia*:

> Ned Kelly walked to his death in the Old Melbourne Gaol in the morn-ing of 11 November 1880. His mother had urged him to die like a Kelly. Some said he looked frightened and morose and only managed to utter a lame 'Ah well, I suppose it has come to this'. Others said he summed it all up in that sardonic Australian remark 'Such is Life'.[1]

Lawson's positives, then, charity, neighbourliness, even madness, toughness and shrewdness, are really the valued arms of strugglers against the hardness of things. Lawson never states despair: he intones something grim. Even 'It didn't matter much – nothing does' is a fluctuation of the voice, rather than a considered conclusion; and it is a voice that is not so much meditating as actually expressing the moment's reaction to a continuing burden. There is an undefined or lost ideal behind Lawson's writing: it is life *without* the hardness of things; it is the relief of that pressure which creates his narrator's burdened tone.

That Lawson, unlike Furphy and Baynton, implicitly uses such an ideal as a gauge of the quality of reality is illustrated by his attacks on the romanti-cism and optimism of other Australian writers. These attacks in fact indicate his self-delusion, because they illustrate *his* romantic longing:

> They put in shining rivers and grassy plains, and western hills, and dawn and morn, and forest boles of gigantic size – everything, in fact, which is

not and never was in bush scenery or language; and the more the drought
bakes them the more inspired they become. Perhaps they unconsciously
see the bush as it should be, and their literature is the result of craving
for the ideal.[2]

The angry bitterness is revealing. It is as though Lawson would really like
to 'put in shining rivers and grassy plains' but the truth prevents him and
makes him angry with those who do. In the phrase 'they unconsciously
see the bush as it should be', he gives himself away, by implying that the
bush 'should be' an Arcadian dream world. Clearly, and ironically, Lawson's
literature is equally 'the result of a craving for the ideal' of the optimists
he attacks, albeit in conjunction with his constant emotional rediscovery
that the world is not ideal: 'And may the grass grow green and tall' ('Andy's
gone with cattle').[3] In Tom Collins's ridicule of *Geoffry Hamlyn* and other
romantic novels, by way of contrast, we find no 'craving for the ideal' and
total scorn of Kingsley's literary concoction, which Tom would never *want*
as a substitute for bush life. The irony in Furphy's superior implication that
life may be more romance-like than Tom perceives does not alter the fact
that neither Collins nor Furphy endorses a romantic literary projection, or
even dreams of 'the' ideal.

Lawson's fascination with ideal and real, and with illusion and reality,
triggers the creative impulse behind several of his best-known stories. It
leads him to examine perspectives on a seeming innocence or state of grace,
a condition in which the hardness of things dissolves or loses its oppressiveness, and in which altruism and generosity are unsullied by hard experience,
and may work as an agent of good. These stories, however, work to conclude
that the hardness of things itself explains or modifies any initial, magical
appearance of innocence or grace, and reduces it to the status of very unmagi-
cal experience. 'That's the way of it', comments Donald McDonald at the
end of 'That pretty girl in the Army': 'With a woman it's love or religion;
with a man it's love or the devil'.[4] That pretty girl, whose initial mystique
is of altruism, beauty and spiritual quality, so far from transcending the

hardness of things through some unusual bestowed grace or inherent innocence or goodness, is eventually to be perceived as simply the product and
the victim of this ordinary hardness of life: apparent innocence becomes an
explicable delusion. Mrs Baker, too, must remain deluded: the hardness of
things is *too* hard for her to be told. The Giraffe, to whom we have begun
to respond for his innocence and natural generosity, is as close as Lawson
gets to sainthood. But in Lawson's world, where there are many martyrs and
no saints, the Giraffe has to start saving his money, and is dispatched on
the train to marriage, which in Lawson is virtually a synonym for Paradise
Lost. 'I wish I could immortalise him!', writes the narrator, longing for the
ideal, but thereby confirming that he cannot.[5] The Giraffe has never really
changed hard-bitten humanity; it has changed him.

The innocent and gregarious potential of the carefully named Bob
Brothers, incidentally, is given a non-human referent. 'The Giraffe' is not
merely a nickname to designate an awkward lanky appearance. The name
becomes associated with naive, gangling, yet noble, taller-than-life generosity: he is, in this setting, an exotic legendary beast, to immortalise – if that
were possible. In 'The Loaded Dog' the device is used in reverse: the dog is
gauche, stupid, blundering, generous, gregarious and innocent; and the dog
is a mate, with a human name, 'Tommy'. And he is 'immortalised'.

'The Loaded Dog' inverts or softens Lawson's characteristic hard reality:
the weight of the hardness of things is taken from the narrator's shoulders.
As such, it is Lawson's most thoroughgoing bestowal of grace upon a super-
ficially recognisable reality – the comic celebration of a dream. The dog is
idealised mateship. Innocent, gregarious, happy, loyal and unworried, he
is accordingly the unwitting instrument of the forces of good in a triumph
over those adversaries of mateship, selfishness, greed and solitary bastardry.
And because he is ideal, he is allowed only to be a dog. He is briefly let off
the chain in a holiday world where the grim workaday forces of the hardness of things are replaced in their regular melancholy rounds by a literary
Providence, who rewards gregariousness and goodness of heart and pun-
ishes bastards. No worries. Those slender-witted, virgin-souled schoolboys

Andy, Dave and Jim experience literary alarm but never a real care; and the ideal, the dog, is incapable of anxiety. The story is therefore more than simply farce or slapstick. It is what happens to Lawson's imagination when he discards his characteristic assumptions. It is not reality, but its yardstick is reality. As a bush yarn that works within the traditional frame of reference of comic romance, it is an archetypal, speculative and, certainly, serious story; and its seriousness is fully definable only within the wider context of Lawson's complete prose fiction.

From the drover's dog to Kerr's cur and the dingo of Ayers Rock, dogs are legendary mates or bastards in Australian bush culture. Lawson's bush is a prodigious literary kennel. Although his dogs are not invariably man's best friend, and his kangaroo dogs are emphatically repugnant and untrustworthy, most dogs in Lawson are the gregarious adjunct and loyal companion, the mate, of their owners. The indefatigable 'Alligator' is coura-geous and loyal; the practical 'Five Bob', though perhaps not the full quid, is a devoted gravedigger's labourer; and that unfortunate poodle who is the victim of an ungracious tonsorial operation in 'The shearing of the cook's dog' is so much his owner's mirror image that the cook is 'narked for three days', not by the indignity of the act but because 'they'll think me a flash man in Bourke' with the dog 'trimmed up like that'.[6] Both versions of the morose 'That there dog o' mine' exploit the received wisdom that the dog is man's close and faithful friend: in the original version, in which the dog eats his dead master, this sentiment is the source of the nihilistic grotes-querie; in the revised version, it is a means of endorsing and illustrating mateship. The moral of 'Two dogs and a fence' is that men, like dogs, will quarrel stupidly over a barrier: 'Yet if those same two dogs were to meet casually outside they might get chummy at once, and be the best of friends, and swear everlasting mateship, and take each other home'.[7] Lawson's dogs, then, are only human, but more so; and sometimes ideally so. The Loaded Dog is gregarious innocence, the epitome of idealised mateship; and his skulking adversary is brooding, selfish, stand-offish bastardry.

The story begins quietly and deliberately, with two pages of down-to-earth detail concerning the technology of cartridge-making and fishing. Lawson's method is not only to establish an authentic if somewhat idyllic calm before the explosion but also to allow the tale gradually to forge and validate its own folk significance; it works slowly at first towards the genre of the apocryphal story and heightened folk yarn, from an initial immersion in genial pedestrian actuality:

> They used the old-fashioned blasting-powder and time-fuse. They'd make a sausage or cartridge of blasting powder in a skin of strong calico or canvas, the mouth sewn and bound round the end of the fuse; they'd dip the cartridge in mellow tallow to make it watertight, get the drill-hole as dry as possible, drop in the cartridge with some dry dust, and wad and ram with stiff clay and broken brick.[8]

The narrator here is confirming his bush credentials. The reader is to assent to this practical mystique, to nod approvingly at the bushmen's and the narrator's know-how, and to perceive the wisdom and rituals of the ethos, 'as bushmen do'.[9]

It is not until after the introduction of the dog that the story transcends the pleasantly mundane. Then the vitality of the imagery, the apocryphal exaggerations of the yarn, the slapstick conventions and the ritualised posturing towards the reader establish a 'do you remember the time' quality which is confirmed by the concluding lines:

> And most of this is why, for years afterwards, lanky, easy going bushmen, riding lazily past Dave's camp, would cry, in a lazy drawl and with just a hint of the nasal twang:
> "Ello, Da-a-ve! How's the fishin' getting on, Da-a-ve?"[10]

That is Lawson's cheerful but certain reminder to the reader that the teller of a tale is licensed to blur reality with the shine of myth: the reader should not necessarily believe that the land of once-upon-a-time is a real place.

Lawson's use of the apocryphal yarn, and of anecdote as a literary device, is diverse and uneven. At his worst his stories are straitjacketed by the boring conventions of tall-tale garrulity, which have lingered into Frank Hardy's Billy Borker yarns and into the futile maundering that still passes for humour on some radio programs. The original version of 'Rats', in which in a final sentence we learn that the little old man is yarning in the pub about 'the way in which he had "had" three "blanky fellers" for some tucker and "half a caser" by pretending to be "Barmey"',[11] is inferior to the final version because, as Brian Kiernan has pointed out, 'the disturbing implications of the sketch are lost in the factitiously well made story version'[12] – or, to extend the point, the reader feels that *he* has been 'had' by the author, since the subtleties of the reader's uncertainty and disturbance are reduced to the engineered certainty and bar-room bravado of a conventional yarn.

In other stories, and in various ways, Lawson deflates the apocryphal and romantic elements of the recollected yarn: 'Send round the hat' and 'The Chinaman's ghost' are examples. In 'The bush undertaker' he demythologises a conventional apocryphal yarn, not by suggesting that it is spurious but actually by confirming that the ordinary ingredients of a seemingly far-fetched tale constitute a grotesquely credible heightened reality: its 'truth' may not be exactly literal, but neither is it apocryphal. Lawson uses certain elements of the yarn to affirm that the story is *not* a yarn.

In 'The Loaded Dog' we work towards the avowedly apocryphal, but from the beginning we respond to glimmerings of idyll:

> Dave Regan, Jim Bentley and Andy Page were sinking a shaft at Stoney Creek in search of a rich gold quartz reef which was supposed to exist in the vicinity. There is always a rich reef supposed to exist in the vicinity; the only questions are whether it is ten feet or hundreds beneath the surface, and in which direction.[13]

Although the narrator is rather cynical about this golden dream, a holiday quest for El Dorado, his tone is indulgent. We are not in workaday reality,

for the mates have gone fishing as well as gold-seeking; and fishing is a traditional literary escape, from Izaac Walton to Huck Finn. Moreover, Lawson's
not-so-good earth has suddenly become bountiful: 'There was plenty of fish
in the creek, fresh-water bream, cod, cat-fish and tailers. The party were
fond of fish, and Andy and Dave of fishing'.[14] The creek is neither in flood
nor in a dry, hard bed; and the weather seems uncharacteristically clement.

The cartridge is 'a formidable bomb'. The emphasis on its destructive
potential is unstinting – indeed, Dave has engineered an elaborate device 'to
increase the force of the explosion'.[15] To argue, therefore, that Lawson even
here tinges his bush humour with the constant threat of crude violence and
destruction is understandable; but I do not believe that we are invited to
respond to the threat of the cartridge except insofar as it is primarily a familiar
comic clowning device, the equivalent of the double bunger of the later Tom
and Jerry animated cartoon. Although there is some sadism within the convention itself, appropriate to the 'sadistic' bush tradition that countless stories
and cartoons in the *Bulletin* of the period unpleasantly exploit, it is remarkable that this element has been greatly softened in comparison with other
examples in the *Bulletin*, and has been transformed in context from 'realistic'
sadistic humour into a distanced, almost comic cartoon stylisation. As we are
to discover, the Providence of Lawson's comedy, unlike the Fates of his reality,
will use the destructive power of the cartridge to achieve a poetic justice and a
happy retributive ending. The dog itself makes a belated *grande entrance*:

> They had a big black young retriever dog – or rather an overgrown pup,
> a big, foolish, four-footed mate, who was always slobbering round them
> and lashing their legs with his heavy tail that swung round like a stock-
> whip. Most of his head was usually a red, idiotic, slobbering grin of
> appreciation of his own silliness. He seemed to take life, the world, his
> two-legged mates, and his own instinct as a huge joke.[16]

The impression is immediate, exaggerated, almost Dickensian, and unfor-
gettable: the sudden juxtaposition of this colourful caricature against the

genial pedestrian rituals of pragmatic bush technology confirms the dog's status as the larger-than-life subject of the yarn. He is not only a mate; he is a gangling, gauche, madly friendly, stupidly generous mate – a caricature of his own masters, and a satirical but delighted idealisation of bush gregariousness. This description together with the action that follows emphasises the vitality of the forces the dog embodies, the reversal of the usual Lawsonian passivity.

The dog is proper instinct, graced by a freedom from all worry and malice; and in his innocence he is necessarily stupid, the archetypal saint and fool, an ideal who cannot be killed off by the immense and random destructiveness of the cartridge. A bush dog, he grins 'sardonically'; 'they loved him for his good-heartedness'; life for him is 'a huge joke': the seeds of the moral allegory are sown, and germinate within the farcical action – all his good-hearted, game-playing, fun-loving, faithful, gregarious responses actually cause the slapstick.

As in an animated cartoon, which the technique anticipates, a series of poses and attitudes makes up a set of ritualised 'frames': Dave and Andy running in divergent directions; Jim shinnying up a sapling; the 'big pup' laying the cartridge 'as carefully as a kitten' at the foot of the tree; the sputtering fuse; Jim hiding in a hole; the dog grinning 'sardonically down at him, as if he thought it would be a good lark to drop the cartridge down on Jim'. Farcical action is pictorialised. The technique may derive from pantomime stage tradition and circus clowning, and from the black and white pen drawing that helped to popularise the *Bulletin*. It is hard to think of examples before Lawson which better exploit it through the medium of the written word.

Providence in the shape of a benevolent Lawson has the retriever arrive at the natural home of mates and bushmen, the pub, where he goes 'in under the kitchen, among the piles': a plausible, Hades-like moral setting in which to find the sworn enemy of mateship and gregariousness, the troll of the Bush, ensconced in selfish solitary brooding. This particular *bête noire* is a *chien jaun*, a nameless, 'vicious yellow mongrel cattle dog sulking and nursing his nastiness under there'. He sounds like the kind of *person* Lawson finds distasteful, a canine Barcoo Rot, 'a sneaking, fighting thieving canine, whom neighbours had tried for years' to put down.[17]

At this stage a mock-epic assemblage of the clan or pack, a sort of grand dog Union, gathers at the pub, and to the fray:

> Nearly a dozen other dogs came from round all the corners and under the buildings – spidery, thievish, cold-blooded kangaroo dogs, mongrel sheep- and cattle-dogs, vicious black and yellow dogs – that skip after you in the dark, nip your heels and vanish without explaining – and yapping, yelping small fry. They kept at a respectable distance round the nasty yellow dog, for it was dangerous to go near him when he thought he had found something which might be good for a dog or cat.

Lawson's dogs here are scruffy, unheroic witnesses, as are his unionists in other contexts; the 'one-eyed cattle dog' of this company is perhaps a counterpart of 'One-eyed Bogan'. The parallel, however, is no more than a suggestion: the essential, and literally redeeming, characteristic of the dogs is that they stick together, gregariously. They are an audience within an audience to be viewed by the drinkers at the pub; both audiences will be viewed by the reader. The dogs, as the story's inner circle, will be required to engage in the ritual witnessing of the central providential purgation of evil and restitution of right. We are told that they are to remember this caution-ary epic ritual all their lives.

> He sniffed at the cartridge twice, and was just taking a third cautious sniff when –
>
> It was very good blasting powder – a new brand that Dave had recently got up from Sydney; and the cartridge had been excellently well made. Andy was very patient and painstaking in all he did, and nearly as handy as the average sailor, with needles, twine, canvas, and rope.

The 'big bang' is narrated with a comedian's timing, but the amusing ironical understatement of 'It was very good blasting powder . . .', protracted within a return to the prosaics of Dave's and Andy's practical credentials, anticipates carefully the sensationally juxtaposed apocryphal exaggeration which insists on the incredible 'folk' status of the yarn: 'Bushmen say that the kitchen jumped off its piles and on again. When the smoke and dust cleared away . . .'[18]

What is happening is that Lawson is insinuating into the narrative the rules and terms by which the Loaded Dog is to remain in our minds: he is to be remembered as legend, as the hero of a happy bush instance in which the hardness of things is overcome and destroyed, in which gregariousness actually triumphs and endures in the imagination. The dogs disperse to go home, to seek their ancestral birthplaces, to remember the lesson and nurse their cautionary wounds; but laughter is restored to all ordinary decent humanity, in hyperbolic quantities of segregated squawks, hysterics and shrieks.

Life resumes with this grand cautionary memory, and with universal good cheer, gregariously established; and the dog will finally be put back on the chain. But the triumph of mateship incarnate, of the Loaded Dog as total gregariousness with Providence on side, of myth as a lingering armament against the workaday reality that must be returned to, is celebrated by the ritual of his final victorious appearance before the reading audience: 'And the dog that had done it all, Tommy, the great, idiotic mongrel retriever, came slobbering round Dave and lashing his legs with his tail, and trotted home after him, smiling his broadest, longest and reddest smile of amiability'.[19]

That 'The Loaded Dog' has become Australia's greatest bush nursery yarn is not only the serious compliment it deserves; it is also the enduring evidence that Lawson's literary instructions and gestures within the story, which require that it assume that kind of status as a popular yarn, have been heeded with an authenticating delight and affection.

'Compounded of incompatibles': The songs of a Sentimental Bloke and The moods of Ginger Mick

Philip Butterss

Norman Lindsay's response to the success of CJ Dennis's *The songs of a Sentimental Bloke* was to erect a cross in his front garden and crucify a copy of the book. But while Lindsay stamped his feet about its popularity and its sentimentality, the rest of Australia loved it. Dennis's verse narrative about a larrikin street-fighter and his nervous courtship of Doreen, a young woman who pastes labels in a pickle factory, is still the best-selling book of Australian verse. Since its publication in October 1915 more than 300,000 copies have been sold in upward of sixty editions. It was followed a year later by *The moods of Ginger Mick*, celebrating the wartime career of Mick, the best man at the Bloke and Doreen's wedding. Although the sequel did not have the longevity of its predecessor, its first print run was almost 40,000, a staggering figure for a book of verse.[1]

For most of his working life, Dennis supported himself by writing mainly poetry, often of a humorous kind. As editor of the satirical Adelaide weekly the *Gadfly* in 1906–07, his humour could have a darker and sharper edge, as in 'The righteous man':

Is Sunday, and the man of prayer,
Of aspect mild and chastened look,
Kneels in the church, and worships there,
And bows his head upon a book;
Reading the lesson for the day,
He bleats devoutly

       Let us pray.

Is Monday, and the man of trade,
Of aspect keen and crafty look,
Sits in his den where schemes are laid;
And bends his gaze upon a book,
Planning the business for the day,
He softly mutters

       Let us prey.[2]

After his editorship of the *Gadfly*, Dennis spent seven years in Victoria as a freelancer, principally writing topical verse for the *Bulletin*, often of a political nature. Between his lampooning of conservative politicians such as George Reid, Alfred Deakin and Joseph Cook were some moments of lighter humour. What later became known as 'The Austra-laise' first appeared in the *Bulletin* in 1908, and in 1909 that journal published a couple of poems that he was to develop into *The songs of a Sentimental Bloke* and its sequel. After the publication of *A book for kids* (1921), generations of Australian children went to bed wondering about the triantiwontigongolope, 'a very funny creature that you do not often spy, / And it isn't quite a spider and it isn't quite a fly'.[3] And Dennis's daily contributions to the Melbourne *Herald* kept readers laughing through the 1920s up until his death in 1936.

In 1915, with the country at war and reports from the battlefields gloomy, the affectionate humour of the 'Bloke' narrative and its happy domestic ending proved just the ticket for Australian audiences. A year later, the stories of Ginger Mick's heroism were to do the same. Much of the success of these volumes comes from the way they provided a fictional world that smoothed over the deep social divisions within Australian society. The declaration of war had come during the bitter 1914 election campaign. Politically, the relatively fluid coalitions of the first decade after Federation were settling into a more clearly demarcated party politics. Conscription, the most divisive issue of World War I, began to emerge as a dispute mid-1915, with some elements of the union movement declaring themselves against compulsory military service in July that year.[4]

When Dennis found that Henry Lawson's draft preface to *The songs of a Sentimental Bloke* contained a mild reference to class difference, he was horrified. In fact, Lawson was just repeating what Dennis had told him was the purpose of the book: 'to prove – amongst other things – that life and love can be just as real and splendid to the "common" bloke as to the "cultured"'. But Dennis felt that any public reference to class was 'likely to jar', and the quote was deleted. He wanted the preface 'to be kindly and coloured with goodfellowship toward all men'.[5] In marketing the book, Dennis intended to appeal to the whole community, but he also wanted the preface to be in tune with the narrative's unified sense of Australianness.

The songs of a Sentimental Bloke begins with these well-known words:

> The world 'as got me snouted jist a treat;
>   Crool Forchin's dirty left 'as smote me soul;
> An' all them joys o' life I 'eld so sweet
>   Is up the pole.[6]

Central to the poem is its attempt to hold together diverse elements, something identified by the literary critic HM Green as its chief problem. Although Green acknowledged that Dennis was 'one of the most humorous, wittiest and most ingenious writers of verse that Australia has produced', he felt that the most 'fundamental fault' in *The songs of a Sentimental Bloke* was that 'the Bloke is a fake, because he is compounded of incompatibles'. To Green, it seemed absurd for a larrikin to be represented as 'an essentially civilized being, capable of sympathies, generosities, refinements, romantic yearnings: one might as well expect him to be a connoisseur of fine porcelain'.[7] Ina Bertrand also identifies the incompatibles in the Bloke's character, but she sees them as crucial to the narrative's impact. In her work on Raymond Longford's silent film version, *The Sentimental Bloke*, Bertrand suggests that 'Bill's function . . . is to bridge social divisions – class, wealth, and particularly gender'.[8] The incongruousness at the heart of Dennis's characterisation and narrative is precisely what made both *The songs of a Sentimental Bloke* and *The moods of Ginger Mick* humorous; but their attractiveness to such a large and diverse audience also comes from a broader compounding of incompatibles: the way both texts smooth over the faultlines and tensions within Australian culture of the time.

The merging of what seems contradictory is immediately evident in the language that so delighted wartime and later readers. Although the semi-scholarly apparatus of the glossary at the end of both books might suggest that the readership needs help in translating an authentic sociolect, Dennis has not really attempted to replicate larrikin speech. The larrikin *effect* is derived from the use of some street slang, a lot of stage-cockney, and various mimicries of non-standard pronunciation, such as dropped initial h's, dropped final consonants, and v's for f's. And the fakeness of the language extends to the Bloke's vocabulary; as Green notes of the opening lines: 'to imagine the abstract word "Fortune" in the mouth of a larrikin is impossible, nor is it possible to imagine a larrikin speaking of anything or anybody smiting his soul'.[9] And to cement the compounding, there is the lovely rhyme of 'soul' with the colloquial expression 'up the pole'. In the glossaries of both volumes, Dennis continues this fundamental juxtaposition of class extremes: larrikinese with what linguists were later to call 'educated Australian'. 'Snouted' is glossed as 'treated with disfavour'. 'Clobber' is not rendered as 'clothes' but as 'raiment; vesture'; 'cobber' is 'boon companion'. The Bloke's and Ginger Mick's language draws attention to the impossibility of the mixture it joyfully represents. And Hal Gye's illustrations are also instrumental in holding the incongruous together: Dennis told George Robertson that he wanted them 'to be aesthetic enough to balance the coarseness of the dialect and emphasise the sentiment'.[10]

The humour of *The songs of a Sentimental Bloke* emerges in a string of situations where the Bloke uses larrikinese when a more formal register would be expected, for example the introduction to the beloved, meeting the beloved's mother, the interview with the parson, and the marriage ceremony. And because he narrates the tale, the other participants in these situations have their voices filtered through his larrikin speech, often incongruously. Best-known is 'The play', where the Bloke and Doreen go to see a performance of *Romeo and Juliet*. The sequence is full of jokes for those with even a passing acquaintance with Shakespeare's original:

> Mick Curio, 'e gets it in the neck,
> 'Ar rats!' 'e sez, an' passes in 'is check.
>
> Quite natchril, Romeo gits wet as 'ell.
> 'It's me or you!' 'e 'owls, an' wiv a yell,
> Plunks Tyball through the gizzard wiv 'is sword,
> 'Ow I ongcored!
> 'Put in the boot!' I sez. 'Put in the boot!'
> ''Ush!' sez Doreen . . . 'Shame!' sez some silly coot.[11]

George Orwell's warnings against the patronising nature of any attempt to mimic working-class speech are relevant throughout Dennis's larrikin pieces,[12] but in this poem the audience is encouraged to inhabit a range of contrary positions. Certainly, readers are invited to laugh at a larrikin and his girlfriend's awkward consumption of high culture, to enjoy the incongruous translation of Shakespeare, and to be amused at the bloke's enthusiasm for the violence (and therefore his inadvertent revelation to Doreen that his reformation is not complete). But in the earthy and vigorous language of the retelling, there is also an undercutting of the pretentiousness of high culture. This element is brought out more strongly in Longford's film, where the actors on stage performing *Romeo and Juliet* are presented, in one critic's words, as 'ridiculous, if well-intentioned'.[13] At the end of the passage just quoted, the audience sympathises with Doreen's embarrassment at the Bloke's interjection, but at the same time agrees that the person yelling 'Shame!' *is* a 'silly coot'. And to underline the ways the text is uniting incompatibles, the Bloke has already convincingly asserted the similarity between high art and lumpenproletariat life, observing that the Montagues and Capulets are 'jist like them back-street clicks, / Ixcep' they fights wiv skewers 'stid o' bricks'.[14]

As well as the incongruities within language and situation, Dennis is having a lot of fun with genre. In the first place, it is surprising to have as hero and heroine in a romance a larrikin who has done a 'stretch fer stoushin' Johns'[15] and a woman who pastes labels in a pickle factory. But more incongruous is the inversion of the sexes, as Bertrand has pointed out. In contrast to a typical 'feminine romance', this narrative is related through a male voice, and is driven by male desire for a partner, but it is still 'resolved through the conventionally female goals of marriage and family'. Bertrand argues that this insertion of the male into a traditionally 'feminine' genre 'allows for shifting gender identifications, and so a closure satisfying to both genders'.[16]

Of the social divisions that *The songs of a Sentimental Bloke* addresses, class is, of course, the most central. The narrative opens with the problem of class difference, with the Bloke pining for women who are unapproachable and who look down on him. By the end, the initially impermeable barrier has been crossed: the Bloke has married above himself, and proudly runs a fruit farm that he is destined to own. The demonstration that class mobility is possible in Australian society is complete when the Bloke has employees of his own, as he says: 'To take me orders while I act the boss'.[17] But to continue the delicate balancing of opposites, Dennis makes clear that the ex-larrikin also retains some of his old values, and when he muses about their new-born son's future career he slips back a little:

I think we ort to make 'im something great –
A bookie, or a champeen 'eavy-weight:
    Some callin' that'll give 'im room to spread.
    A fool could see 'e's got a clever 'ead.[18]

The tension between the desire to elide class difference and the *reality of* class difference is played out often – for example in the somewhat over-determined poem where Doreen takes her beau home to mother. To the Bloke, Mar represents a higher class, a different generation and a different sex, and he pictures her as a 'stern female in a cap / Wot puts the fear o' Gawd into a chap'. He suffers terribly from his new clothes, and puts his foot in it a few times, but Doreen's mother likes her future son-in-law, and the two unite to talk about household matters and to encourage Doreen to set the date. On the other hand, the text counterbalances this too-easy smoothing over of class, generation and sex differences with a reassertion of some of those boundaries. Dennis can't resist some standard mother-in-law jokes: the bloke worries that Doreen might turn out to be a 'fat ole weepin' willer like 'er Mar', and the poem finishes with a rejection of the mother-in-law's attempt to have him called the more pretentious 'Willy' instead of 'Bill'.[19]

In a society where sectarian divisions were profound, Dennis manages a careful balancing act in questions of religion. Although clergymen in Syd-ney and army chaplains in Egypt were to preach sermons on *The songs of a Sentimental Bloke*, the book avoids overt expressions of belief, allowing for a range of views in its audience. The parson is gently mocked, but is characterised as decent and approving of the union with Doreen. The Bloke initially proposes a registry wedding, and doesn't understand the clergy-man's talk of 'jooty an' the spiritchuil life', but in the final poem expresses a belief in the creation, announcing: 'I am blest, becos me feet 'ave trod / A land 'oo's fields reflect the smile o' God'.[20] None of the characters are assigned any denomination, but Ginger Mick's name neatly allows the pos-sibility that a Roman Catholic of Irish descent is best man at a Church of England wedding, without actually saying so.

Much of *The songs of a Sentimental Bloke* is concerned with the compounding of the incompatible models of masculinity labelled 'masculinist' and 'domestic' manhood by Marilyn Lake. Although the book's final chapters add up to a strong endorsement of the latter type, the transition from larrikin to good husband and father has moments of equivocation, allowing both models to co-exist. For instance, in the fourth poem, 'Doreen', the Bloke says:

> Fer 'er sweet sake I've gone and chucked it clean:
> > The pubs an' schools an' all that leery game.
> Fer when a bloke 'as come to know Doreen,
> > > It ain't the same.
> There's 'igher things, she sez, for blokes to do.
> An' I am 'arf believin' that it's true.[21]

In this romance with the sexes reversed, the Bloke's rise in status and financial position depends on marriage, as would a traditional heroine's. But to prevent any emasculation that this role reversal might entail, the text demonstrates that Bill's upward mobility is not just dependent on a woman. Instead, the bonds between men are crucial to the process. Uncle Jim's decision to bestow property on the young couple hinges on his feelings towards the Bloke:

> 'I got no time fer wasters, lad,' sez 'e,
> > 'Give me a man wiv grit,' sez Uncle Jim.
> 'E bores 'is cute ole eyes right into me,
> > While I stares 'ard an' gives it back to 'im.
> Then orl at once 'e grips me 'and in 'is:
> 'Some'ow,' 'e sez, 'I likes yer ugly phiz.'

And this blokey communion between men is also a bridging of urban and rural, another social difference that the text manages to span. When the

Bloke first sees him, Jim is 'A cherub togged in sunburn an' a beard / An' duds that shouted "'Ayseed!" fer a mile'.[22] But in Uncle Jim's befriending of the Bloke – and particularly in his decision to call him 'Bill' rather than 'Willy' – the text shifts its emphasis from difference to similarity. Rural man adopts city larrikin as his heir as part of the narrative's overall movement from city slums to rural Arcadia. And this transition has implications for other strategies for consensus; as Les Murray suggests, the farm is 'away from the restraints of the city and, by implication, of class itself'.[23]

Ginger Mick may have been born as a convenient rhyme to 'shick',[24] and may not have had much more than a walk-on role as best man in *The songs of a Sentimental Bloke*, but Dennis saw the prospect of developing the character, and began publishing poems about Mick in the *Bulletin* in May 1915, several months before the first book was published. Angus & Robertson released *The moods of Ginger Mick* in October 1916, a year after its predecessor. By 31 December, the first printing of almost 40,000 had been followed by a second impression of 15,000,[25] and the pocket edition was popular among the troops.

Where the humour of its predecessor *emerged* from the incongruity of a larrikin in love, the very project of *The moods of Ginger Mick* – humour about warfare – is a compounding of incompatibles, and, not surprisingly, this is much harder to pull off. In *The songs of a Sentimental Bloke*, Dennis could get away with a joke about Doreen's mother's response to her husband's death, but being funny about battles and casualties in a book focused on a real war is much more tricky. There are some aspects of the conflict that Dennis attempts to make light of: he heavy-handedly explains that the war began 'Becos a crook done in a prince, an' narked an Emperor', for example. Referring to the Dardanelles campaign, Mick writes jauntily, and perhaps not entirely accurately, of 'the day we walloped Abdul o'er the sands o' Sari Bair'. And, in a precursor to *Monty Python and the Holy Grail*'s image of a knight gradually losing his limbs, Mick warns off a potential rival for the affections of his girlfriend, Rose, by threatening that, if when he returns from the war his arms and legs are lame, he'll '*bite* the blighter'.[26]

The moods of Ginger Mick repeats much of the fundamental material of its predecessor, generally in a more laboured and less polished fashion, but its different subject matter necessarily means some alteration to its uniting of incompatibles. For example, the demands of writing about war meant a different male image; as Gye records: 'There was nothing of the cupid touch about those illustrations; they had to be of men – real men; and yet, as Den said, to be drawn lightly'.[27] Clearly Mick's transition from larrikin to soldier contains nothing of the incongruity in Bill's transition to domestic man, but the reference to lightness indicates a desire to soften the toughness of the larrikin-soldier. William Routt argues that in Gye's drawings Ginger Mick is 'rough but wholesome',[28] perhaps also hinting at an attempt to balance what could have been an extreme representation of masculinity.

Historians of World War I have often described Australia as a 'divided nation',[29] and many of the divisions were crystallised in the conscription debate. Although the first of the referenda was held in October 1916, the month in which *The moods of Ginger Mick* was published, conscription had begun to emerge as an issue more than a year earlier. Dennis was at the time working as private secretary to EJ Russell, a Labor senator, and he had trouble making the final corrections to the second book because, as he wrote to his publishers in September, 'Things are so mixed and so distracting in the political atmosphere in which I live, that "Ginger Mick" . . . and everything else have gone temporarily into the background'.[30]

In keeping with his desire to provide a story that unites its readership, Dennis sidesteps the issue of conscription in *The moods of Ginger Mick* by not mentioning it, but he covers some similar ground in rehearsing the arguments for and against enlisting. Again the book allows multiple positions for the audience by refusing to endorse any of the views that are expressed. At first Mick refuses to be involved in what he sees as a fight to protect the rich's cars and diamonds. The Bloke repeats some of the contemporary propaganda about Germans burning homes, killing children, and 'comin' it reel crook wiv decent tarts'. Mick still disapproves of going to war and says that it is none of his business, but then asks what soldiers get paid. And the text finally fudges the issue by beginning the next chapter with him in Cairo, and the Bloke saying that he did not understand his mate's motive. When a reason is finally given, it is that Mick has felt 'the call of stoush', an ancient and evidently unexplainable feeling deep inside men.[31]

The moods of Ginger Mick continually returns to images of harmony and consensus among the Australian troops. For example, one poem, 'The singing soldiers', presents singing together as the digger's distinctive contribution to the war:

> Now, the British Tommy curses, an' the French does fancy stunts,
> An' the Turk 'e 'owls to Aller, an' the Gurkha grins an' grunts;
> But our boys is singin', singin', while the blinded shells is flingin'
> Mud an' death into the trenches in them 'eavens called the Fronts.[32]

Like its predecessor, the book vacillates in its representation of class difference, but in presenting images of class unity among the troops it goes much further than *The songs of a Sentimental Bloke*: 'So the lumper, an' the lawyer, an' the chap 'oo shifted sand, / They are cobbers wiv the cove 'oo drove a quill'.[33] The book depicts 'pride o' class' being replaced by 'pride o' race'; the communal bonds of nation explicitly replace the divisions of class. When he dies, Ginger Mick's most significant epitaph is that 'He was a gallant gentleman', and what is surprising is the text's respect for the source of these words: Trent, 'an English toff wiv swanky friends'.[34] The final arbiter of value is not even Australian-born; at this point the text's depiction of unity has expanded to include not only the Australian nation but the whole Empire.

Not surprisingly, the inclusiveness established in the fictional world of Dennis's larrikin books is incomplete. The Egyptians are referred to as 'niggers',[35] and their exclusion is set out at length in 'The Battle of the Wazzir', a poem about rampaging Anzac troops supposedly cleaning up Cairo, that was refused publication by the censor.[36] At home, the 'chows' in 'Duck and fowl', the opening chapter of *The moods of Ginger Mick*, are outside the community established by both books, and Indigenous people are not mentioned in either.

Apart from these exclusions, the two books work hard to construct a sense of the Australian community as, in Benedict Anderson's words, 'a deep horizontal comradeship'.[37] The Bloke's voice continues almost unchanged through both, and is joined by Ginger Mick's in the second, so that a boss can sound like a larrikin, domestic man like masculinist man, farmer like resident of the inner city, nationalist like larrikin. *The songs of a Sentimental Bloke* and *The moods of Ginger Mick* are open texts, with the situations explored and the overall narrative structures allowing the audience multiple positions that encourage inclusiveness. Class distinctions, sectarian differences, the divide between the city and the bush, popular culture versus high culture, the clash between different models of masculinity, even gender differences, are all smoothed over or accommodated. Dennis was proud that letters of praise for his books had 'come from men and women of all grades of society, of all shades of political thought and of many religions'.[38] For a society that was divided within and felt threatened from without, *The songs of a Sentimental Bloke* and *The moods of Ginger Mick* were deeply unifying texts. In humorously compounding incompatibles, they produced a vision of social consensus that was perfect for their time.

Humour and culture

'Aussie' humour and laughter: Joking as an acculturating ritual

Jessica Milner Davis

Defining the essence of Australian humour in popular jokes and humorous tales is like chasing a will-o'-the-wisp. Despite conventional wisdom that typical 'Aussie' jokes and yarns do exist, the contents of many volumes whose titles endorse this idea are ambivalent. Diversity in subject matter, style and form is more striking than any characteristic pattern or flavour. In introducing the 1989 special issue of *Thalia* devoted to 'Australian humour', Turcotte observed that Australia has 'an undeniably heterogeneous or diverse humorous tradition' and noted that 'Australia's humorists are still laughing as part of a survival process'.[1] This suggests that focusing on the social functions and conventions surrounding Australian uses of laughter and humour may prove more fruitful than seeking definitive topics and structures.

When collectors such as Keith Willey (1984) or Bill Wannan (1954) nominate a favourite Australian joke, they select a wry narrative, often with an outback setting, reflecting traditional 'Aussie' self-image.[2] Yet in all Australian joke collections, universal topics (such as relations between the sexes, family members, rural and city, civility versus self-indulgence) outnumber local topics. Confronting this problem, the editors of *The Penguin book of Australian jokes* (part of a 1994–2001 series) recorded their 'failure to find any jokes that are authentically, unequivocally Australian'.[3]

Like others,[4] Adams and Newell acknowledge one characteristic of the jokes collected – their offensive nature (including outright racism). They hazard the possibility that poor taste might define Australian jokes, reporting, 'whenever we found a joke that might have been regarded as tasteful, it failed another important test – it wasn't funny'.[5] Such distinctive crudity is also noted by Davis and Crofts, contributing an Australian chapter to a comparative study of national humour styles.[6] Comparative archival studies of joke collections around the world also confirm this trait: Christie Davies found a uniquely large Australian category of 'dirt' jokes, which defy normal social conventions on obscenity and filth. He noted that these are only recorded post-1970, after Australian publishing escaped rigid censorship laws, suggesting prior, unrecorded existence. The category includes a significant subgroup reflecting, in Davies' immortal words, 'the dingo-like tendency of Australians to return to their vomit for humour'; in other words, a preoccupation with 'chunder humour', well exemplified by Bazza McKenzie's comic behaviour in *OZ Magazine* and related films.[7]

Should this kind of crudity be designated 'quintessentially Australian'? With Joseph Furphy's famous descriptor of *Such is life* as a guide ('Temper, democratic; bias, offensively Australian'), it certainly qualifies as 'offensively democratic'. However, the rest of the Anglo-Saxon world has emulated this attribute in recent years, courtesy of politically incorrect British comedies like *Men behaving badly* and *Little Britain*,[8] and, in North America, 'shock-u' comics (for example Bill Hicks, Andrew Dice Clay and Mike Marino, 'New Jersey's Bad Boy of comedy')[9] and even TV cartoon-series such as *South Park*, with its figure of Stan, the compulsive vomiter.[10] In fact, writing about 'The progress of Australian humour in Britain', Davies acknowledged the inroads chunder-humour was making in the United Kingdom, noting, 'When the British laugh about the Australians, they are laughing about themselves'.[11] Furthermore, given permission of time and place, other cultures can indulge in (to Anglo-Saxons) even more offensive and disgusting comic topics, for example some Japanese popular stage-comedy.[12]

Davies' comparisons of regional and national joke collections (including ethnic 'put-downs') also showed that jokes targeting particular figures or sub-groups recycle common formats from one culture to another, interpolating locally recognised names or stock character-types to suit varying environments and belief systems.[13] Australian joke collections certainly bear this out, casting Australia-specific concerns and locations in joke formats shared with other cultures and times.[14] Adams and Newell challenge: 'Show us an Australian joke and we'll show you an English, an American or a German joke that has been on a long journey'.[15] Jokes against backwoods Tasmanians or stupid New Zealanders share formats with Canadian jokes against Newfoundlanders and English against the Irish, with local features interpolated (for example for New Zealanders: excessive attachment to sheep[16] and the distinctive 'Kiwese' accent).[17] Similarly, the universal formulae Davies identified as 'stupidity jokes', 'canny jokes' and 'dirt jokes' recur in other national collections, *mutatis mutandis.*

Since it is difficult to draw firm distinctions between the joke proper, the tall tale and the short, humorous narrative, the same definitional problems with jokes affect 'Aussie yarns' and short stories. Like most editors, Bill Wannan, who recorded Australian folklore and humour from the 1950s to the mid-1980s, collated tales with jokes and often included cartoons or funny sketches, as well as more literary extracts.[18] Although his titles usually label the published material as 'typical', 'classic' or '100% Australian', this is no reliable guide. 'Classic', for example, merely privileges more traditional (therefore more remote) Australian locations, times, characters and themes. Even including the outback, the bush, icons such as 'the little Aussie battler', the 'underdog', notions of a 'fair-go', 'mateship', the cultural cringe, the Australian dream-home, beach and sport and so on, the majority of material in these collections still escapes this net.[19] And as with joke collections, so with tall tales and short narratives: what is nominated as 'typically Aussie' reflects personal selector preference.

Moving beyond topics and structures to the purposes and social effects of humour may allow more valid conclusions to be drawn about what is specially Australian. Most surveys assert[20] that humour functions as part of

an 'Australian democratic tradition' of irreverence and anti-authoritarianism
and some of the themes rehearsed above support these notions. Davis and
Crofts reported subversion as a characteristic of the (especially male) Australian vernacular, or Strine, seeing its richly inventive range of metaphor
and word-play as 'a form of abuse, particularly against people in authority'.[21] 'E-facts' about Strine appearing in the 'National Cultures' section of
Wikipedia (although rather meagre on the topic of Australian humour as
opposed to a rich entry on New Zealand humour) include:

> [I]t combines a mocking disrespect for established authority, particularly
> if it is pompous or out of touch with reality, with a distinctive upside-
> down sense of humour. For instance, Australians take delight in dubbing
> a tall man 'Shorty', a silent one 'Rowdy', a bald man 'Curly' and a red-
> head, of course, is 'Bluey'.[22]

While slang and metaphor are not formally jokes, they can perform a joking
function, and examples are often included in humour collections. Davies[23]
reviews some colourful examples of Australian comic insults and vulgarities,
with a useful source list.[24] Davies agrees that Australian joking exchanges are
still marked by the use of Strine and inventive metaphors, involving either
exaggeration or meiosis (or both). The unwritten rules of engagement,
which exempt neither friend nor foe, seem to demand competitive ratings
for colourfulness and creativity from participants and witnesses alike.

Besides such licensed, democratic self-expression, Australian humour
can also serve as a valuable survival technique in hard times, a function
providing the title of Keith Willey's 1984 survey, and noted by others.[25] Discussing literary humour, Dorothy Jones emphasises that significant recurring
motifs extend beyond the settler/survivor battle to include landscape and
geography.[26] These themes abound in popular collections like the bookstore-
counter 'Little Aussie joke-books',[27] which tug at national pride as well as
tourists' wallets. Jokes about the scale and brooding presence of the land, its
distance from anywhere and the difficulties of making a comfortable living in

and on it manifest a sense of unease. Perhaps, like most humour, they assist by acknowledging and releasing tension. While to some extent contemporary city-life deflects it, the Australian experience of isolation in a geographic 'vastness' is common to all inhabitants, felt particularly by the newly arrived and especially by first-time visitors to the outback. The scale and (to unfamiliar eyes) strangeness of the continent diminish individual stature, tending to provoke for some a spiritual response and for others a joking response (the two are not mutually exclusive). Joking offers a way, if not of overcoming this sense of personal diminution, at least of learning to live with it.

Humour's value in distancing and counteracting stress is well known from survivor accounts of disaster zones and concentration camps, as well as from those coping with ongoing handicap. Changi survivors, polio sufferers and emergency volunteers have all provided luminous examples of the creation and enjoyment of survival humour;[28] and Australian research has demonstrated the local role of humour as a moderator of stress and trauma.[29] Such studies validate speculation from a literary standpoint about how Australian humour assists 'individuals manipulated by circumstances, or a destiny they are unable to control, [to] wryly resign themselves to their own powerlessness'.[30] In isolated, rural Australia, where people still battle in the settler tradition against a harsh environment, fine examples are to be found that illustrate Watson's observation: 'Defeat is the essence of Australian rural humour. It is nature mocking our intentions'.[31]

Among the most wryly resigned to powerlessness are many Australian Indigenous communities. Elsewhere in this book, Lillian Holt remarks how little focus there has been on the important survival role of humour in Indigenous life. One exception is Ruby Langford Ginibi, who has written of its importance in her life and illustrates a rich tradition with her account of using humour against unwanted visitors to one of her sons, Nobby, ill in hospital after his release from jail:

The police were always checking him out and wouldn't leave him alone. Not believing he was sick, they pushed past me. I didn't say anything till all four of them were in the bedroom, when I said, 'I hope you've all had your shots, he's got contagious hepatitis.' You should've seen those dicks [policemen] fly out of the room, asking where the nearest doctor's surgery was. I fell about laughing and so did Nobby.[32]

Humour as effective retaliation, but also as good therapy for the patient.

Although written records are still sparse, there is a long tradition of such joking being played defensively by the original inhabitants of the land against their dispossessors. Examining the first cultural exchanges between British arrivals and original inhabitants, historian Inga Clendinnen has remarked, 'I think many British doings must have brought rich amusement to the Australians, along with the anxiety and the anger'. Taking the diary of Watkin Tench (1788), she describes how Colbee and Boladeree, guides for Captain Phillip's exploration party, took 'special delight' around the campfire 'in miming the more spectacular British slips and stumbles of the day "with inimitable drollery"'. Today we might see here the first seeds of what has now become a common Australian function of humour as an identifier of newcomers unfamiliar with the terrain, called 'taking the mickey'. Clendinnen tentatively concludes:

> . . . through processes I do not yet understand, we are now more like each other than we are like any other people. We even share something of the same style of humour, which is a subtle but far-reaching affinity. Here, in this place, I think we are all Australians now.[33]

Humour can be dangerous, however. It is not always used gently in taking down another group or individual (especially those, like Phillip's men, experiencing the 'shock of the new'). Much aggressive Australian humour has not been directed (respectably) at *self*, but rather at 'new-chums', that is, new arrivals, wave after wave.[34] That this may be hurtful, even deeply offensive, seems of little social concern. Davies' findings on dirt-jokes show that Australia lacks many restrictive conventions or taboos on joking (until the advent of political correctness, a movement that sparked its own counter-revolution as comedians protested limitations on their work).[35] Even Adams and Newell were surprised by the absence of reader-outrage at the many offensive (and racist) jokes they printed, concluding that Australians 'fear the "other", what we deem to be foreign or alien, and so tell savage, uncivilised jokes about Aborigines, Jews, migrants . . . Jokes that are bigoted, blasphemous or phobic outnumber all other categories'.[36]

The butts of such jokes are comic stereotypes, whether newly created ones or inherited (as from Anglo-Celtic rivalries). Their defining characteristics are usually invoked, in both jokes and colloquial speech, by brief, derogatory labels, such as Abos,[37] Micks (Irish, especially Roman Catholics), Poms (British, especially the BBC-accented ones), Frogs (French and inherited, but renewed in vigour during diplomatic tensions over French Pacific nuclear testing in the 1970s) and, especially, Wogs (an elastic group).[38] Recently, some of these titles and stereotypes have been deliberately re-appropriated by their Australian 'owners' as comic, defiant badges of honour, a phenomenon Roberta Sykes explained as driven by the need to 'jump in first and call ourselves something like "nigger" or "bastard" because it leaves them with nothing to call us'.[39]

Appropriating humour and insult used against oneself and one's group is not new: even in 1905, Freud described how the best, witty Jewish jokes emanated from the Jewish community, choosing itself to subsume the clumsier barbs of others.[40] Although it thus shifts the comic perspective, appropriation is not a fundamental challenge to the permissive nature of joking: rather it reflects the attitude that 'if you can't win, you might as well join them'. However, as retaliation it is certainly effective, as is demonstrated in a personal narrative shared with me about Sydney in the 1970s, when a new teacher, Mr Leong, brought his maths class under control (including several rowdy Italian-Australian wog-boys) by announcing his name, writing 'W O G' in large letters on the blackboard, and spelling it out as 'Wonderful Oriental Gentleman'. Class ensued peacefully. Similarly today, for professional Australian comedians (the successful, self-styled 'ethnic comics' discussed below), appropriation and turning back the joking may represent some cause to celebrate the achievements of an Australia which now embraces many diverse, cultural communities.[41]

In 2000, I was invited to speak about Australian humour at a conference convened in Osaka.[42] Trying to convey to a Japanese audience the nature of this anti-authoritarian and levelling humour, and also grappling later with the complex, restrictive social conventions that conversely surround all uses of humour in Japan,[43] I realised some truths. The most confronting thing about Australian humour for non-Australians is not its obscure, colloquial references (swagmen are not hoboes, billabongs and creeks are different bodies of water, a dunny is not found indoors, and so on), nor even its crudity and offensiveness, but rather its ubiquitous and unavoidable occurrence, regardless of time, place and social space/s. For Australians, using and appreciating (or at least tolerating) humour is not so much permitted as compulsory. This is a culture that deploys humour openly as a weapon to identify those who are truly 'at home', in both the land and the society. In this sense, it is the style and conventions of the 'jok(e)-ing' rather than those of the jokes that indicate 'Australian-ness' – that is, how Australians *use* humour rather than the nature of the humour used.

Collections of Australian jokes and humour routinely assert that embracing such aggressive humour is part and parcel of being Australian. Hunt remarks ironically: 'To live in Australia, Aussies have to have a sense of humour. It's a cheap form of entertainment and helps pass the time'.[44] The Aussie custom of taking the mickey (effectively, baiting others, particularly the obviously 'other', with joking, teasing and insult) enjoys such broad permission that objecting to it is totally ineffective. Hidden rules decree that when the victim either rejects the baiting or 'doesn't get it', by definition the joke has succeeded. The only effective response is to accept, appreciate and reply in kind. Peter Ryan observed, in a *Quadrant* article on tenacious Australian traditions, that taking the mickey is effectively a national civil liberty.[45] Unlike British and many other cultures, Australian culture gives social permission unquestioningly for this comic challenge to be applied not only to friends and colleagues but also to strangers and senior figures. This is true even in seriously hierarchical organisations, like the army or business enterprises. For those hailing from more formal societies, this is quite challenging – intentionally so.

Arriving as a schoolchild in 1950s Australia, I rapidly discovered how to survive having the mickey taken, especially via the customary licence for offensive name-calling (despite being a girl, I was 'a pommie bastard'). To be accepted, we European kids were expected to assimilate these attitudinal standards, and so, in the playground, as on a battlefield, we learned to survive this practical and linguistic joking, and then (cautiously) to use it on others. Later, these experiences were illuminated for me by reading (under the desk, risking detention) a fictional account of such acculturation. Written by the very Australian John O'Grady as 'Nino Culotta', *They're a weird mob* (1957) recounts the mocking treatment meted out by Aussie workmates to Nino, a 'new Australian' migrant-labourer from northern Italy. He arrives in Sydney speaking the Queen's English but unable to understand the Strine responses he receives, so becoming an irresistible mickey-target for his builder's-labourer mates – until he learns the rules. The book is cheerful, sentimental comedy, and a sequel, *Cop this lot* (1960), allows a classic turning of the tables on Nino's tormentors/friends, who accompany him back to Italy only to find themselves in need of his help to survive Italian daily life and language. O'Grady's series illustrates well how mickey-taking operates as an Australian acculturating ritual, ensuring that people (especially new arrivals) do not give themselves airs and graces but rather accommodate themselves to an established set of social norms.

As a former Australian Army officer, Ryan experienced mickey-taking within a formal hierarchy more seriously than among friends and playmates. Significantly, in the case he describes, good intentions compete with malicious incompetence, and victory is won by mischief, not by power and righteousness. He recounts how, on becoming a keen, young officer, he finally gained the longed-for seniority needed to reform a lazy sergeant and his totally unhygienic cookhouse:

On my first day as an orderly officer, and backed by the regimental sergeant-major, I strode on my rounds of inspection into that greasy kitchen. The sergeant-cook (known to the troops as 'Poisoner') was at least twice my size. Bare, hairy arms were folded, and a dead cigarette dangled from his lip . . . 'Now look here, sergeant,' I began sharply, 'you've got too many flies in this kitchen!' 'Izzat so? Well, if you're so f— smart, tell me how many I ought to have!'

In the long run, of course, by nagging insistence and relentless inspections, I won the battle. But the victory was hollow, and ashes in my mouth. The mickey had been taken in the first round, and I knew it. So did 'Poisoner'.[46]

Evidently, the rules of mickey-taking make it possible to baulk authority without risking retribution even in a machine bureaucracy like the army. Most Australians would agree, saying it's their democratic right to challenge in this way their elders, betters, enemies and, of course, their friends. Many popular acts and TV shows, such as *The Chaser's war on everything*,[47] are built on this premise and take delight in pushing the limits.

Despite this, mickey-taking against authority figures does not constitute serious, revolutionary challenge. Rather, in line with Jones and Andrews' observations on Australian humour in general, its licence is a condition imposed on acknowledgement and acceptance of the status quo.[48] Recognition of power and position is qualified by assertion of a common status *at the level of humorous interplay*. Thus, Australian joking is permissive, but operates as a great, levelling assertion of conformity to group norms, addressing the familiar dichotomy of 'us' and 'them' and asserting the power of the 'us'. This is a far cry from conventional views of 'larrikin Aussie rebels' and celebration of the rugged individual. Australian humour seems rather to serve an aggressively normative and socialising function, to break a number of civilised conventions on obscenity and filth, and to underpin the egalitarian but conformist nature of Australian society. It is this combination of functions that is uniquely Australian.

Keith Cameron has observed how national identity can become synonymous with certain activities and customs, whether or not these are unique to a culture (for example, bullfighting for Spain):

> From an individual point of view, national identity seems to be a conscious and often an unconscious identification with a symbol, be it language, political system, gastronomic activity, religion etc, which is within that person's perception common to the small or large community to which he or she belongs. [49]

Having 'a good sense of humour' is something most societies and cultures pride themselves on. It is, however, often hedged about with qualifications ('we laugh at ourselves', or 'we appreciate wit') and restrictive rules. Australians' pride in their permissive use of humour is largely unencumbered: joking of all kinds can be targeted at all social levels and, while witty is good, crude will also pass. Making Australian national identity synonymous with taking the mickey staves off the many would-be censors, both external and internal. Even recent hesitations about cultural sensitivities in the context of religion, diplomacy and terrorism have not much dented Australia's customary broad licence. Politicians of all stripes still accept (with as good a grace as can be mustered) being pilloried in cartoons, comic repartee and hoaxes; and, as we will see, new generations of comedians continue to earn their living without much limitation on text or performance.[50]

Examining European and North American multicultural, multi-ethnic communities, Robert Putnam identified diminished senses of trust, connectedness, and hence common community, which are directly proportionate to the degree of ethnic diversity in a community. These qualities are aspects of social capital that his earlier studies (1993) show to be prerequisite for economic success, making his findings of major concern.[51] Since one such study (2001) showed that ethnic diversity contributes positively to the future of modern nations such as the United States and Canada (and, by extension, Australia), methods of redressing such 'unconnectedness' clearly need special attention. Hence, Putnam's latest work stresses the importance of 'popular culture, education, national symbols, or common experiences (like national service) in building a broader sense of "we" '.[52] His 2006 Skytte Prize lecture made it clear that humour has a role in this.[53] It seems plausible therefore that for many generations in Australia the informal common experience of having the mickey taken (whether gently or otherwise) has provided such an adaptive, unifying experience.

Thus, during the postwar period when successive generations of 'new Australians' from strongly diverse cultural traditions have settled, they and their descendants may well have adopted this kind of joking as a social norm. Apart from anecdotes, this is difficult to document for interpersonal exchange, but the record of public entertainment certainly bears it out. During the 1990s, the first Australian-born generation from non-English-speaking families (who endured worse challenges at school than I did) began to enter the professions and the arts. As John McCallum pointed out, they included notable successes in comedy.[54] As confident young adults, they joked back publicly against the former established majority of the school playground which had mocked them and their 'otherness' to conformity. In doing so, they replicated the tradition, joking not only against their earlier tormentors but also against their own family communities and those succeeding them.

Many of these comic voices emerged from the Melbourne International Comedy Festival.[55] Pioneers include Nick Giannopoulos, Mary Coustas, Simon Palomares, Mark Mitchell, George Kapiniaris, Wendy Harmer, John Barresi, Ernie Dingo, Magda Szubanski, Hung Le, Ian McFadyen, Shaun Micallef, Eric Banadinovich (Eric Bana), Rachel Berger, Akmal Saleh and Anh Do, some of whom have appeared in collaboration, some solo. Their performances range from stand-up comedy to radio and TV, theatre and film. Many developed comic scripts and personae based on their life experiences, which inevitably reflect the tensions of the 'them and us' divides through which they navigated, growing up in Australia. This is as true for Ernie Dingo, with an Indigenous background, as for Rachel Berger (Jewish diaspora), Nick Giannopoulos, Mary Coustas, George Kapiniaris, Simon

Palomares and John Barresi (Greek-Australian) and Hung Le and Anh Do (Vietnamese-Australian). All are recognisably and confidently Australian performers, while never denying their heritage.

The team that became known as 'Wogs out of Work' (WOOW) was the first to enjoy big commercial success. Its leader was Nick Giannopoulos, and its 1989 origins and history have been described by McCallum and Bramwell and Matthews.[56] The Wog label was deliberately adopted and was opposed to 'Skip' (from 'Skippy the Bush Kangaroo', a popular children's TV program), a retaliatory label for Anglo-Celtic Australians.[57] Giannopoulos's comic 'mask' (persona) was a social worker's nightmare, a high-school drop-out on the dole, with leather jacket and slicked-back hair, hanging out in cafes – and more attached to his souped-up Holden Monaro car than to any girlfriend.

The original *Wogs out of work* stage show toured in 1989, with a sequel, *Wog-a-rama*, playing to enthusiastic Melbourne and Sydney audiences. A TV comedy series followed, *Acropolis now!*, set in 'The Acropolis', an inner-city Greek-Australian café, starring Giannopoulos, Mary Coustas as Effie (or 'Iphigenia', teenage rebel with would-be-blonde hair teased out to shock) and George Kapiniaris as Memo ('Agamemnon', frenetic waiter, with a nod to Manuel and *Fawlty Towers*). The 2000 film comedy *The Wog boy* had a commercial success that entered Australian film history. The plot combined melodrama with broad comedy, using stock character types – bad boy turned good, good girl tempted to be bad, and a wild caricature of a power-hungry, sex-crazed female Minister for Unemployment Benefits (disclaiming resemblances to historical Ministers). The pejorative labels Wog and Skip were eagerly anticipated by audiences, as the film shared its jokes out equally to migrant communities and the establishment, culminating in a sentimental reconciliation as the 'bad Wog boy' unselfishly assisted old folks from both communities at a bingo session.[58]

Thereafter the group disbanded. Giannopoulos's career moved into film and TV,[59] but two others, Palomares and Kapiniaris, continued as a comedy duo, 'The Tiboldi Brothers'. The Hysteria Theatre website explains their conscious mission as 'ethnic comedians' to promote cross-cultural understanding in Australia. At the 2006 Melbourne Comedy Festival, Palomares 'skilfully worked the room, showing how laughing at people's differences could unite them, regardless of background'.[60]

Comedian Le Trung Hung ('Hung Le', co-star in *The Wog boy*) escaped Saigon by boat with his family at the age of nine. Mary Coustas described him as 'a lanky, skinny, yobbo, dreadlocked Vietnamese classical violinist who's also a comedian. And shy'.[61] While others in *Wog-a-rama* announced themselves as Wogs or Skips, Le appropriated the label 'Ching-chong', in both script and direct address to the audience when the actors stepped out of their roles. He subsequently articulated the WOOW intentions:

> To emphasise the ugliness of a lot of old migrants towards the new migrants. To show that they were dealing out the same intolerant attitude to new arrivals that they themselves experienced when they first arrived – flexing their superiority muscles and baring their battle scars.

The shows achieved a social phenomenon, as Le reported in his inimitable style:

> People of mostly Southern European descent – or whoever gets to be called 'Wog' – would come to the theatre in packs, and keenly wait to hear the piss being taken[62] out of their nationality . . . the bigger the abuse, the crazier the response. After the show people would complain if their country HADN'T received equal piss-take time . . . No matter what you were, Skip, Wog, Chink, Boong, Spic, Nip, Arab, Shmarab . . . whatever, Nick [Giannopoulos] gave it to ya, straight at the jugular.

Thus:

> When packs of boys in Monaros roared past me in the street yelling abuse, they meant it as a sign of affection and appreciation of the show.

For two years and five hundred shows, 'Hey Ching Chong' meant 'love ya work . . . China!!' Bizzzaaarre.[63]

Although Hung Le's work evolved to create 'a persona less overtly reliant on his racial identity and cultural positioning',[64] in 2001 and 2004 at the Sydney Opera House he joined with Indigenous performer Ningali Lawford to create comedy shows *Black and Tran* and *Black and Tran 2*, seeking to make a comic virtue of combining Asian and Aboriginal experiences.

In view of the ambivalence towards multiculturalism that emerged in Australia, as elsewhere, after 11 September 2001, the standing ovations achieved by a 2002 comedy show called *Habib on parole* were remarkable. Although it featured the eponymous Habib Halal, a comic (Australian-Lebanese) drug dealer from the popular SBS TV series *Pizza*,[65] the role was created by Tahir Bilgiç, who calls himself 'Australia's only Turkish stand-up comedian'. At Sydney's run-down Enmore Theatre, Habib and friends drew a largely Australian-Lebanese and Australian Serbo-Croatian audience, at a time when divided feelings within – and against – the local communities were running high. The Milosevic trial was being conducted in The Hague,[66] attention was focused on threatened Islamicist terrorism, and members of Lebanese communities in Sydney were complaining about a racial backlash as a major court case involving gang rape was being heard.

Nevertheless, the youthful, packed houses enthused in true WOOW tradition about the 'piss-take' accorded their different local communities. An eager show of hands responding to the query 'Anyone here from Campbelltown?' met the rejoinder 'Have you got any shoes on? Well, hey, bro, that's cool!' (Campbelltown possesses low socioeconomic status.) 'Anyone from Marrickville? Try to take a shower once a week, willya?' followed. Joking issues about adaptation to life in Australia included style (video-tour of the mini-palatial Habib family home featuring a ghastly indoor fountain surmounted by a stuffed peacock), tension between adolescents and 'Mum' (rap-dancing male comedian in drag), and ambivalent attitudes to the law (parole-breaker as hero). Reviewing the show, Paul Comrie-Thomson wrote,

'The audience squirmed and groaned', recognising reality with embarrassment as well as laughter.[67] Those with a Serbian background were invited to
mock those with a Croatian background, and vice versa. The show embraced
the Aussie imperatives to 'let others have a go at you' and to 'have a go at
yourself before they do'.

Many of these ethnic comedians have enjoyed commercial success,
whether they stayed with ethnic comedy or not. Bilgiç with Hung Le and
others, toured Australia in 2003 with *Lord of the kebabs*, and hosted a popular, stand-up comedy production *Show us your roots* in 2005. Ethnic comedy
is available in video/DVD, TV, radio and stage formats, and has dedicated
websites.[68] It seems to have evolved some social conventions for taking the
mickey. These may reflect issues of credibility and authenticity, and perhaps
shadows cast by political correctness. In conducting a public 'piss-take' of
one group (whatever the basis, ethnic or otherwise), a prior requirement
seems to be to attack oneself and/or one's own group first, before targeting
others. Many stand-up comedians automatically favour this technique, bas-
ing material first and foremost on their own life-stories, before venturing
further afield.

Australian audiences are also less likely today to believe that comic insight
into the ethnic experience can be rendered vicariously, as John O'Grady
attempted for his fictional Nino in 1957. Even interpretations of ethnic
migrants popular in the 1980s (such as Mark Mitchell's popular impersonation of every suburb's Greek greengrocer, 'Con the Fruiterer', in *The comedy
company*) seem effectively superseded by today's authentic community artists.[69] Perhaps such delineation of territory is natural, given the stand-up
origins of most current-generation comedians: stand-ups are notoriously
possessive about 'their' own material. But contemporary audiences may be
drawn to the authenticity of a comic 'other' voice.[70] These caveats may be
even stronger in the case of Indigenous Australians. Although in 2001 Ernie
Dingo publicly admired Louis Beers, a Townsville Anglo-Australian who
performs black-face as 'King Billy Cokebottle', Beers's act does not enjoy
a national profile, nor is it likely to.[71] Whatever the reason, laughter flows

more easily when the comic baton is firmly held by a genuine 'ethnic' come-dian. The WOOW team and its successors thus possess natural advantages in carrying out resistance to the 'flexing of superiority muscles' and per-forming comic payback.[72]

Besides comedy performances, Australia's generous licence for mickey-taking also underpins rich offerings of newspaper cartoons debunking politicians and others, and, as in the theatre, it refuses social permission for cartoon-victims to feel aggrieved, despite Australia's (in)famously restric-tive defamation laws.[73] Cartoons, novels, joke books and dramatic scripts all distance their aggression with context and stylisation. But in daily life, private jokes and even scatalogical abuse of friends and public figures are also socially protected, even to the extent of sometimes disrupting formal occasions. Taking the mickey can even be a welcome corporate event, as in the hoax-impersonations pioneered by Campbell McComas (deceased) and by Rodney Marks (both highly professional actors commanding substantial fees).[74] The business leaders who hire them regard their acts as valuable educational development, enhancing flexibility of thought and discourag-ing gullibility in belief systems and judgement on the part of managers and employees.

The success of mickey-taking as an acculturating experience is neverthe-less driven by the fact that it is not high-minded but pleasurable (eventually). Far from being an official part of education or citizenship qualifications, mickey-taking simply occurs as an inevitable part of living in Australia. The advantages of such a near-compulsory, socialising experience should not be underrated by a nation seeking to accommodate many disparate groups, with different backgrounds of race, language and religion. Humour and laughter may constitute a two-edged sword, but more often than not they promote the cause of humanity and cultural integration, appealing beyond ethnic divisions to the common Australian-ness of 'taking the piss'. And if comedians and humorists can earn a decent living in the process, then good on them. ·

'This is serious':
From the backblocks to the city

John McLaren

A quintessential example of Australian verbal humour, as it has been defined by Keith Willey in 1984 and the duo of Dorothy Jones and Barry Andrews in 1988, is the final line of Lawson's 1899 story 'The Loaded Dog': 'El-lo Da-a-a-ve! How's the fishin' getting on, Da-a-a-ve?' The epitome of visual humour is Stan Cross's 1933 *Smith's Weekly* cartoon, 'For gorsake, stop laughing: this is serious!'. Neither is particularly characteristic of the author's work, but both have shown a capacity to move out of their immediate context to stand for a moment in Australian life that, in seeming to resolve the competing pressures of their time, becomes of universal significance. Yet they raise a number of questions: What view of Australia do they stand for? How does this view change between the two dates of publication? Are they in any case distinctively Australian?

The last question is problematic and possibly unanswerable, so it is worth pondering it first. Both jokes depend on a potential tragedy that becomes farce and is turned to humour through verbal wit. This goes back in the English language at least as far as Chaucer's lovelorn clerk kissing his lady's arse, or to Shakespeare's Titania making love to an ass. If we reject love as being delusory rather than tragic, then we have the clear case of that 'tun of man', Falstaff, whether being cruelly dismissed by Hal as a mere 'trunk of humours' or himself dismissing the role of honour in battle with the remark that 'if honour pricks me on . . . how if honour pricks me off when I come on'. But these are narrative jokes that do not have an impact outside the highly mannered context of their telling. More to the point, perhaps, is Dickens' eternal optimist, Mr Micawber, always waiting for 'something to turn up'. But English humour, even in Shakespeare and Dickens, depends on class, the upper class condescending towards those who vainly try to join its ranks, or the middle class laughing at the unworldly ways of their betters. The true parallels to Henry Lawson and Stan Cross will be found in other settler societies, where the humour is, as AD Hope remarked of Steele Rudd's *On our selection*, like reports from the trenches of World War I, 'comic relief from a life that was usually bitterly hard and often heart-breaking'.[1] This is the source of the knockabout humour in Brett Hart or Mark Twain – although not of Twain's ironic satire. We find it in Australia in the stories in Steele Rudd's *On our selection*, or in Banjo Paterson's tall tales of the battling Saltbush Bill, and his successors in the bush yarns of Alan Marshall or Dal Stivens. Lennie Lower brings the tradition into the city. One common element is the overturning of pomposity, whether of love, valour or class. A second is the defeat of circumstance by embracing it. The English master of wit and absurdity, Frank Muir, remarks that, compared with American humour, this humour is 'kinder to women, and unashamed in its appreciation of the value of "mateship"'. He claims that it lacks both the cruelty and the political edge of the Americans: 'all ordinary Australians were so implacably against authority in the shape of Australia's politicians and police that there was hardly any mileage left in writing about it'.[2] The absence of politics did not, of course, extend to black-and-white humour.

Ken Stewart, in an essay characteristic of his scholarship, humour and appreciation of the distinctively Australian, celebrates Lawson's achievement in 'The Loaded Dog'. Stewart identifies the story's 'central and formative position in Australian popular literary culture', as the dog 'grins and slobbers and wags his tail with the ineradicable certainty of a figure in a nursery rhyme'.[3] Lawson's fiction itself provides the context that gives the story its meaning, as, without his characteristic sombreness, it displays his affection for his gregarious bush workers in the face of the general hardness of their lives. Stewart shows how Lawson's typical response to this hardness, a resigned 'Ah well . . .', although lacking the intellectual complexity of Furphy's 'Such is life', signals not acceptance but a way of coping. The 'Loaded Dog' takes this weight from the narrator and invests it instead in the dog itself, a symbol of mateship who, 'because he is ideal, is allowed only to be a dog'. The story's style, he points out, anticipates the animated cartoon with its series of ritualised poses, attitudes and incidents, culminating in the 'big bang' of its climax, narrated with a comedian's sense of timing. Its protracted and understated ending insinuates the way we are to remember the incident – as a 'happy bush incident in which the harshness of things is overcome and destroyed'.[4]

Lawson's story represents one of the commonest narrative patterns – a plan for easy gain is thwarted by the contrariness of events, only for balance to be restored by fortunate accident. This is the plot of Jack and the beanstalk, with the giant acting to thwart Jack's intentions and Jack's fleetness of foot serving to restore balance, albeit that Jack retains his unearned profits. It is vastly different from the humour of Paterson's 'Saltbush Bill' ballads, which celebrate the battler's use of skill and cunning to defeat those complacent about their own abilities or standing. In a yarn like 'The ironbark chip', Dave Regan does use his bush cunning to outwit the landowner. This is a favourite theme of bush humour in ballads, yarns and cartoons, but 'The Loaded Dog' goes further. Like the stories behind 'The drover's wife' or 'Water them geraniums', it has (as John Barnes and Brian Matthews have suggested) the marks of a story that becomes folklore as it is passed down within a family or by mates in the pub.[5] But in 'The Loaded Dog' the wealth he seeks is no more than a few fish. His intentions are thwarted by a silly dog, 'a big, foolish, four-footed mate', and balance is restored by a mean and ugly dog, 'a sneaking, fighting, thieving canine', that in an act of restorative justice blows itself up and so removes the danger from the rest of the community. The remark at the end takes this fleeting episode and makes it co-extensive with Dave's whole life, conferring on him the unalterable characterisation of the man whose modest ambition will never be either fulfilled or subdued. He becomes the eternal bushman, asking little but insisting on his right to ask, just as his mates insist on their right to laugh at his attempt even as they endorse its value. Their world is reduced and enlarged to the worthy pursuit of fishing. This is what their pursuit of independence, through gold-seeking or fencing or stockriding, has come down to.

Lawson apparently wrote his story in Australia, but it was published by William Blackwood & Sons in London in 1901.[6] English humour at this time was dominated by the London *Punch*, with elaborate satire of parliament, caricatures of eminences from the law and politics, whimsical accounts of society, mock music-hall dramas and carefully drawn joke cartoons about the absurdities of sport – 'le kick-ball' – or city gents and girls. A sad rhyme sympathised with the miners for their poor conditions but condemned them for taking strike action to remedy the conditions. One cartoon boasted of the superiority in engineering of the Forth Bridge compared with the Eiffel Tower. Another showed the imperial eagle swooping on blacks who are vainly protesting amid their palm trees and grass huts. In 1890 it published six cartoon panels portraying the comedy that occurs when 'A colonial friend pays me a visit'. The panels show a stereotyped bush horseman startling the other huntsmen with his bush garb of beard, broad-brimmed hat and leggings. In covert, his 'method of amusing himself was unusual' (he fired off a gun) and his riding-style was 'a trifle reckless' (he caused others to fall and rounded up the domestic cattle with his stockwhip). But, the commentary assures us, 'all this wouldn't have mattered as much, if he hadn't galloped through the hounds – And murdered the fox with his infernal whip'. The tone is not malicious and is even affectionate, but it is condescending. The colonists are all right, it implies, if only they would stay in their place and not offend English practices, which by implication are the sole standard for judging right conduct.[7]

The Australian cartoons of the time have the same characters as Lawson's stories – the bushmen, prospectors, the women washing clothes, the publican and his wife – but the source of their humour is different. Earlier Australian black-and-white humour in, say, the Melbourne *Punch* depended on the incongruities of colonial life. Its particular targets were the new chum, the Chinese and the Aborigines, and their failures to accommodate the language and reality of settler society. Alongside this is class humour, where the swaggie uses his wax matches to turn the tables on the squatter, or the larrikin's pretensions betray his ignorance. These themes continue in the *Bulletin*, which is probably more racist than the London *Punch*, but its sympathies are clearly with the worker and with resistance to authority and respectability. The priest, the parson and the preacher remain objects of derision in the *Bulletin*, where artists like Livingston Hopkins caricature alike their piety and their distance from reality, although occasionally giving them the last word at the expense of the Irish, as in this 1890 contribution:

'Is it going ye are, yer riverince? Sure an' ye haven't seen my last baby.'
Father Cassidy: 'No, Mrs Maloney; an' I niver expect to.'

Such artists as Frank Mahony and Ambrose Dyson give variations on the Saltbush Bill theme in cartoons that show the irreverent bushman putting the squatter in his place by threatening to burn his paddocks or making him responsible for their supplies, as in the following joke printed in 1900. To the boundary-rider's query about missing stock, Mahony's swaggie replies: 'No; only wish I did. Haven't had a bit of mutton these four weeks.' This is comedy of stereotype and situation, of realities in conflict. Some contributors, like DH (David Henry) Souter, drew cartoons that could have appeared in the London *Punch*: the society girl confides to her companion, 'He said my beauty intoxicated him', only to receive the reply, 'My dear, some men get quite tipsy on one small whisky'.[8] More, however, keep to those on the margins of Australian society – drunkards, publicans, swaggies, larrikins. Yet, although the cartoonists are incisive and appreciative observers, they view their subject matter from outside.

In contrast, Lawson writes as a participant who, however much he may embellish, recalls the events he describes. His comedy goes beyond slapstick to character. Although the element of slapstick was to become the staple of writers like Steele Rudd (Arthur H Davis), who use the same narrative structure of high expectations constantly undermined by fortune, Rudd also, in his best work, shows an appreciation of characters under stress. Rudd's first story appeared in the *Bulletin* in 1898, the year before Lawson composed 'The Loaded Dog'. Like Lawson, he writes from family memories and as a participant, as signalled by both the first-person narrative and the identity between the writer's nom de plume and the name of his fictional family. If the family finds a way to plant the wheat, the seed is destroyed by drought or the crop is blasted by heat or the market fails when the harvest is sold. Typically, the characters react with comic retreat. We understand these responses from within, because the narrator has shared the hopes that have been destroyed. The moral centre of this world is endurance. Dan leaves home in a fury at Dad's rejection, only to return with a cheque that keeps the family going. Dad erupts in fury or drinks in despair, but he always turns back to the work. This is a different world from Lawson's deserted and despairing wives and travelling men. Some of its settlers will survive against all the odds. Although they help each other in need, they also charge good rates, in cash or kind, for their assistance. Their ethos is one of individual achievement rather than of mateship and, unlike Lawson's desperate selectors, they eventually succeed. They represent the change of the Australian image from bushmen to pioneer to farmer that Richard White first identified in *Inventing Australia*.[9] Dad eventually goes into parliament, and his adventures became softened into a radio serial, a country soap-opera that lacked the original knockabout comedy. We cannot imagine either fate for Dave Regan.

Although Rudd gives little physical description of his characters, this was supplied by his illustrators, who drew on the visual traditions established in the *Bulletin*. Leigh Astbury shows how this tradition derives from the commercial photographers and newspaper illustrators who, in the later part of the nineteenth century, produced bush images for an urban public.[10] The familiarity of these images facilitated the shift of Rudd's characters from the page to general folklore. Hope argues that this transition was facilitated by the illustrators, who included Frank Mahony, Percy, Norman and Lionel Lindsay, and George Lambert. He further likens Rudd's art to the comic strip, including among its successors 'Wally and the Major', created by Stan Cross, artist of 'Stop laughing . . .'

Just as the selectors of Lawson's youth were driven from the bush by the depression of the 1890s and became his enthusiastic readers in the city, so the bushmen of his fiction migrate to the city and become the desperate poor of Elderman's Lane or the unlovely larrikins of 'The captain of the Push'. These characters find their chronicler in Louis Stone's *Jonah* (1911), but although there is high comedy in his description of Mrs Yabsley's party, it does nothing more than lighten for a moment the dark world of destruction that engulfs Jonah and his bride. This was a world rarely entered by the artists, although from the 1890s they found the larrikins a rich source of comedy. Tom Durkin's cartoon 'In "Push" society', for example, shows slab-faced gents in elaborate garb pushing equally poshed-up girls around a dance-floor. The caption reads:

CHOPPER MARKS [addressing the assembly at the 'Rocks' dance-room]: 'Ay! They's going to be a benefit for Jago – ye all know Jago –'im as is just done 'arf a annual for surgery on his bride. Blokes a deener, girls a nod.'

The same combination of sexism and violence appears in Alf Vincent's *Bulletin* cartoon 'Premature stoush', where Eileen admits that Bill had stoushed her. 'Gawd, the cur!' Mrs Muldurney replies, 'He mighter waited till he married yer.' Whereas the Chopper Marks cartoon distances the reader by portraying the larrikins as almost subhuman, certainly beyond sympathy, Vincent's drawing (of kids scrabbling for jam, the girl in genuine distress, and sympathy marking the haggard woman who questions her) contradicts the comedy of the words.[11]

The digger humour of World War I brings together the larrikin and the bushman. A literary link is proved through CJ Dennis, whose *Songs of a sentimental bloke* appeared in 1915. In this the larrikin turns from thug into a gentler figure who, while he still enjoys stoushing cops, is ready to allow a woman's hand and the sentiments of love to lead him to a more respectable life. In the following year, in *The moods of Ginger Mick*, he took the Bloke's mate off to war. Otherwise, however, writers like Lawson, Brennan and Paterson preferred the heroic or elegiac modes, or fell into polemic, and little comic writing emerged. There is digger humour in works published later by writers who actually served, like Leonard Mann or Frederic Manning, but it appears only in sardonic scraps of dialogue that reinforce the futility of the whole enterprise. Typical is the remark, in Manning's *Her privates, we* (1930), of a soldier watching his comrades, exhausted in battle, pretending to a smart military dismissal: 'They can say what they like', he said appreciatively, 'but we're a bloody fine mob'.[12] This sardonic humour, inherited from the contributors to the *Bulletin* and its contemporaries, provided a rich vein for the cartoonists, although few achieved the same savagery.

Stan Cross's cartoon, published in *Smith's Weekly* in 1933, is even more emblematic – a moment, not an episode. Yet the moment implies an episode and a whole history.[13] The artist achieves this not in words but through his drawing, which endows his two workmen with both individual character and the stereotype of the ordinary Australian that goes back to the lanky bushmen of Lawson, through the diggers of World War I and forward to Wally and the Major and Bluey and Curly in World War II. *Smith's Weekly* played a significant part in this transition.

The conscription debates that had split the Labor Party and exacerbated sectarian divisions in society at large had led to the *Bulletin* shifting its loyalties from the workingman and the unions to the settled society of the suburbanites and the small farmers. By 1933 it had changed its motto from 'Australia for the Australians' to 'Australia for the white man', and an editorial comment in that year, signed 'Tacitus', was full of praise for Hitler who had recently become German Chancellor. He is described as an 'Honest, straight-forward, clean-living man, fervent patriot, great organiser, a man of vision' and is praised for his 'relentless' fight against Communism. His plans for the Jews are not mentioned. Norman Lindsay, who was able to cloak his conservatism beneath his anti-wowserism, was less enthusiastic, drawing a cartoon that shows distrust alike for Hitler and the New Guard's Eric Campbell. The paper was uncertain whether to support or oppose Japan's invasion of Manchuria, believing that, although Japan was a 'useful' ally to the British Empire, both China and Japan were equally 'good parasites' and 'poor colonists'. Its cartoonists poked fun at middle-class respectability, drunks, flappers and Jews, and a Percy Leason kept alive the image of Dad and Dave. It serialised Henrietta-Drake Brockman's novel *Men among pearls*, set in Broome, in which romance is complicated by business troubles.[14]

Smith's Weekly, established in 1919 in the aftermath of the war, was in a similar populist mode to the early *Bulletin*. It carried more news than the *Bulletin*, and its stories were exotic or gruesome histories or romantic fictions. In 1930 its lead story declared that the federal Labor member for Hunter, Roland James, was unfit to remain in parliament because early in the century he had been convicted of a string of minor offences and was now fomenting revolt among striking miners. The headline, 'Old Time Enemy of Law and Order Incites Miners to Violence', gives no indication of the fact that all his offences, except one of drunk and disorderly, were of the kind that could well be associated with strikes and picket lines – resisting arrest and using offensive language. Yet the inflammatory nature of this story is offset by the Stan Cross comic strip, 'Smith's vaudevillians', printed immediately below it. This shows a drunk rejecting the kind words of a respectable busybody with the observation that they are 'like water to a drowning man'. This tone, mocking authority, respectability and the wowser, dominates the paper. It is embodied in the figure of the digger that appears in its weekly feature 'The unofficial history of the AIF', and links it back to the writers and artists in the earlier *Bulletin*.

By 1933 Australia was struggling with the Great Depression. Joseph

Scullin's federal Labor government had split and had been replaced by a conservative administration under Joseph Lyons, while the New South Wales Labor premier, Jack Lang, had been dismissed by the Governor. The British banks were in control and in 1931 the ranks of the unemployed had grown to 30 per cent of the workforce. *Smith's Weekly* attacked Jack Lang and his communist associate Jock Garden, but it also attacked the British banks and poured scorn on Lyons and his predecessors, John Latham and Stanley Bruce. But the staple of its news was not so much politics as gossip and scandal. During the 1930s Kenneth Slessor began publishing his light satirical pieces, first in prose, then in verse. He mocks all pretension when he gives his recipe for converting cream into 'an indestructible, non-corrosive and everlasting hunk of rubber', which in one case has been so effective that his friend 'got a Royal Commission out of it'. While this may be anti-authoritarian rather than distinctively Australian, like most of the cartoons, it demonstrates the urbane cynicism of a sophistication that might be found anywhere. There is more Australian content in the tales of romance and horror that the paper also published, but these use fact and fiction purely to entertain with the frisson of the exotic.[15]

This is the milieu that Stan Cross, a committed socialist, helped to construct with his regular contributions. His characters included the accepted types of the bush family, with the bearded father, the lanky son, the over-worked mother and the cheeky nippers, as well as city slickers and down-and-outs. Into this standard fare he interpolated his famous 'Stop laughing . . .' cartoon. Its drawing and the humour are in keeping with the rest of his work, and the paper as a whole, but they also stand apart. The only stereotype they recall is the one given by Joynton Smith in his weekly column 'Why I publish *Smith's Weekly*', where he wrote that it celebrates the 'miraculous energy' shown by Australians in their adversity. The energy in Cross's cartoon comes from the humour with which the workmen greet their disaster. As Lindesay comments, the cartoon contains 'an assault on dignity' and 'there is no situation more undignified than to be caught with your pants down'.[16] This particular indignity separates it from the London *Punch* 'collapse of stout party' joke, offering rather a characteristically Australian attitude to the general absurdity of life.

This is not the kind of trench humour that AD Hope writes of, for there is no sense in which the audience can identify with the situation. Rather, the cartoon takes the common lot of adversity to an extreme from which there can be no recovery, and therefore no future memory, and has its victims return the laughter of the gods. But if the readers cannot identify with the situation, they can identify with the men caught in it – men who are recognisable descendants of Dan or Dave Rudd, the diggers and, ultimately, Lawson's lanky bushman Dave Regan. The drawing makes it clear that they have migrated from the bush into that maelstrom of urbanism, building construction, and have brought with them not just the determination of the Rudds but also the fatalism of the trenches. Because the situation of the cartoon is outside the experience of most readers, they must infer the story it implies, of how the builders got themselves into their predicament. They could be unemployed and forced to take a job outside their capacity, or experienced men led astray by a moment's inattention or, more likely, by incompetent management of the work-site. They are workers, not larrikins, but they would find Joynton Smith's praise of their type ludicrous: they refuse to accept even the authority of circumstance and laugh at the fate that cannot defeat them. This laugh is also at the expense of the reader, for we can never be sure what the man clinging to the trousers finds funny, or what his sledge hammer will strike. It may well be us, for unlike the readers of Lawson or Rudd we remain outside the comedy, implicated in it only by potential. Read in this way, Cross's joke lends support to John Marsden's argument that Australian humour is based on an arrogance directed at the ignorant outsider.[17]

While this may apply to some cases, particularly the cartoons directed at Aborigines, new chums in the bush and the ignorant bushwhacker in town, it is not the dominant characteristic. In most cases, the intended reader could easily be in the situation of the swaggie, the selector, the digger or the housemaid. Even more recent examples, like *Kath and Kim* or (aptly) *The Memphis trousers half hour*, depend on this recognition. We may like to think we are superior to Kath and her family, but we know that we are all victims of the same society of consumption and celebrity. We just watch the ABC and use our markers differently, but our distinction is precarious. Meanwhile, *The Memphis trousers half hour* recalls the famous episode where the great and aloof lost his strides and so brought himself down to our common level, thereby starting a rise in his popular standing that continues to this day.[18]

Cross explained that the idea for the situation of his scaffolders had come from a drawing submitted to *Smith's* by a student, but the humour was his own. He said the cartoon had left readers with such a 'sense of disquiet in the reality of the inevitable disaster that they wanted a happier ending'. He obliged by drawing a sequel that depicted a rescue. The man with the trousers is now almost naked, but he still holds on to his hat, to preserve his dignity and perhaps to emphasise the phallic ambiguity of the original. The joke line reads: ' "Cripes, that was a narrow squeak." "Yairs – we were lucky to get out of it" '. This may satisfactorily conclude the episode, although despite the rescuers at hand the situation remains precarious. Cross recalls that the second cartoon got the louder laugh at a lecture by a psychiatrist on the medical value of humour, but this may have reflected the release of the audience from their anxiety.[19] The sequel, however, lacks the proverbial force of the earlier remark which links it back to Lawson and an Australian folk tradition. Another phrase from this tradition, the idea of a 'fair go', suggests exactly what none of these characters either receives or expects from life. The hammer is always falling and there is nothing we can do about it except laugh.

Of the names of horses

Peter Pierce

In the Introduction to *From go to whoa: A compendium of the Australian turf* (1994) – a book that in its turn introduced me to provisional tax – I wrote this:

> Thoroughbred racing, whether in Australia or in many other countries, offers drama without parallel. Rich in legend and superstition; replete with transitory triumphs and intense disappointments, it is an activity – a sport, an industry, an obsession – whose participants plumb depths of meanness and perfidy, but also reach heights of courage and grandeur. No other business offers such scope for idiosyncrasy, or for the cruel play of luck on the best-laid plans. No other forgets less and forgives more, so thrives on extreme reversals of fortune, and better mirrors the society in which it is enmeshed.[1]

What do the names that have been bestowed on horses in Australia for nearly two centuries have to tell us about that society at various periods in its history?

Another way of asking this is to inquire into the relation of Australian racing, and the names of its horses, to supposed elements in the national character – not only the self-congratulatory sardonic sense of humour but something that is perhaps more intrinsic. This is a deep nihilism that speaks its name in action rather than words. Its obverse, or perhaps its complement, is sentimentality. The sharper focus of these reflections concerns the naming of horses, the whimsy and the historical contexts that this reflects, the apparently less than casual linkage between signified and signifier. Trying to see what might be in a name will expose some of the history of Australian horseracing and the society within which it has flourished.

Let me begin with the call of the card for the first two races on the Brisbane Cup program at Eagle Farm on 13 June 2005.

And let me add this caution: some levity follows, even though I am aware
of the simile 'solemn as a sports historian'. The first race was the Club Conrad Handicap. The naming of races is a sideline that might also have been
followed, not least because of the way that it dissolves the identity of 'time-
honoured events' for the sake of brand names that change in their turn,
making a historian's tracking of the names of the same races at different
times an irksome one. That is not to mention how risible it is to find a
Group Two event called Harrolds 101 (a shop and its address in Collins
Street, Melbourne) or a Group Three called the Dodo Sprint. But back
to the Club Conrad Handicap. The names of the horses that lined up in
it had an ecumenical feel. Going to the stalls were Abdullah, Poetic Papal
and World Peace. Then came Goodfella and Katabatic, the first saluting a
long-lost Mafia don perhaps, the latter named for a violent Antarctic wind.
More secular in spirit was number six, Unite and Prosper. As it happened,
this was the horse that won, beating Poetic Papal, although that went on to
win a much harder race at 80/1 the following week.

Race Two brought us Hello Possums, thanks to Barry Humphries, Bos-
worth Field, in melancholy remembrance of Richard III's last stand where
he wanted a horse, and – an atrocious pun – Ears to Victory. At least that
horse missed a start, remaining one of the emergencies. I want to begin
my general remarks with horses from each of these races. First, number
two in the Cafe 21 Handicap: Dead Cat Bounce. My category this time is
politically incorrect horses' names. Now, Dead Cat Bounce refers to what
happens when a cat is dropped from a sufficient elevation. Metaphorically,
it indicates a deceptive and temporary rise in a faltering stock market. Not
to a crazed animal activist, however, who objected not only to the registra-
tion of this name but to another – Kill the Cat. Indifferent to where names
may come from for horses, he or she evidently did not know that Tale of
the Cat (presumably an inoffensive name) was the sire in question for each
horse. To a fanatic, one supposes, the disconnection between signifier and
signified in horses' names does not matter.

Back to Race One. Abdullah might be the name of an Afghan camel driver out Broken Hill way in the nineteenth century. Now it sounds vaguely Muslim. Seemingly this name was not so offensive to the ears of the faithful as the Colin Hayes-trained Mohammed back in the 1970s. Objections eventually led to its being renamed, presumably on the principle that one would not want to hear a race caller coping with Jesus Christ losing ground in a maiden at Traralgon. More on a horse called The Wandering Jew shortly.

The Eagle Farm races suggest a couple of other trails in this tale of names. Lord Rupert went around in Race Two, reminding us of a vanishing fashion whereby the titles of royalty dignified the participants in the Sport of Kings. We can list Sir Dane, Sir Blink, Lord Dudley, Princess Eulogy, Princess Talaria, Poetic Prince (this was a New Zealand topliner that had to race in Australia with 'Our' in front of its name because there was a local nonentity that was already called Poetic Prince). That is to mention only some of those who have gone around in Australia since World War II. But when we find Lord Rupert – or, more egregiously, Sir Breakfast or Sir Les – we are likely to suspect parody, or republicanism.

The next category is signalled by Grand Filante (which might also feature under such a heading as 'names that mean nothing'). The mangling of languages other than English has a long and inglorious history in the naming of racehorses in Australia. In the winter jumping season of 2005 in Melbourne, Le Thief met Le Colonel. Now if the second is French, more or less, and by accident or design, the first could hardly even be dignified as macaronic. Indeed, that name is the more odious because the sire of the great and beautifully named Melbourne Cup-winning mare Light Fingers was actually called 'the thief' in French. This was Le Filou. He also sired the drolly named The Dip (see later for horses with names that begin with the definite article). And what of the five times Group One-winning horse that campaigned stoutly in 2004, Grand Armee? There was no article and no agreement between noun and adjective. Maybe that is why the horse was doomed to fall just below the very top line of performers in the last decade.

Now we move to a contentious category. It may be the case that, for the owners of the horse, there never can be a bad name. After all, the champion staying mare Makybe Diva took its name from the first two letters of the Christian names of five of the owners' female staff. On the other hand, can a horse with a bad name win a good race? Think, first and by contrast, of the resoundingly named champions of the Australian turf – Archer, Carbine, Let's Elope, Phar Lap, Tranquil Star, Vain. But then think again. What of Big Philou, whose name means nothing and which won the 1969 Caulfield Cup – but on protest – or of Beldale Ball, trained by Colin Hayes and owned by Robert Sangster, but the worst Melbourne Cup winner of the 1980s. And then there are the Asian champions of recent years – Fairy King Prawn from Hong Kong and Bubblegum Fella from Japan. Their names suggest a disdain for all those who might be stressed by the sonority of the names of horses.

It is time now to turn to some technical matters. Sometimes the element of whim or bad taste is reined in, as it were. Trotters and pacers in France, so far as I have seen in a couple of visits to Vincennes (the track, not the chateau), are all allocated an initial letter for the year of their birth. Thus they must race as A, or H, or whatever. This is another inscrutable manoeuvre from within the world of the 'red hots' whose peculiarities in France outdo our own. Thus I got odds of 14/1 on a pacer called Abbon which was a well-beaten third at Vincennes only to be happily elevated to first because the first and second horses had galloped at some stage during the race and were disqualified.

In Australia the names of horses can be used again after seventeen years have passed since the horse ceased to race. Thus we have had second editions of Snub and Iga Ninja (the latter a speedy rogue that won an Oakleigh Plate in the 1960s). There have been two thoroughbreds in Australia named Abstainer – the first by Tippler, the second by Noalcoholic. The names of classic winners and the winners of other nominated races are protected from being bestowed again. However, in 2005 one temporarily got through. In 1976 Colin Hayes trained the Victoria Derby winner Unaware. The New

Zealand-bred horse that had initially been given that name a year or so before will race in this country, cheekily, as We're Unaware.

Some horses' names seem to predestine their fate, but let me detour for a moment. When, back in the late 1970s in Sydney, a jockey and three owners were rubbed out for pulling a horse, one of the owners, a Mr Calvin, declared that 'we are three innocent men and a boy'. A colleague of mine reflected of Mr Calvin how 'that would teach him to think that predestination had any place in a game of chance'. But what of Vain, who had every right to be? Or of Classic Mission? The latter – from New Zealand – gave George Moore his last big race win, in the 1971 Victoria Derby, for all the controversy that raged about whether, upon close inspection of his teeth, the horse was in fact a four-year-old. Some names are redundant, but we forgive that redundancy for the calypso lilt in the name of the champion Kingston Town. Other names are accidental. Century, the first horse to win three Group One sprints down the Straight Six at Flemington, was allegedly named after the first ninety-nine names suggested for him had been rejected. And some horses simply have unpropitious names. In June 2005 a lightning bolt killed a horse in a paddock in New Zealand who had tempted such a fate by being called Rainhailorshine.

There are horses' names that have passed into the Australian vernacular. And, sadly perhaps, passed from it, as is the case with Barry Humphries' majestic simile for drunkenness, 'full as two race trains'. But consider these: 'a heart as big as Phar Lap's'; he 'jumped that like Mosstrooper'; or he 'finished like Bernborough'. Sometimes the usage is not an honorific. Drongo was the most famous non-winner in Australian turf history, even after thirty-seven starts which included a second in the Victoria Derby of 1923 to the elegantly named Frances Tressady. Now a drongo is a mug, or rather used to be, for drongo is another of those words that are slipping out of the vernacular.

Horses acquire nicknames as well as names. There was 'Old Jack' for Carbine, the greatest Australian racehorse of the nineteenth century and the sire and grandsire of English Derby winners; there was 'The Red Terror' for Phar Lap, although this is a sobriquet that has not lasted; and there was 'Irky', because he was so ill-favoured at birth, for the brilliant front-runner Vo Rogue. What did his actual name mean? 'The Goondiwindi Grey', Gunsynd, was also honoured in popular song, warbled by the Sydney race-caller Johnny Tapp: 'They cheer him from the grandstand / They cheer him from the flat / They cheer a little beauty / A real aristocrat'.

Some horses' names have been, or appeared to be, lubricious. There was a hurdler in the 1970s called Tsipura, until someone went to the trouble of spelling its name backwards. Do authorities sometimes connive in letting such names through the vetting agency, or are their educations deficient? Dr Geoff Chapman's two-year-old Merkin was good enough to win a Silver Slipper in Sydney in the 1970s and campaigned for a while longer before sufficient of the righteous deemed that the name for a pubic wig did not fit a thoroughbred.

Thriving on superstition as it does, racing lore informs us that horses cannot win with 'The' in their names. Yet The Wandering Jew raced on to victory, without protest, in the Queensland Derby of 1892. A century later, The Phantom and The Phantom Chance performed stoutly, but the profusion of names so formed is long gone. It was in 1887 that the equine representative of the bunyip aristocracy, The Australian Peer, won the Victoria Derby. Melbourne Cup winners have included The Barb (1866), The Pearl (1871), The Quack (1872), The Assyrian (1882), The Grafter (1898), The Victory (1902), The Parisian (1911) and The Trump (1937), most recent of all of them.

The Night Patrol was named with the Great War in mind, as was the Melbourne Cup winner of 1919, Artilleryman. A radio journalist mused that the winner of four consecutive country cups in the 1940s, of whom he had read in *Miller's Guide*, must have been a good horse, until it was pointed out to him that 'Abandoned War' referred to the suspension of the race, and not to a horse. The names of horses have something to say of the social history of the eras in which they raced. Warworn won the Goodwood Handicap in Adelaide in 1944. Prophetically, on the eve of a depression,

The Crash won the Western Australian Derby in 1891. Admittedly this was a race in which it was the only starter. England's Dust saluted in the 1958 renewal of this event, perhaps as a portent to England's dismal Ashes tour of 1958–59. Some names are simply incongruous. Hobart won the Launceston Cup of 1885. Others are meant in jest, especially as plays on the names of a sire and dam. Thus we have Gallops and Stays (by Fast Boy out of Corset Girl), Shotgun Wedding (by Double Bore out of Bridal Stream), The Stutterer (by Talking out of K-K-Katy) and Who-am-I, by an unidentified sire out of an unidentified dam.

What do these examples tell us about the connections, if any, of the names bestowed on Australian racehorses during the last two centuries, and of the society that evolved in that time? These are some provisional responses. That dignified names have dwindled. That whimsy has been indulged, often at the expense of good taste (if that is part of a game of chance). That sire lines have dictated many names, but not to much poetic effect when a Danehill begets a Danewin. That the names of great horses in modern Europe are not necessarily grander than ours, more meaningful, or euphonious. Think of Falbrav, Rakhti, Bago. I saw the latter win its maiden at Longchamp in 2003 and predicted that it would prove a Group winner, despite its name. Indeed it has won at Group One level at two, three and four, including the 2004 Prix de l'Arc de Triomphe back at Longchamp.

On with the names: England might recently have had a Rock of Gibraltar and a Horatio Nelson (by Danehill) in more senses than one, but Australia has had a Fastnet Rock that failed to train on in England. Some names that seem to have been chosen at random resonate – as Johannesburg does, but Dubbo would not. Briseis (Achilles's slave girl in Homer's *Iliad*) won the Melbourne Cup as a three-year-old filly in 1876, but mythology as a source of names in Australian racing has now nearly faded away, not only because of a lack of classical education among our race-callers. The beautifully named filly Mnemosyne won its first start as a two-year-old by six lengths, but was then reduced for public consumption to Nem-o-sin.

In a country where nihilists fortunately still outnumber evangelicals, the very randomness of horses' names seems right. On the other hand, so does the unabashed sentimentality that greets great horses, whatever they are called. That points me at last to maybe the most significant thing about the names of horses. They constitute a communal memory of a precious kind – a bond between members of various generations who might remember a Tulloch, as I barely can, or a Tobin Bronze or a Vain, as I certainly can, and indelibly in my own recollection through the calls of Bert Bryant. Great races are cultural highlights in the nation's history, almost irrespective of which horse one backed: Octagonal and Mahogany in the Cox Plate, Vain and Daylight in the Craven A Stakes (or whatever it is called now – then at least and clearly the sponsor was the turf world's fag of choice), Crisp in the two Hiskens Steeples that he won and in the English Grand National where he gave Red Rum twenty-three pounds and just lost. Red Rum, by the way, is 'murder' spelled backwards.

Retailing these examples among scores suggests a more personal example of the context of the names of horses. Two more stand out for me, talking through my kick for a moment, Social Upstart at 100/1 in a mid-week at Randwick in 1977, and Oxford Prince at tote odds of 174/1 at Randwick again in 1994. Their names are among the signal signposts in one's own life story, cherished punctuation marks in the storehouse of one's recollections. The randomness and the whimsy of the names of horses dissolve as we appropriate them autobiographically; make them a well-loved part of our own past, as much, and besides, that of the nation.

Risus sardonicus

Fran De Groen

Chapter 8 of *The survival factor* (1989), by ex-POW medico Dr Rowley Richards with journalist Marcia McEwan, recounts the sufferings of 'Anderson' and 'Williams' Forces on the Burma–Thai Railway during outbreaks of smallpox and cholera. Titled '*Risus sardonicus*', it takes as its theme the 'scornful smile' deriving from the Latin *sardonius*, a fabled Sardinian herb which, if eaten, produced facial convulsions resembling horrible laughter. According to Richards, this unsettling grimace contorted the visages of prisoners dying of 'dry' cholera.[1] He noted the same smirking snarl on the lips of allegedly healthy men who 'had learned to keep their hands at their sides when slapped or when watching a mate take a bashing'. Describing it as 'a faint shrug . . . a carefully contrived mixture of apparent good humour with a slight curl of the upper lip that stopped just short of being a recognisable sneer', he interpreted it as the prisoners' last defiance and only defence against 'the steady piling up of misery, of mud and toil, bashings and starvation'. 'There was nothing to do but grin and bear it.'[2]

Richards' brilliant verbal snapshot of the sardonic smile aptly illustrates HW Fowler's analysis of 'the sardonic' in the taxonomy he devised to differentiate between eight frequently confused gradations of humour. For Fowler, the distinctive motive or aim of the sardonic is 'self-relief', its province 'adversity', its method 'pessimism' and its audience 'the self'.[3] Like the grimly controlled sneer that Richards observed among Australian prisoners of the Japanese, the instances of sardonic humour discussed below suggest a struggle to attain control over the self through the cathartic relief of pessimistic laughter in circumstances of great adversity. Although not the only kind of humour in Australian texts documenting captivity under the Japanese, the sardonic is both prominent and pervasive and aligns, moreover, with what some scholars have identified as the central national tradition, where 'irony predominates and individuals manipulated by circumstances or a destiny they are unable to control wryly resign themselves to their own powerlessness'.[4] Springing from 'the disjunctions of colonial life', notably including 'an assertively male view of the world which sought to render women peripheral',[5] the sardonic tradition coloured Australian military humour of World War I.[6] Not surprisingly, it flavoured Pacific War captivity texts that were produced by men who had lived through the Depression and into the early 1940s in what remained a relatively homogenous male-dominated white Anglo-Saxon society.[7]

Stan Cross's celebrated Depression-era cartoon, 'For gorsake, stop laughing: this is serious!', belongs to the sardonic mode, embodying as it does 'the notion "you can't win"'.[8] Mirth in circumstances of extreme adversity is disconcerting and can appear inappropriate. It can also threaten to break into hysteria or tail off into catatonic silence. Whether the mirth you have when there is nothing to laugh about is a peculiarly Australian response remains an open question. A preliminary survey of English and American texts documenting captivity under the Japanese, however, suggests that the sardonic mode is less common in the humour of other nationalities.[9]

Reports of the *physical* manifestations of the sardonic among prisoners of the Japanese are not difficult to find in Australian captivity literature and the following three examples are fairly typical. Kenneth Harrison, who survived Pudu Gaol, Changi, the Burma Railway and the Nagasaki dockyards, commemorates the 'bold sardonic eyes' of a brave though unlucky comrade, trucked off to execution by the Japanese for joining an escape party.[10] At Bandoeng (Java), Edward 'Weary' Dunlop's response to the threats made by his captors while issuing instructions for the conduct of captivity is a variation on this theme: 'Much stress of death to CO (me), but all very friendly with much laughing. I, of course, *laughing more like a man with a brick dropped on his toe*'. Later, at Hintok Mountain he notices how he and his fellow human wrecks 'trod for a time along the Nipponese railway, the cause of it all, and *smile with bitter humour* at its crude and snake-like course'.[11] In a somewhat similar context, Ray Parkin celebrates POW medico Major Corlette's wily circumvention of Japanese demands that sick men work on the Railway. Parkin had a minor shoulder wound that did not merit time in hospital. By bandaging him up so that he resembled an Egyptian mummy, Corlette fooled the Japanese medical corporal into thinking the injury was serious enough to permit Parkin to remain in camp: 'I could see Doc. Corlette give a sardonic leer behind the Jap. *It is this twisted smile* that has endeared him to the men who call him The Gangster because of it'.[12]

A survey of the better known Australian captivity texts reveals the pervasiveness of the sardonic grin not only as a reported *physical response* but also as a distinctive *tone* in the writing, suggesting clenched jaws, gritted teeth and a 'slight curl of the upper lip that stops just short of being a recognizable sneer'. Evident on almost every page of *The survival factor*, it is also prevalent in the recorded oral accounts of captivity and lends them a characteristic piquancy.[13] Bob Davis, for example, was with a group of prisoners who had come straight from the tropics to Moji (Japan) in winter and lacked warm clothing. They were marched to a large unheated shed with a concrete floor, fed one rice ball and left there overnight. Davis's caustic aside, delivered as if from the corner of his mouth, exemplifies the sardonic attitude: 'there was no dancing I assure you'.[14] Richards records a comparable throwaway line, delivered on board a prisoner transport vessel close to the Japanese coast. Lindsay Savage's conversation with a fellow captive about surfboard riding at Manly Beach was interrupted by a torpedo attack from an American submarine: 'Pity the Yanks missed', he quipped. 'We could have swum to shore from here. Done a bit of surfing, eh Jimmy?'[15]

The ability of Australians POWs to pass sardonic remarks ventriloquially was renowned. Donald Wise, a British officer with a big moustache discovered this when they made him the target of their scorn in Thailand. The first time he went on parade they mocked him mercilessly: 'What is it?' 'I don't know, never seen one like this before.' 'Jesus, do you reckon it fucks?' 'Looks like a rat peering through a broom.' Wise was unable to identify the culprits because all the sniping was 'from men who apparently weren't moving their mouths'.[16]

The terse almost shorthand entries in Weary Dunlop's *War Diaries* evince the distinctive sardonic tone. A master of understatement, Dunlop notes at Bandoeng that 'slapping is rather in vogue again'. Members of a returning work party had been 'slapped down for bringing in cigarettes, though this is often permitted . . . The Nipponese who slapped them was very short and had to swing wildly, far uphill. The results were rather devastating actually – a ruptured eardrum, a broken tooth plate and a tooth knocked out'. Later, at Chungkai (Thailand) the Japanese distributed questionnaires about treatment of POWs, asking such things as: '"What is the most detestable, deplorable etc incident that you have seen?" "What is the kindest action you have seen by a Nipponese soldier?"' Opinions on all matters of camp administration were invited. 'As regards kindest act by Japanese soldiers', Dunlop drily notes, 'one officer offered the following: an occasion when, before beating him, the soldier let him take off his spectacles and did not use a crowbar!'[17]

Ray Parkin's derisive account of the 'special Japanese brand of humour' at Hintok Road camp depends, like the example from Dunlop, on ironic dissonance ('a light job') and laconic, matter-of-fact expression that offers a modicum of bitter self-relief:

They gave twelve light-dutymen a light job. It was to roll a forty-four gallon drum of petrol out to the compressor: eight kilometres along that black road of slush – down that Hill which, day after day, wet and dry, has half-killed us – then down a deeply mudded jungle track.[18]

In Donald Stuart's thinly fictionalised memoir of captivity under the Japanese, *I think I'll live* (1981), the proletarian dialogue of the private soldiers, coarse and often scatological, is the chief source of the novel's bleak humour. An unlettered POW, for example, reports a comrade's sardonic comment on the cost of survival: "'Fraid his ole' dial's a bit lop-sided and his left eye's never gonna open more than halfway, but as he says, he'll scare the tripe outta the general public when he gets back"'. Elsewhere, 'a good poor silly soft-hearted bastard' would 'give you his arsehole an' shit through his ribs if need be' and 'these fuckin' Japs wouldn't wake up if a man was to piss in their left ear'ole'. Stuart's diggers regularly strike pungent notes in sardonic response to the hardships of the notorious Burma–Thai railway. As the following example demonstrates, their ribald pessimism provides momentary relief from anxiety about the progress of the devastating 1943 cholera epidemic:

'. . . but it'll slacken off soon, you'll see.'

'Listen feller, just how do you know it'll slacken off, eh?'

'Well it stands to reason, doesn't it? If it keeps going there'll be none of us left will there?'

'Hell, that's a great bit o' logical bullshit, if ever I heard any. Do you honestly believe the cholera wog gives a twopenny upright root whether there's any of us sees it through? Don't kid y'self sport, your name's in the hat along with the rest o' them, and mine's there too.'[19]

Where Stuart relies on working-class slang for sardonic effect, Dunlop depends on an artful control of formal registers and a genteel, educated vocabulary of impeccable precision, even when discussing bodily functions and indelicate medical procedures. Attending a concert in camp at Tarsau (Thailand), Dunlop recorded the following details: 'An orchestra (very good) and a fair stage, but no lights were allowed owing to blackout restrictions! *Rectal swabbing by a Nipponese party was going on lustily, dealing with twenty at a time!*'[20] Like Parkin, Dunlop rarely resorts to profanity when quoting

fellow prisoners and, although attuned to (and amused by) the cultural differences between nationalities, eschews racist abuse.

The sardonic humour of many captivity texts arises out of the brutal and, to the Western mind, irrational behaviour of the Japanese. This
humour is markedly evident in Richards' account of the grimly entertaining antics of the hard-drinking Japanese superintendent at Kunknitkway
(Burma). Otherwise know as the 'clown prince', Lt Naito so terrorised
his own troops that they would run away and hide in the jungle until
he caught and punished them with heavy drill and training manoeuvres
at all hours. His most memorable foray resulted in the capture of the
POW latrines, a military victory worthy of 'the Fifteenth Order of the
Flying Kite'.[21] Fellow POWs, however, could also be a source of scornful
amusement. When Dunlop makes note on 2 February 1943 that his party
has arrived at Konyu (Thailand) to camp alongside a British contingent
already established there, he is singularly unimpressed by the way things
are being run by the captive English top brass. His account of how, after
'a lot of preparations as though setting out for an all-day journey', he is
escorted by the English CO to the camp's cemetery, a mere 150 yards
away, is vintage dead-pan:

> The Colonel seemed to come into his own and dilated on the whole
> show with the pride of a sexton in a village churchyard. He showed
> great enthusiasm (for him) and wished to know if we desired to share in
> the cemetery (Yes); if so, did we want a separate part made as an exten-
> sion? Not if it would take up too much of the accommodation. Then he
> waxed keen again and said 'Oh no, I want to fill up this part first – but
> there is plenty of room here.'[22]

Australian prisoners, too, can elicit Dunlop's sardonic grin. His entry for
5 March 1943, introduced under the heading 'Evening: many troubles',
adopts the dramatic mode, latent in the previous passage, by developing
a shorthand dialogue that underscores the absurdity of the culture clash

between fervent Christian captive and equally dedicated Japanese captor. One of the 'troubles' involved the well-loved Roman Catholic padre, Gerard Bourke, who had been 'arraigned before blotch-faced [camp commandant] Osaki sword in hand':

O: Why do you disobey the orders of the Japanese Army?
B: I take my orders from a much higher authority than Japanese Army.
O: (More angry) Nunda! Nunda! Higher authority – where?
B: (Pointing to sky) My orders are from up there!
O: (Perplexed, then explosive) Bugero! (raising sword)
B: (Face happy at prospect of martyrdom)
I intervened, tapping my head. 'Kristian priests very eccentric men!'
O: (Mollified) Ah, 'eccentric' man.[23]

The anxious respect for madmen, shown here by Osaki and commonplace in traditional Asian cultures, emerges again in another sardonically amusing episode, this time at Chungkai, where Dunlop records 2 June 1944 as being:

[c]hiefly notable for the escape of Skillycorn, the acute mania, who eluded his watchers, swam the river at a rate of knots and escaped stark naked! Eventually he was apprehended paddling a Thai canoe along the river gaily. Everyone was given a fearful rocket by Okada. It is commanded that a very strong 'box house' be made in one of the wards to contain three lunatics with six guards to be posted day and night. Jack Marsh asked why a 'box house' for three, since only two lunatics, and was told that the other place was for him (Okada)![24]

Passages featuring a sardonic tone are more common in the documentary textual forms of the diary, the memoir and the oral histories than in the fiction and verse addressing captivity under the Japanese. George Sprod's compilation of amusing cartoons and verbal sketches, *Bamboo round my shoulder*: *Changi: the lighter side* (1981), for example, rests, as its subtitle announces, on the sardonic premise that captivity's privations should be minimised (even celebrated) through self-mockery: *Are we downhearted? YES!* A memoir, *Kurrah! an Australian POW in Changi, Thailand & Japan, 1942–1945* (1991), by FW Power and *You'll never get off the island: prisoners of war, Changi, Singapore, February 1942–August 1945* (1989) by Keith Wilson both maintain a wry tone throughout, while Russell Braddon's *The naked island* (1952) and Douglas McLaggan's *The will to survive: A private's view as a POW* (1995) manifest it more intermittently. In the early stages of his narrative, based on the diary he kept in captivity, McLaggan laconically plays down his suffering (asides such as 'belted to leg by another attack of malaria' and 'winning the yak lottery' are common). And his title for Chapter 9, 'We died in Singapore and this is Hell', quotes a comrade who had 'summed up the position adequately by reckoning that we were killed in action on Singapore Island and that this was Hell, although we did not know it'.[25] In documenting the mounting wretchedness he and his fellow 'other ranks' endure, McLaggan's grim derision modulates into pity (and self-pity), returning only when he exposes the selfish behaviour of certain (unnamed) Allied officers.

Writers who discuss (rather than perform) sardonic humour, including in particular Roy Whitecross, a veteran of the Burma Railway and forced labour in Japan and the author of *Slaves of the son of heaven* (1951), generally echo Richards in reading its significance mutually as grinning defiance (of the enemy and all his ways) and self-soothing in adversity ('bearing it'). Both elements may be seen jointly to contribute to the 'self-relief' that Fowler identifies as the 'motive' of the sardonic. The 'defiance' element, loudly proclaimed by Whitecross but muted in Parkin's *Trilogy*, is affiliated to the 'big-noting' theme in Australian war writing diagnosed by Gerster (1987) as negatively aggressive, boastful and xenophobic. In contrast, the element of 'self-soothing', prominent in Parkin, constitutes an admission of the prisoner's fear, vulnerability and pain and undermines heroic self-aggrandisement.

The defiance element is probably most conspicuous in the insulting nicknames prisoners gave to their Japanese and Korean guards.[26] A selection from the vast array of these sobriquets includes the following: 'Rigor Mortis' and 'the Blind Boil'; 'Bird on the Bough' for a smooth-voiced English-speaking Japanese with European features who had 'a habit of fluttering the eyelids in a sort of ecstatic spasm' and 'the High-Breasted Virgin' for an 'outwardly effeminate one-star private'; 'Scrap Iron' for a guard with gold teeth; 'Willythe-Wop', who resembled 'a little gangster straight from Damon Runyon'; 'the Ice-Cream Man', aka 'Mr Peters', who always wore 'snow-white clothing like that of ice-cream boys in cinemas' and 'Mr Cunt', whose name needs no explanation. Wilson tells us that the lowly guards, whose grasp of English was minimal, were often openly if 'politely' addressed by offensive names, including the ubiquitous 'Bastard'. Newly arrived POWs sometimes laughed when they heard the old hands behaving in this way and had to be educated not to.[27] A sardonic variation on the work chant accompanying pile-driving conformed to this same principle. The normal version, which involved counting off in Japanese ('itchi–ni.i.i–san–YONG'), was changed by the POWS to 'Horseface–the ee ee–baaars–TED'.[28]

The spirit of defiance in sardonic humour has been singled out for chauvinistic celebration by Roy Whitecross who attributes to it the capacity of Australians to survive their travails on the Railway more effectively than other nationalities. To sustain hope, all prisoners performing slave labour for the Japanese needed to set feasible goals. 'Of all the troops in Burma the best at this game were the Australians. *Their sense of humour carried them on past every time limit they set themselves.*' The Dutch, however, allegedly came crashing down into the 'very depths of despair' because they set their goals too high. Shipped to Japan in an unseaworthy hulk that lacked any markings identifying its cargo of captives, Whitecross's contingent knew that their chances of arriving alive were slim. To compensate, they indulged in 'much sardonic banter in the usual Australian style': '"What do you do when you meet a shark, mate? Try and hypnotise him, swear at him – or stick out an odd arm or leg as a peace offering?"'[29]

The defensive element of the sardonic response, inextricably implicated as it is with the spirit of defiance, proves more difficult to pinpoint. An incident recounted by Ray Parkin, however, may offer some insight into the way that silence and inappropriate, sometimes hysterical laughter relate to the self-defensive operation. In this instance, Parkin's squad failed to heat the Japanese engineers' bathwater to the correct temperature and, despite Parkin's display of extreme contrition, the Japanese corporal insisted on punishing the entire work party. He took a thick piece of bamboo, drew a cross on the ground, formed the g-string-clad POWs into a queue and, as each stepped onto the cross, administered four or five 'lacerating whacks' across the buttocks, thighs and back. The Japanese guards, 'enjoying the slapstick', helped the corporal to turn the occasion into baseball batting practice. This resulted in several broken arms and horrendous bruises: green, red, blue, purple and yellow, 'intermingled like the daubs on a painter's palette'. Initially dumbstruck, the victims' unscathed comrades who inspected them for damage suddenly 'all burst into roars of laughter . . . "Blue-arsed monkeys!" someone yelled'.[30] Spontaneous scornful laughter that seems inappropriately to mirror the sadistic mirth of the Japanese who inflicted the suffering in the first place replaces shocked sympathetic silence. Verging on hysteria, however, like the excessively high-pitched laughter and constant chatter that Richards noted among fellow 'disaster happy' prisoners who had survived being torpedoed,[31] it belies the grim stoicism that is the hallmark of the sardonic.

Such inappropriate laughter at life-threatening misfortune recalls the 'screaming merriment' of the terrified crew in Conrad's novella *The nigger of the Narcissus* when, during a typhoon, they watch the perilous efforts of the boatswain to rescue the eponymous 'nigger', Jim Waites, from his deck-cabin while the ship is listing almost horizontally in the water:

> In our extremity nothing could be terrible so we judged him funny kicking there, and with his scared face. Someone began to laugh, and, as if hysterically infected . . . all those haggard men went off laughing, wild-eyed, like a lot of maniacs up on a wall.

Two seamen, however, refuse to participate in the hilarity, judging it to be inhuman: 'Laughing at a chum going overboard. Call themselves men, too'.[32] Not surprisingly, Whitecross notes that prolonged captivity under the Japanese drove his Australian compatriots 'to be callous about death' while at the same time maintaining 'a humour which nothing could quench' that helped them endure the unendurable. This humour 'became an understanding between us. It could not be called a code as this understanding was never expressed. But it was almost universally adhered to and the few who broke down and moaned were scorned and shut out from the comradeship of other men'. Towards the end of their three and a half years as prisoners, scornful mirth appears to have been swallowed by silence. '[W]e were Aussies and we didn't moan', asserts Whitecross, but there was 'little laughter': 'Laughter had given place to tight-lipped dogged determination not to give in.'[33] Dunlop, however, looking inward rather than generalising chauvinistically about his countrymen, acknowledges the cost of captivity in the 'avoidance symptoms' common to cases of post-traumatic stress: apathy, loss of joy and a feeling of detachment from others:

> Somehow, I seem to have lost all emotional depths these days and am living in a drab way without much thought or feeling or reaction to anything. Worst of all one's sense of beauty and appreciation of beauty seems to suffer . . . These must have existed but one can't feel very much any more. Further, I can't react much to physical suffering or death.[34]

Whereas Whitecross celebrates adherence to the pitiless Australian code of stoicism, Dunlop's self-confessed lack of affect exposes the code's limitations, underscoring the fact that the sardonic imperative is maintained by a ruthless repression of emotion and ostracism of those who express it. Such insights suggest the proximity of the sardonic to the *in*humanity of extreme individualism that brings to mind the ravaged psychological terrain of the starving Ik tribe of north-western Uganda, studied by Colin Turnbull in *The mountain people* (1974). Otherwise abnormally silent and affect-less, the Ik laughed only when they witnessed human misery: if a toddler burned itself on live coals, for example, or an emaciated man who had not eaten for three days fell to the ground and could not rise. Even the elderly who, regarded as already dead, were refused food or, if found with it, were robbed of it, 'joined in the merriment' at their own expense. 'They knew it was silly of them to expect to go on living, and, having watched others, they knew that the spectacle was quite funny. So they joined in the laughter.'[35]

It is also the terrain of Shakespeare's *Titus Andronicus*. For Manfred Pfister, Titus's lengthy silence, followed by mirthless barks of laughter ('Ha, ha, ha!'), when presented with the decapitated heads of his two sons and his own severed hand, involves 'laughter beyond, or at the far side of tears'. Like 'being struck dumb, to which it is closely related and which it disrupts', such laughter articulates 'utter helplessness and the most radical protest against the horror of existence and the failure of language to express it discursively'. Read in this perspective, Shakespeare prefigures 'post-Enlightenment laughter' that ranges in the absurdist plays of Samuel Beckett from bitter, mirthless laughter to the '*risus purus*, the laugh laughing at the laugh, the beholding, the saluting of the highest joke, in a word the laugh that laughs – silence please – at that which is unhappy'. For most if not all prisoners of the Japanese, this was the only kind of laughter possible.[36]

Aboriginal humour:
A conversational corroborree

Lillian Holt

Paul Kelly, famous Australian musician, was quoted by Rachel Perkins, film-maker and daughter of the late Aboriginal leader Charles Perkins, as saying on ABC radio, 29 October 2001, 'I've never met an Aborigine without a sense of humour'. Obviously Kelly had been around Aborigines long enough to recognise how important a sense of humour is to us.

I decided to share that statement with fellow Aboriginal people around Australia and asked them to comment on the topic of Aboriginal humour. There was much agreement with Kelly's view, and this article is, in part, the result of those conversations with Aboriginal people about how they see humour. In that sense, it is a sharing of the insights of the interviewees, as well as my own as an Aboriginal person.

It would be a fair assessment to say that Aboriginal people see the necessity of humour as a tool of everyday existence and narrative, and for survival. And yet humour is one of the less documented areas of Aboriginal life. (The impact of a history of racism, conflict and oppression on the health and well-being of Aboriginal people, on the other hand, has been well documented and much researched.)

Recently a whitefella approached me and suggested making a documentary on Aboriginal humour. In his opinion, most white Australians did not equate humour with Aborigines, and would thus find it an intriguing, albeit incongruous, theme.

Intriguing? Incongruous? I laughed at the thought that whitefellas could possibly think this way, as most blackfellas know what an important part humour plays in our daily existence. As a blackfella myself, I've always intuitively known the importance of humour in everyday life.

And this was stunningly reinforced in the interviews I did with other Aboriginal people, who demonstrated no reticence in talking about this topic.

To the interviewees and myself there is nothing 'intriguing', nothing 'incongruous'. That's just the way it is. Integrated into everyday existence. Everyday conversation. Everyday survival. It's about the collective. The community. Humour is shared within the group. Which is probably why there aren't too many Aboriginal comedians, because it all happens 'on the ground', locally, so to speak. It's spontaneous and part of ordinary life, happening in the here and now!

As I sit reflecting on and writing about this topic, surrounded by other blackfellas in an Aboriginal organisation, I'm reminded of the intoxication of humour and laughter. I've missed this kind of free-flowing, spontaneous humour and laughter, having only just arrived back in Adelaide after working in a remote community – Melbourne University! – for the past seven years.

Humour happens everywhere in the Aboriginal community, but for me it happens particularly in my workplace, in the arena of Aboriginal adult community education. Right now, as I sit writing this piece, I am reminded of many instances of Aboriginal humour – my own and others – some of which I will share with the reader. So I ask you to bear with me for a moment, as I give you some of my impressions of and encounters with that very wry and dry humour.

For example, I was thrown into the thick of it when I first came to Adelaide in 1973 to work at the newly created College of Aboriginal Education, as it was then known. In the latter part of that year, a whole lot of us blackfellas were sitting around waiting for a bus to take us on a planned field trip. The bus should have turned up at 9 am, but it didn't arrive until after lunch, and when it did it was ancient and battered. On seeing the state of the bus, people cringed, cowered and scattered, and said things like, 'Shame, I'm not getting on that old bus'.

I happened to be standing next to an Aboriginal man in his mid-thirties, a Vietnam veteran. Without blinking an eye, he said: 'Look at that old, battered bus, Lillian. You'd think those whitefellas would have given us blackfellas at least a new bus to wreck'.

This comment cut the shame surrounding the bus, for it contained that tension between truth and stereotypes of both blackfellas and whitefellas. And, as with all good humour, it brought perspective and relief. All of us blackfellas just burst out laughing and got on the bus.

That incident is a good illustration of Aboriginal humour. It's a spontaneous spoofing of the stereotypes, both black and white. It's incisive and to the point. It's about laughing at ourselves and at others and then letting it go.

Later on in my career in adult education I asked an Aboriginal employee why he had lasted so long working at the same institution, which was an Aboriginal community-controlled organisation. He said to me:

Well, Lill, it's like this. In the early days the principal [a white man] got in his car and he pulled the wrong lever and instead of moving forward he was thrown backward in his seat. In offering my hand to help him pull himself up (a hand–up not a hand–out!), I made a decision that I would stay until white people could stand on their own two feet. They still can't stand on their own two feet, which is why I am still here.

In such a statement of humorous irony, the expressive face says it all. Such was the case in this instance, accompanied as it was by a chuckle at having reversed the stereotypes.

Walking into the same organisation this week, after working in a large and monolithic whitefella organisation like a university, I am taken by the amount of laughter around the place. It is something I missed terribly when I went to work in academia. There was not much humour to be found in the university's hallowed halls. Indeed, at times I was acutely aware of its absence, for in my view humour is an essential lubricant of life. And I had taken it for granted working in Aboriginal organisations for more than thirty years.

I reckon that if we are to progress through the thorny terrain of race relations in this country, 'humour' is one of the Five H's, the others being History, Honesty, Humanity and Hope. I see it as essential to our spiritual awakening – to ourselves and others – and for me it is part of our spiritual survival.

Humour lubricates. It moistens. Indeed, the word 'humour' comes from the Latin *umere*, to moisten. In moistening and lubricating, it often brings relief from the pressure of one's own pomposity and also brings a new perspective.

Humour, for me, belongs in the realm of the spirit. I can't prove that and I don't intend to. But I was speaking to a whitefella in Melbourne who is involved in humour on an everyday basis. He said to me: 'Lillian, comedy is physical, humour is mental, and laughter is spiritual'. I thought at the time, 'Wow!' I was excited, because in my findings from interviews with my mob around Australia, laughter was the dominant word to emerge and a factor in all the conversations.

I was so excited by this white man's statement about laughter being spiritual that I told one of my older academic friends, whose response was: 'Well, that is only opinion. Where is the proof?'

I have no proof. And therein lies the problem: I am not an expert. But if any topic was likely to elude the purview of an 'expert', I would wager that it is humour, given its elusive, ethereal quality. Yet, despite this, it hits its mark in spoofing sacred cows, including the idea of 'experts'. And so I share a joke about an expert. It goes like this:

A plane that is about to crash has five people on board: a flight attendant and four blokes. However, there are only four parachutes. The
flight attendant grabs one and says as she jumps out, 'Work it out
amongst yourselves, fellas. There are four of you and only three parachutes.' Without hesitation the first male jumps up and says as he grabs
a parachute, 'I'm the PM of the country. The country definitely needs
me, so I'll take a parachute.' He then jumps. The next male jumps up
and says as he takes a parachute, 'Well, I'm an expert. Surely, the country needs ME!'

There are now two men left, an old priest and a young hippie. Without hesitation, the old priest says to the hippie, 'Hurry up and take that
last parachute. I've had my life. Yours is just beginning. Hurry. Take it
and go.'

'Oh, that won't be necessary, Father', says the hippie. 'Didn't you
notice? The "expert" took my backpack.'

Over the years I've seen an endless array of 'experts' who have been brought
in to solve 'the Aboriginal problem'. We've been researched to death by
experts. Dissected, labelled, studied ad infinitum. And still it goes on as they
search for the magic formula in order to work us mob out.

Being 'studied' so much – even our own people are jumping on the
bandwagon – is reason enough for one to need a sense of humour. It is
needed in order to survive the labelling that has come out of the avalanche
of research. There is a joke to illustrate such labelling. I first saw this joke as
a cartoon when I went to live in the United States in 1979. It immediately
resonated with me, for it was humour that could be applied to the Aboriginal experience as well as the Native American one. It illustrates the power
of definition and how we are often inadvertently limited by the whitefella
definition of 'otherness'.

There's an old Indigenous fellow sitting on a slag heap, reflecting on his
life. He says to himself: 'Well, first of all, they said I was primitive. Then

they said I was uncivilised. Then they called me a heathen, a pagan and a savage. Then I was handicapped, deficient, deprived, disadvantaged, marginalised, a victim, blah, blah, blah'. He continues with the definitions imposed on his mob. Suddenly, he stops and says: 'You know what? My position hasn't changed in life, but I sure have one hell of a vocabulary.'

When I tell both of these jokes, in my speeches or elsewhere, everyone – mostly whitefella audiences – laughs. Humour is a brilliant vehicle for conveying those unpalatable truths that we all would prefer not to confront in ourselves. Ultimately, humour's great power is that it is invariably invested with a sting of truth. For me, as a blackfella who has survived sixty years of uninterrogated white supremacy, humour helps to relieve the racism in this rich but racialised land we all call home.

I'm glad to know I am not alone as an Indigenous person in feeling this way. Tom King, a Native American comedian, states:

Those things that hurt in life, those things that continue to hurt about being Native in North America, I can handle those things through humour. I can't handle those through anger because, if I get angry about something, it just gets away from me. It just consumes me. I've got to keep coming back to humour as my sort of safe position. And I think I can make more of an impact.[1]

I can relate to those remarks of King, and, on first hearing the jokes about the expert and the labelling of Indigenous people, I laughed heartily. I also laughed as I sat around and listened to blackfellas talk about their ideas of humour, willingly and wittily, and as they illustrated the issues of Aboriginal existence with humour.

It was impossible to sit around with a bunch of blackfellas with a tape recorder and not join in their laughter, not join in the conversation. It was beyond my skin to do so. And this blackfella did not want to be left out of the fun. That's another thing about humour. It's infectious!

And now that I am at the end of my own comments for this piece, I can confess that I did the interviews originally with the idea of doing a PhD on Aboriginal humour. But I reckon that, instead, maybe I should write a book and call it 'On my way to my PhD I nearly lost my sense of humour'. As I couldn't be so-called 'objective' enough about it all, I would write in a conversational manner that made it accessible to everyone. Isn't that what humour is or should be about: accessibility? Personally, I would prefer to *use* humour rather than analyse it, as it is something one detects rather than defines. And as Henry Spalding, the author of the *Encyclopedia of Jewish humor*, states in his opening lines in the Preface: 'The surest way to destroy the humor of a funny story is to analyse it'.[2]

In speaking to the different Aboriginal people around Australia, it was obvious that humour was appreciated and honoured. There was no angst or analysis paralysis in sight. I can give them no greater accolade than to share some of the conversations and comments I collected along the way.

Most of the interviews were in groups, for I was advised by fellow Aboriginal people that blackfellas would probably share more in a collective conversation than a solo one. But there were some excellent one-on-one conversations that I will also share. For the purposes of privacy and protection I will ascribe each comment to either an individual or a group, depending on the particular source.

Individual 1

In common with the type of sense of humour that you'll find among virtually all dispossessed, oppressed Indigenous people in the world today, I think that the self-deprecating sort of humour that I'm talking about, that has to do with oppression and is used by people who are oppressed, is one mechanism for easing that oppression. I think that that's clearly evident in modern-day Aboriginal humour, humour that makes fun of the adversity that you suffer, humour that makes fun of and pinpricks the blues of pomposity of your oppressor; all of these are sort of in every element of modern-day Aboriginal humour. I think that today's Aboriginal humour has very much been historically affected by the oppression that Aboriginal people have suffered, the dispossession they have suffered. It has been used and is used still to a large extent as a means of countering, subverting or defusing the racism that they experience within the Australian society.

One of the many classic examples of that style of Aboriginal humour is the joke that was contained in the film *Backroads* (1977), where Trickydicky Sullivan from Dodge City Reserve in Brewarrina is sitting by the side of the road and Bill Hunter, the white actor guy, was driving a big flash car and leans out the window and says to the blackfella, 'Hey Jackie, can I take this road to the pub?'; and Trickydicky Sullivan's response is, 'You might as well, you white bastard, you took everything else'. I mean, that's a classic example of the sort of style of Aboriginal humour that distinguishes it from other forms of contemporary Australian humour.

And let's face it, virtually all of the great Aboriginal leaders who I knew in my day were people who had a very sharp and highly developed sense of humour.

You know, I think that those with the greatest ability to satirise and ridicule and laugh at the situation were those who seem to have survived the longest. In other words, a sense of humour was a fundamental and vital component of your personal character if you were to survive as an Aboriginal leader or just as an ordinary Aboriginal person through the greater part of the twentieth century.

Group 1

I think it's gentle humour. You know like C was talking about American humour, I think American humour is really aggressive and it's abusive. I think some of the British humour is class-oriented; it's about, like, 'find the difference'.

The thing about Aboriginal humour is it's gentle, because what it does is there's great mimics, do you know what I mean? People do great mimicry. But to laugh at everybody, not just one person: everybody. So it unites us because everyone's got something but we're still drawn together in the human. I don't think people are isolated, so that gentleness is probably a great gift because it's about including people.

Individual 2

But the important thing about humour is it is a philosophy, it isn't something which is superficial; and it's also about wisdom. If you look outside the Aboriginal community, you'll find that to see the comical side of something, to be able to deflate pomposity with humour, or pretence with humour, it's something we find in some Eastern cultures, Islamic cultures. And the best humour is gentle. It's mocking, it's sly, but it is gentle. It doesn't seek to destroy people.

I think we have quite a crude notion of humour in the Western world; we're used to people being denigrated or brought down or put down. True humour is always about humanism and I think probably this is an Aboriginal philosophy. If you look at it, it is about a humanism that people are all ultimately gifted and flawed; or ultimately the only thing that is the saving grace of most people is that other people put up with them. We don't have the rights, we don't deserve anything: it's actually the generosity of other people that allows us to get along and get by and survive. When I'm thinking about humour too – it's hard to get it down; we shouldn't think of it in terms of a specific joke. I think it's a disposition. When Aboriginal people meet, you often see gentle teasing, because people tease each other just to sort of bring people in. Sometimes it's a non-destructive way of gossiping. Someone is acting up a bit and people laugh at him; instead of moralising it becomes humorous. It's a way of bringing people in: someone seems a bit distant, a bit powerful or important and humour identifies the flaws in their character, the little failings that make them a human being.

Group 2

I reckon it's fun taking off people. I like taking off people and making other people laugh. It's not being nasty or anything to the person. It's just a humour thing, I guess.

Yeah, and see I think a lot of humour is . . . we often laugh at things that others would find quite deadly serious. We tend to joke more about one another, and our community, and our blackness, than we would about white people or something, hey? We sort of tend to, well, throw off more about each other.

Group 3

Well, I might share something like, for instance, you know, blackfellas do funny things. I mean, when you think about it they're not really funny; but I must share because these are my views. When I was living in Port Augusta I was walking down the road and as I was going across the street my knee gave out on me and I fell down in the middle of the road, and one of my girlfriends was walking up to me and she had seen me fall and she stopped dead in her tracks; she didn't know what to do.

So I could see her thinking over in her head, 'God, what am I going to do?' She was thinking in her head, you know. And at the same time, the expression on her face just made me crack up laughing. You know, and even though I'm in pain, and in a dangerous situation, I just couldn't help it, I just cracked up. Because she's come up to me and what she did was actually so confusing. She says, 'How dare you laugh at me when I'm trying to help you!' But I just thought it was so funny. But you see, that's what I think Aboriginal humour is about; it's about taking a pretty stressful situation and making light of it.

Individual 3

I think it's is a survival thing for our mob. It's survival and we sort of use it to laugh, but I think it's also used to cover up a lot of pain sometimes. Like we use our mob to, you know, pretend everything is okay when it's not. I mean, it's good to be able to laugh even in a stressful situation, and we're certainly good at that. But I think sometimes it's like some of our mob they just take that on as a coping mechanism and so everything in life becomes a joke. You know, my brother used to be like that. They say that with the adult children of alcoholics, one of the roles people take on is the joker – you know, making a joke out of everything. Sometimes I think people have to be able to sort of cry when they need to too. And our mob are pretty good at grieving, I reckon, considering. I mean, there's a lot of blocked-up people, but I think we do an okay job, like we still respect funerals and things a lot. With humour, it is a gift that we've got to survive, but if we weren't dispossessed or weren't invaded, I suppose we would have still had as much humour but it wouldn't have had that edge of sort of covering things up every now and then. We don't cover things up all the time, but every now and then I think it is just covering pain up, and that's okay, but sooner or later that pain has got to come out. So it can be a positive thing or, sometimes, once in a while, it's not really the best thing. But yeah, I think it's good. I just think humour is also like a spirit. It's like a thing we've got that, you know, makes us really able to see the funny side of things and see it from completely different perspectives. A lot of black people are really quick-witted and it sort of just comes out of nowhere. It's almost like they're drawing everything together, you know, what they can see, what they can taste, touch and feel about that particular moment, and they say one little thing and it just breaks that situation and completely changes it, you know, completely makes it live. It's like a spirit. It's like something comes through us and makes that moment what it is. And without that humour, if that thing wasn't said, it would be like the moment might just sort of pass and the wisdom in that humour might be lost, you know. It's like the opportunity might be lost too, actually, because sometimes it's just that combination of things, the time, the weather, the where you're sitting, the who you're talking to, how many people, what the conversation is – all those things conspire and at that very, very magic moment, humour. That's why I say I think it's a spirit, it's like it makes people aware, it opens people's hearts and minds to something, another way of seeing. And it takes the mickey out of ourselves as well, you know, makes sure we all stay down to earth and don't sort of, you know, big-note too much. I mean, it's okay to do well and that, but not to think you're better than the next sort of thing. So I think humour is used like that to cut every one down to size but not really in a negative way, not like tall poppy syndrome, just like making you laugh at yourself too, that's what it is really for, yeah.

Individual 2

I think for most of my life I've been upwardly mobile. I've been in strange and foreign environments with white people. I've been really concerned, I suppose, to make sure I'm treated with respect, that I have dignity, and it does make you in a sense humourless. And I think it is a bit of a dilemma in an upwardly mobile Western world. We're all trying to maintain the façade. A lot of us are quite unhappy and almost find it a relief when someone gently sort of just eases some of the protective stuff off us, so we can be human again. It's interesting, because if you think of people who don't mind telling a joke against themselves they have to be people who have a great deal of confidence, who don't mind telling a story which actually shows them as a bit of a fool. We often sort of relax because we can identify with them in that dilemma. We feel that somehow the things we repressed, our weaknesses which we try to hide, can be externalised and we're also part of the human race again.

The comments of this final interviewee resonated with me as a 'once aspiring' and hence 'sometimes perspiring' blackfella whose stilettos got stuck on the rungs of the ladder of success. That was when I had my feet firmly planted in mid-air, but humour often brought me back to terra firma. That humour invariably came in the form of a good zen slap in the face from another blackfella when I was being too serious and thus endeavouring to exert control.

Furthermore, Individual 2's comments reminded me of something I read many, many moons ago, which said words to the effect that often the most oppressed people have the best sense of humour. Now whether that is true or not is not my intention to debate. Suffice to say that I had a wonderful time laughing, joking, sitting around and yarning with members of my mob around Australia about this most elusive of topics. It was essentially an exercise in detection rather than definition – and still is, for me.

In some ways, I'm rather glad that Aboriginal humour evades definition and control – and that dire need we seem to have in this society to control or tame everything we encounter, for example the land. I say hoorah for elusiveness, mystery and awe in life. And maybe that is where humour fits into it all. Hence, I say hoorah for humour.

Maybe that is why humour is one of the least researched areas not just among blackfellas but among whitefellas also. Edward de Bono says that it belongs in the area of 'water logic' – elusive, flowing – rather than the 'rock logic' of Western academia, which tends to set out to quantify and measure things.[3] I agree with him.

In this sharing of some of the comments of the interviewees, I have chosen to honour their words by letting them speak for themselves, rather than analysing and defining yet another aspect of Aboriginal existence. One thing that came across loud and clear is that humour is alive and well in the Aboriginal community. Part of the collective, the communal and the conversational corroborees of everyday life, humour is detected rather than defined. It's present and yet eludes categorisation.

In eluding definition, it cannot be captured. For, as one of the interviewees said of Aboriginal humour, 'Well, it's the only thing that they haven't stolen from us, because we have kept it safe and alive in our hearts'. That is not to say that it can't be shared with others, as any whitefella who has taken the time to be with Aboriginal people would attest to. Just ask Paul Kelly!

So is Aboriginal humour akin to other aspects of Aboriginal existence that are hard to document? Is Aboriginal humour like tribal or customary law? Victoria Laurie, writing in the *Weekend Australian* magazine in 2001, said: 'In many Aboriginal communities around Australia, the influence of tribal or customary law is alive and strong. The problem is trying to put it down on paper in whitefella terms, or even finding a consensus on what to call it'.[4]

I hope that this is the case with Aboriginal humour. So let's salute it and go with its ethereal flow – especially the essence of that which eludes us. For maybe humour, be it black or white, lets us know that, in our arrogance of all-knowing, all-controlling, all-defining, we are not always in command.

Humour in Australian fiction

'We are but dust, add water and we are mud': The comic language of *Here's luck*

Peter Kirkpatrick

Here's luck has long been seen as a classic of Australian humour, Cyril Pearl going so far as to describe it as 'pre-eminently Australia's funniest book, as ageless as Pickwick or Tom Sawyer'.[1] Since it first appeared in 1930, the novel has never been out of print.[2] Its author, Lennie Lower, has thereby accrued a mythical status. As the title of Bill Hornage's biography of Lower would have it, *He made a nation laugh*. Barry Dickins, who wrote a play about him in the 1980s, claimed that 'Lower's palette was the people, he used drink for a brush, and he drew their ferocious features with Temple Bar ash'. Taken together, such comments situate Lower and his work ambiguously between the universal and the local; between a canon of cultured literary humour and what Dickins called 'the wisdom of the shitkicker'.[3]

Let me begin, then, by invoking one of my favourite Lowerisms from *Here's luck* – by way of mood-setting, but also to start thinking about the particular ingredients of Lower's humorous style.

Jack Gudgeon, the middle-aged public-servant hero of *Here's luck*, is describing the glorious breakfast prepared for him by Estelle, girlfriend of his gormless son, Stanley; a breakfast that appears like manna from heaven in the midst of a diet that seems largely to consist of baked beans, tinned fish

and alcohol. Jack describes his breakfast of grilled chops as if it were a landscape painting, and concludes: 'Fried tomatoes furnished the background.
No poet has ever written a sonnet to fried tomatoes. And yet they are supposed to be able to discern beauty and capture visions'.[4]

In this ironic comment Lower situates his text in terms of both high and
low culture. Clearly his readers are not poets, or even the kind of people who
might read poetry. (Early in the novel Jack makes fun of verse by capping
Stanley's poem to Estelle with 'Her little nose she loudly blows'.)[5] He makes
his point against such high literary values, and offers instead an affirmation
of the pleasures of the everyday and the familiar. Poetry, on the other hand,
is about the unfamiliar; it's about beauty and visions. This is the romantic
sense of poetry which Jack invokes, at any rate. But very evidently he knows
something about it in order to be able to say this. In fact he knows at least
as much about poetry as he does about fried tomatoes.

Needless to say, Jack doesn't give us a sonnet about fried tomatoes. It's
enough to make that backhanded reference to high culture to suggest the
value and attraction of fried tomatoes. They are *worth* a sonnet, but you
don't have to write one because everyone *knows* what fried tomatoes look
and taste like. Lower's readership is complicit with him in this appreciation,
this acknowledgement of common wisdom. The idea of writing a sonnet to
a fried tomato is funny, it's a joke, partly because no poet *would*, but also
because there's no need to. Fried tomatoes and poetry traditionally inhabit
different spheres of culture. Bringing them together challenges the way we
see both things; in a sense it inverts them. Fried tomatoes are more important than poetry because they are a more basic part of life: not everyone
reads poetry, but everybody eats. But poetry has its uses. It comes in handy
in situations like this because it enables you to allude to things about fried
tomatoes that you otherwise couldn't.

I labour this point in order to highlight the relentless comic inversion of
cultural values in *Here's luck*. The topos of a world turned upside down from
its usual cultural and power relations relates to an impulse that the Russian
critic Mikhail Bakhtin famously labelled the 'carnivalesque'. Throughout

the novel the normal rules of society are suspended. A typical bloke of his generation, Jack Gudgeon – 'Jack', a name for everyman, while 'Gudgeon' is quite literally a small fry – becomes the focus of a picaresque exploration of contemporary society: society seen, as it were, from the other side, from a subversive, carnivalised perspective. Jack and Stanley enter a world whose rules have been effectively reversed. Instead of abiding by what Freud called the reality principle, the pleasure principle has gained the upper hand: they are briefly permitted to live for desire alone, seemingly without social responsibility. For example, money won by gambling is not 'earned' by productive labour, and through gambling the Gudgeon males quickly and miraculously acquire large sums of cash. This brief class inversion allows Jack, the chubby folk hero, to take an anarchic journey way above the poverty line.

It's not my intention to consider the meaning of that journey, but rather to examine the language in which it's related. *Here's luck* is told from the sardonic first-person perspective of Jack, but his language is inflected by a host of other 'languages' – call them discourses – from early twentieth-century Australian culture, both high and low. In Bakhtin's terms, the language of the novel is dialogised and heteroglossic[6] – but then so is the language of Lower's other comic writing, as I will show. By being ordered through the controlling consciousness of Jack Gudgeon, however, deeper and more sustained levels of irony come into play to create a comic achievement unique in Lower's work. The genre of the novel didn't simply offer Lower a larger canvas for his talents, but actually directed them onto different paths along which – to invert Louis Sullivan's architectural maxim – function followed form. As Ronald McCuaig once said, distinguishing Lower's only published novel from the brilliance of his more ephemeral writings, *Here's luck* contained 'an excellence of character and situation' that the author 'never again attempted'.[7] My focus, though, won't be on the comic events at the level of plot, but on the representation of speech at the level of narrative.[8] There's a reason for this.

An early, unfavourable reader's report for Angus & Robertson on the manuscript of *Here's luck* noted: 'Mr Lower's style glitters with facetiousness.

There is real wit and humour too; but they are swamped by a flood of farce and buffoonery'.[9] This response, while negatively couched, reflects a common emphasis on the novel's 'buffoonery' in its later, highly popular reception (Angus & Robertson disregarded its reader's views and proceeded with publication). What little serious commentary the book has received has also tended to stress Lower's destructive farce at the expense of his wit. This suggests that it is more the slapstick element of *Here's luck* – its male-centred anarchy and comic violence – rather than its linguistic energy that constitute its classic status. Indeed, the novel's knockabout action has been closely associated with the nationalistic claim that it is 'Australia's funniest book'.

The earliest extensive study of *Here's luck* is contained in Keith Willey's *You might as well laugh, mate: Australian humour in hard times* (1984), which, like the reader's report, similarly focuses on the physical over the verbal comedy. While acknowledging the novel's comic brilliance, Willey reads *Here's luck* as a critique of its times, 'turn[ing] Australian society upside down in a masterpiece of alcoholic nihilism'.[10] In this way, Willey extends an idea from a 1963 essay by Alexander Macdonald on 'The melancholy of Lennie Lower', which noted 'a never too distant undertone of actual cruelty' in Lower's humour, and saw that 'glint of the callous streak' as characteristically Australian.[11] Peter Edwards' 1992 essay comparing *Here's luck* with Steele Rudd's *On our selection* offers the best critical analysis – and the only academic study – though it focuses on the book's farcical elements, seeing the escalating destruction of the Gudgeon house as a form of symbolic violence towards women. More recently, a 2001 review in American *Publishers Weekly* (reproduced on Amazon.com) notes little verbal energy in Lower's style and, by assuming that the main springboard for humour is the plot, finds common ground with the Angus & Robertson reader:

First published in 1930, this reissue of what has been hailed as 'Australia's funniest book' will leave modern American readers asking, 'Says who?' Lower's pursuit of irony and folly is tireless. But with a trifling plot line used primarily as a vehicle for the jokes the comedy soon grows tiresome. So do the cantankerous characters who inhabit nondescript settings and whose emotional states are frequently reduced to adverbial phrases.[12]

Evidently, older insistence on the exceptionalism of *Here's luck* can now prove counterproductive. Partly for this reason, I want to shift away from the novel's anarchic take on Australian suburbia to look more closely at Lower's verbal humour and how it works. This takes discussion of the book beyond concerns about its national status and relocates it within a larger tradition of comic writing in English, to which – as Pearl's comparison of Lower to Dickens and Twain implies – it also rightly belongs.

But before I return to *Here's luck*, here is one of Lower's early newspaper pieces that was collected in his second book, *Here's another* (1932). It points to the difference between Lennie in journalistic mode and Lower the novelist. This is the opening of 'Lonely sardine':

Electrocardiogram!

   Phantasmagoria!

   Not that we bear any malice. Simply that we occasionally run short of curses. As Edison once said to the Governor of South Carolina, 'Inspiration is one-tenth perspiration and nine-tenths exasperation'.

   We shall, therefore, talk to you to-day, children, about sardines.

   The sardine lives in a tin slum and, due to its environment, there are many feeble-minded sardines in our midst – unaccustomed, mark you, as they are to public speaking.

   Environment, said he, throwing his cigarette-butt into the waste paper basket in an earnest attempt to burn the office down, is a strange thing. In a very short time, a cat caught in a rat trap becomes distinctly like a dead rat. Given time, the cat may even become deader than the rat. As the poet described the electric chair, 'That burn from which no traveller returns' – that's where it goes.

Speaking of electric chairs, we understand that they are most uncomfortable. A man told us that the accommodation in the electric chair department was shocking. Apart from that, he explained to us that it was one of the few occasions when he didn't have to strap-hang.

The humour in this piece comes, in part, from its word-play – notably puns, of course – but more consistently from its rapid-fire code-switches: absurd juxtapositions that create the dominant effect of comic surprise. The piece begins with an unusual take on what HW Fowler called polysyllabic humour, 'electrocardiogram' and 'phantasmagoria' presumably appearing in lieu of expletives. There follows a comic misquotation of a popular maxim of Thomas Edison's before Lower launches into a mock lesson in the manner of a 'radio uncle' that makes absurd fun of contemporary eugenic theory about slums. Faux, would-be aphorisms – 'Environment . . . is a strange thing', 'In a very short time, a cat caught in a rat trap becomes distinctly like a dead rat' – are followed by another misquotation, this time from Hamlet, which is part of a segue into a punning account of electric chairs. The rest of the column jokes about Christmas puddings, raisins and iron – the links are made through puns and freely associated metonymies – until it returns to sardines by way of closing:

> And if you must have something about sardines, they have no heads, but they carry tales.
> Mean to say, they repeat on us.
> Abyssinia later.[13]

Against the wild surrealism of 'Lonely sardine', compare the following passage from *Here's luck*, in which Stanley, Jack and Uncle George are leaving the country town where they've spent a night in the lock-up and are heading back to Sydney. Jack muses:

Almost, I was sorry to leave. Seated in the side-car with George straddled across me, I wondered how long I would survive the machinations of Woggo Slatter's gang in Sydney. As we rushed along the road, we were leaving behind us a place of quietness and peace where the cows browsed placidly on the footpaths and even the flies buzzed in a minor key. And for what were we leaving it? For a roar and a shriek and the sound of hurrying feet. Back to the smoke and the clatter and the pale faces. Back to the place of lightning shaves, half-eaten breakfasts, bundy clocks, and stand-up luncheons.

Progress we call it, this manifestation of group lunacy. What is the use of all this vaunted progress? Jones builds a bungalow with a sliding roof, rotary floors, disappearing gate, electric window-wipers and an automatic bath-room and thinks he has said the last word. But he hasn't.

Smith comes to light with an aeroplane catapult on the roof, escalators to the front door, a revolving porch, illuminated key-holes and a verse from the Koran inscribed on his doormat. So determined are we to live as close as possible to the stench of business that we live on top of each other in flats and have to wait our turn to cross the road. What is the use of it all? How much deader than a dead stockbroker is a dead potato-grower, when all is said and done?

Had it not been for the fact that I cannot bear the dullness of the country, I would have ordered Stanley to turn around and go back.[14]

This is another example of carnivalesque inversion; in this case, of the literary trope of pastoral, in which country life is classically praised above city life. Correspondingly, Lower brings in the discourse of bush balladists like AB Paterson and Henry Lawson: 'For a roar and a shriek and the sound of hurrying feet' evokes 'Clancy of the Overflow'; 'Back to the smoke and the clatter and the pale faces' is an echo of 'Faces in the street'. Unlike Paterson, however, Jack then immediately dismisses the vision splendid.

Here's luck and 'Lonely sardine' both play fast and loose with other discourses, carnivalising them via humorous recontextualisation and juxtaposition. But the passage just quoted is a different kind of comic writing than that of the newspaper columns, one grounded in characterisation. Because as readers we inhabit his mind space, we can follow Jack's musings and empathise, even as his parody of modern technology becomes more and more absurd (I'm reminded of the ultra-modern house parodied in Jacques Tati's *Mon Oncle*). In his essay 'Discourse in the novel', Bakhtin observed that 'In the English comic novel we find a comic-parodic re-processing of almost all levels of literary language, both conversational and written, that were current at the time'.[15] In *Here's luck*, this 're-processing' is enacted through Jack's highly literate consciousness, which is why the novel – despite its popular appeal – never entirely dispenses with high art.

Thus, rather than reject Shakespeare out of hand, Lower simply revises him. For example: 'The slings and arrows of outrageous fortune were descending on me in matted clumps'; 'What a wonderful thing is sleep! Knits up the ravelled sock of care, restores the tissues; the greatest post-jag pick-me-up ever shaken together' (note the transposition to the lower bodily stratum, from 'sleeve of care' to 'sock of care'). 'There's a divinity that shapes our ends, rough-hew them as we will' is similarly transformed into a Lowerism: 'Man, rough-hewing his destiny with the blunt axe of Reason, sees the head fly off his axe and his destiny bashed into a shapeless lump'.[16]

As a representative of the common man, Jack adopts an everyday perspective, with a lexicon to match. As Bakhtin suggests: 'the primary source of language usage in the comic novel is a highly specific treatment of "common language" . . . taken by the author precisely as the *common view*, as the verbal approach to people and things normal for a given sphere of society, as the *going point of view* and the going *value*'.[17] In this regard, it is worth noting that Lower makes fun of popular genres more often than high ones. For example, as Jack is reluctantly dragged along to the racetrack, he picks up a verbal cue from Stanley and transforms the scene into a cliché from a detective thriller:

'Randwick!' [Stanley] cried. 'Drive like hell!' and the car leapt forward.
    'Keep close to that car in front,' I added, 'and if it stops, shoot to kill.'

I struggled out of the hat, which was much too small and jammed down on my ears.

'What are you talking about?' said Stanley. 'What car in front?'

'There's always a car in front,' I replied testily. 'A black closed-in car, and it winds in and out streets until it pulls up at a deserted house and they all get out and carry the unconscious girl into the cellar and we surround the house and capture the Master Mind who turns out to be the butler.'

He stared at me.

'You're mad!' he said.[18]

Jack's utterances are often ironically self-directed like this – directed, that is, somewhat against what Bakhtin called 'the going point of view and the going value'. This point is worth emphasising, because one reason that *Here's luck* has failed to attract academic interest has probably been its perceived sexism, or, to be more precise, its apparent celebration of a male separatist ethos that sees ockerism as a liberation theology for domesticated man. In that spirit, the *Publishers Weekly* review sourly described Jack as 'a middle-aged, unemployed male chauvinist and part-time drunk'. Evidence for the prosecution might be provided in Jack's famous description of his mother-in-law:

> In this description of my mother-in-law's mode of life I think I have written with a certain amount of tolerant restraint. She is an old lady and the age of chivalry is not dead while a Gudgeon lives. Perhaps a different son-in-law might have described her as a senseless, whining, nagging, leather-faced old whitlow not fit to cohabit with a rhinoceros beetle. But I wouldn't.

Passages like this can make Lower's humour appear very un-PC, and yet the joke is as much based on class as on gender. Agatha's mother lives in the 'earnestly genteel' suburb of Chatswood, where 'respectability stalks abroad adorned with starched linen and surrounded by mortgages'.[19] Jack picks up on this middle-class pretension by making fun of 'chivalry' in a backhanded assertion of his own failure as a gentleman. In any case, the build-up of irony at this point is overwhelmed by that extraordinary metaphorical leap of 'not fit to cohabit with a rhinoceros beetle', whose absurdity provides the real punch-line.

For the fact is that Lower doesn't necessarily equate ockerism with 'the going *point of view*' at all, but rather satirises it and, in doing so, also satirises the patriarchal pretensions of everyman. Indeed, the deflation of fatherly authority is a prominent theme in *Here's luck*. Take, for instance, the following passage, when Jack talks about his fearlessness:

> The only way I ever discovered what fear meant, was by looking it up in the dictionary, when I found it to be 'a painful emotion excited by impending danger', and that is all the knowledge I have of fear. I have been called a brave man. Modesty permits no discussion of the matter, but I have lived with Agatha and Gertrude, I have seen the hotel door shut in my face on Saturday night, and I pinned an Orangeman's badge on a drunken Irishman. The Irishman was colour-blind, of course, but I took the risk with his instinct. I was not afraid of [Woggo] Slatter; he was something tangible that could be dealt with. It was the dreadful feeling of impending trouble that perturbed me.[20]

Words slide off their objects and relocate themselves very easily in Lower's humour. In this case, Jack rejects any experience of the dictionary meaning of fear only to recognise it in his own paraphrase a few sentences later.

The whole novel can be seen to work towards the destruction of Jack's illusions of his masculine power and independence. At the end he's doomed to a suburban ham-and-beef shop – what we'd now, in a more pretentious age, call a delicatessen (or, if we lived in gentrified Woollahra, site of the former Gudgeon home, a 'providore'). And although the ham-and-beef shop seems a demeaning fate, given the comic exuberance of Jack's brief period of born-again bachelorhood, the emotional disorder of the spree was starting to get to him. At one point he declares, 'I always think that in humouring a man who has made the Great Mistake [marriage], one should adopt the tone usually reserved for children and half-wits'.[21] But that's after the disastrous journey to Chatswood to make it up with Agatha, where Jack manages to kill his mother-in-law's parrot, brain her dog with a picket fence and smash her front window. Later on he announces to Stanley and George, 'Love! . . . You think it is the door to the palace of romance, when it is only the fire-escape exit leading out to a back lane'.[22] But already one senses that the cynicism is that of the frustrated romantic rather than the misogynist. As Edwards has written, for all its apparent male chauvinism the novel 'emphatically puts paid to the great Australian myth that a man without women, a man among men, is more a man'.[23]

The main instrument in the deflation of Jack is his son, Stanley, who is what Bakhtin might call a 'parodic double' of his father. Edwards suggests that Stanley's unbridled larrikinism is a realisation of the spirit Jack would seek to liberate within himself,[24] but in the image of Stanley and his misdoings it all appears callow and grotesque. It also sparks a homicidal rage – as in the chase across the roof with a cleaver in chapter 7 – which can be read in Freudian terms. Jack's concluding letter to the Department of Navigation, seeking a job for Stanley as a remote lighthouse keeper, thus expresses his wish to remove the third member of the Oedipal triangle. But lighthouses themselves are phallic symbols, and in seeking Stanley's banishment Jack is also banishing the dream of male independence and self-containing power.

It is the demolition of that myth of heroic individualism and the acknowledgement of social bonds – symbolised by marital bonds – that ultimately give the novel its comic structure and meaning. Returning from the disastrous mission to Chatswood, Jack consoles himself with a self-melodramatic and therefore parodic version of lonely male triumphalism:

It is the last defiance of a manly soul to quaff the bitter cup of fate and fling the dregs in its face. How I have sometimes yearned to stand on a

peak where the wind howled, and bare my teeth and laugh. Laugh! Or
drive a ship through whistling spray into the very jaws of a gale while the
splintered rigging thrashed on the heaving deck. And all that. To fling
aside the petty considerations, the conventions, the saving, the sordid
cares, and hoist myself to a seat beside the gods in one wild, glorious
burst.[25]

That Jack is retailing a set of adventure story clichés is signalled by the
addition of 'And all that'. It's like Stanley's frustrated notion at the start of
the book to go hunting elephants in Africa after he's been jilted by Estelle,
an idea that Jack can't take seriously because it is announced by his parodic
double, his son:

Stanley was [in the drawing room], standing with arms folded and a
look of hopeless determination on his face – or determined hopeless-
ness. Properly blasted. He was gazing out the window as if he already saw
the elephants advancing with writhing tentacles . . .

'Ah, Stanley!' moaned the wife, warming up to the work. 'Don't go
to South Africa!'

It made me mad to see her pretending to take him seriously.

'I will. I am. I shall – must!' said Stanley.

I could see that with all the encouragement he was getting he had
become rather taken with the idea.

'But, Stanley – it's so far away! Couldn't you go to the zoo?'

'Zoo!' hooted Stanley. 'Zoo! What zoo! . . . I don't want those lop-
eared, peanut elephants! I want elephants that are wild! That crouch
ready to spring and tear one limb from limb with their claws! Elephants!'
he concluded with a shout of triumph.

'But, Stan; elephants don't have claws,' said Agatha.

'They'll wish they had before I'm finished with them,' said Stanley
fiercely.[26]

Here's luck climaxes with the party to end all parties, the party as *Götterdämmerung*. Jack's penultimate vision of a green elephant of delirium striding from the charred ruins of his house recalls Stanley's dreams of Africa, only now the dream has turned into an alcoholic nightmare. Jack awakens from that nightmare into the harsher and more terrible reality of the ham-and-beef shop. Temporarily off the grog, well might he say, as the sozzled politician Mr Sloove says, raging against the sodden ecstasies of water-drinking rectitude, 'We are but dust, add water and we are mud'. But his last words are to welcome once again Flannery the publican and the prospect of an alcoholic resurrection: 'Thank God!'[27] The title of the book *is* a toast, after all.

Lower's creation of Jack Gudgeon was his masterstroke, in that it allowed his characteristic word-play a novelised 'common language' and a coherent, organising consciousness within a closely observed social milieu – things often lacking from his hit-and-miss funny columns. (Brian Penton, his editor on the *Telegraph*, 'used to say that all they wanted from Lennie was three good sentences a week'.)[28] This is why *Here's luck* is one of the great novels of Sydney. Alexander Macdonald made a point about Lower's newspaper work that applies equally, if not more, to his only published novel: 'Lower was expected to – and *did* – furnish a sort of readers' common room, to be shared with equal pleasure by fans of Mr FJ Thwaites [a popular romantic novelist], readers of the *Sporting Globe*, and earnest students of Feodor Mikhailovitch Dostoievski'.[29] As the voice of the common man, Jack Gudgeon accommodates all of these implied cultural values, in a sustained ironic dialogue with each other, within himself.

Why men leave home:
The flight of the suburban male in some popular Australian fiction 1910–1950

Michael Sharkey

'Married?'

'Aren't I a man?' he said angrily. 'Aren't I a man? I mean blind. Like everyone else before me, I fell headlong into the ditch. I married. I took the road downhill. I became head of a family, I built a house, I had children-trouble. But thank God for the *santuri*!' (Nikos Kazantzakis, *Zorba the Greek*)[1]

Late nineteenth-century Australian fiction is rich in naturalistic and tragic disquisitions on marriage; the twentieth century is rich in comic recensions that begin to signal a gradual cultural shift towards reconciliation of gender roles. The *Boy's Own* world of late nineteenth-century Australian frontier fiction posited a sphere where sterling chaps battle against natural forces, including the feminisation of society, for an independent place in the sun where they can settle down with a 'good' woman to spend their autumn years reflecting on their high adventures. While many of these tales, from *The recollections of Geoffry Hamlyn* (1859) forward, might strike us as unconscious parody of masculinist concerns, women authors took another turn, frequently subverting the masculine romance.

Ada Cambridge's serialised novels – among them *Dinah* (1879–80), *A girl's ideal* (1881–82), *Mrs Carnegie's husband* (1884–85), *Against the rules* (1885–86) and *A marriage ceremony* (1894) – critiqued the institution of marriage in tales of physically and psychologically battered wives, whose brutal or uncaring husbands leave them for more beautiful, stronger women.[2] Rosa Praed, who made a career as a novelist following the collapse of her Australian marriage, also portrayed the grim side of the marital frontier, in novels that pricked the bubble of women's dreams of ideal husbands in outback or metropolitan society. Like Rosa Praed's heroines, Jessie Couvreur's fictional women attempt on occasion to take in hand the education of men into higher principles than male bonding, horse-racing and gambling. Some of Couvreur's women are horrified by the idea of marriage; Laura Lydiat, in *Uncle Piper of Piper's Hill* (1889), declares to her suitor George Piper, 'I abominate the system of marriage . . . I think the yoking of two people together without a chance of release – as if the yoke mightn't gall them any day – perfectly barbarous and absurd'.[3] Much of the writing is far from comic, though Cambridge, Praed and Couvreur employ irony and, at times, humour to suggest the difficulty of the task of schooling men to abandon their 'cranks', much less adopt egalitarian principles.

Parallel with this trend, late nineteenth- and early twentieth-century popular masculine fictions reluctantly, if at all, surrendered romantic ideals about women; and herein lies a tension and source of comedy for emerging comic writing about the urban and suburban male. Whether it was always perceived as conscious comedy is another matter: the *esprit de sérieux* often carries the male writers into unconscious contradictions and absurdities.

In 'Challis the doubter: The white lady and the brown woman', a story in Louis Becke's first collection of stories, *By reef and palm* (1894), the title character one day walks out of his house after a tiff with his wife concerning her admirers. He visits a lawyer and sets off for a cruise of six months among the islands of the North-west Pacific. At the story's end, four years later, he is ensconced with a brown woman, whom he discovers he loves when he is on the point of sending a letter back to 'the woman with violet eyes'.[4] Challis tears up the letter, gives his brown woman a ring, and she declares she will bear him a son. Challis's flight is at once an escape from bourgeois conformity and a trajectory towards sexual and emotional stability that leaves unexamined the ramifications of re-establishment of the 'couple'. In this respect, Becke's story reprises a traditional comic theme, encapsulated in Byron's formula 'All tragedies are finish'd by a death,/All comedies are ended by a marriage'.[5]

Becke's formula is neither the first nor the last such expression of male desire in Australian fiction, and the comic potential of such a theme was later exploited in a deal of popular fiction written by men and published throughout the period between the two world wars.

An extraordinary proportion of the popular authors of the first fifty years of the twentieth century were male journalists whose out-of-hours comedies drew on their suburban and inner-city roundsmen's experience, and provided the vehicle for a critique of institutions that they could not so directly question in their diurnal reporting. The individual's solutions to problems are those of the freelance observer of the social farce. Daydreams and alcohol are the preferred modes of their Walter Mitty-like vacationers from mundane torment. The dream of flight is put into action, only to break on the rock of recognition of life's circularity. How can the awakened characters make life bearable for themselves? The fiction rarely pushes so far: comic fugue is all-in-all. Reading such fiction, we do not encounter social realism but a type of best-selling formula. Reality is invoked only to point up its insufferable heaviness.

The male romances took various guises. Some of Ernest 'Kodak' O'Ferrall's short stories celebrate the solo male boarder, whether as fallguy of others' intrigues – such as the hapless Bodger, namesake of his first collection, *Bodger and the boarders* (1921) – or active instigator of his own holidays from constraining logic – as in 'Balloons and sausages', where two happy drunks attach a string of sausages to a stolen haul of balloons and thereby break up a dignified civic ceremony.[6] O'Ferrall's stories have something of the tone of *Monsieur Hulot's holiday*: a gentle, if not genteel, whimsy bordering on absurdity. O'Ferrall's sketches are more congenial than such fantastic tales as the English writer Dornford Yates' unmediated escapist 1926 folly *The stolen march*, chiefly because O'Ferrall tempers his observation of working-class manners with a democratically based satire of the sort of pretentiousness exemplified in his snobbish contemporary.

O'Ferrall's sense of the pitfalls of confusing actuality and art is illustrated in a short story, 'The escaped hero', concerning a cliché character who has taken leave from a romance writer's imagination to torment the first-person narrator of his tale in a public garden.[7] Another story, 'The lost bishop', concerns a shipwrecked bishop and a female impersonator who, upon their rescue, take to the stage as 'a male team of tanglefoot dancers and cross-talkers'.[8] In a twist to the theme of male escape, O'Ferrall's 'All at sea' recounts a woman's flight from her domineering brother's influence: she fetches up as a steward on a coastal steamer, onto which she smuggles her eloping nephew and his newlywed bride, to the uncomprehending confusion of her brother.[9] O'Ferrall's sympathies extend to frustrated spirits regardless of gender; and while the stories variously locate their characters in New York, South Pacific islands, Indian seaports or Sydney offices, those dealing straightforwardly with male fugitives focus on individuals who live within the districts with which he is most familiar, the suburbs of Sydney and, occasionally, Melbourne.

In Norman Lindsay's fictions an adolescent or young male hero is shown poised on, or in, the act of flight from a suffocating family at the head of which stands 'Ma', symbol of societal conformity and restraint upon masculine exuberance. In *Halfway to anywhere* (1947), Lindsay traces the emergence of his ingenuous hero Bill Gimble from a state of 'incompetence, disguised as boorish scorn for the graces . . . a state of celibacy', to self-reliance. In his half-aware pursuit of this end, Bill attempts flight from influence by parents, schoolmasters and his own sexual ineptitude into what he imagines is a world of adult independence characterised by the opportunity to booze at will. In illustrating where power resides in

Bill's family, the narrator points up the paradox of Bill's efforts to seduce a girl:

> Bill was much better off than [his friend] Waldo [whose father thrashes him for attempting to seduce a housemaid], having an old man who never oozed anything about the house except a smell of booze, and who never took any part in Ma's domination of the home. This may also have been due to coming under her castigations himself, especially after arriving home so inked up that Ma had to put him to bed.[10]

Bill's first encounter with booze enables him to see the world in a new light; in the course of an inking-up with his friend Waldo, he makes several discoveries:

> In fact, it was now discovered that beer stimulated a state of mind the reverse of the befuddlement of intoxication. It bestowed extreme clarity of thought, disposed of life's ills as mere trifles after all, gave an enlarged perception of life itself, and, above all, stimulated the ennobling emotion of friendship.
>
> As Bill put it, 'Girls may be bonzer enough for doing a bear-up to, but they don't come up to blokes as friends.'

Waldo agrees: 'Properly speaking, girls ain't friends at all. Admitted girls are bonzer for doing a bear-up, how do they treat a bloke, supposin' he gets going with them? Nine times outer ten gets his face pushed trying it on with them'. As the pair become more intoxicated, Bill goes further: 'Can't say absolutely girls have brains because a bloke can hardly think of a thing to say to them. With a friend bloke can think of millions things to say'.[11] Lindsay does not leave things in this state, of course; the narrator portrays the likely results of a lifetime's dedication to voyages in the glass canoe by the 'booze-oozing intimates of the Royal Hotel back-parlour': 'hearty, back-slapping good fellows whose stentorian joviality was strangely stripped from them the moment they reached home, the mere clicking of a front garden gate turning care-free roisterers into exhausted breadwinners'.[12]

Halfway to anywhere combines moral fable and escapism: biographically minded readers, recollecting Lindsay's Methodist antecedents and upbringing, and his personal abstemiousness, may perhaps see no contradiction in such a conjunction. Lindsay's 1970 autobiography, *My mask*, traces the beginning of antagonism between himself and his own Ma to her discovery of his efforts to persuade a small girl to reveal what it was that was different about girls and boys: Ma gave young Lindsay what he called 'a hell of a jawing'.[13]

Lindsay's novels early establish a dichotomy between Ma and the desirable alternative, a pattern reprised in the fiction of Lennie Lower and WS Howard. In all three writers' works, an Eve-figure (mother, wife, mother-in-law or aunt) is contrasted with a Lilith-type who, if she doesn't actually take the sexual initiative, can be persuaded to comply with the male hero's desire. Lindsay and Lower write ambiguously of the result of such a liaison: Lilith may be transformed into a new Eve, and the cycle of bliss and disillusion recommence.

Lindsay portrayed the simultaneous sexual reluctance and fascination of young men and young women. For the most part his focus is on the young man, who is no untutored innocent like Bazza McKenzie, but an inquiring, even bookish hero. In *Redheap* (1930), for example, young Robert Piper is introduced by the ramshackle scholar Bandparts to the romances of Boccaccio, Rabelais and Byron. Robert duly plans to escape domesticity, the family business and the looming prospect of marriage to a parochial female denizen of the small-minded town of Redheap; at the novel's conclusion he is poised to depart.

This dream of escape to a wider world outside, familiar from the character's experience of imaginative reading, is what differentiates these Lindsayan heroes from the later, ockerish heroes of Australian comedy, like McKenzie, whose capacity for conceptual growth is hardly at issue. Bohemianism may attract them, and Lindsay accordingly employed it to comic effect in *A curate in Bohemia* (1913), *The cautious amorist* (1932), *The age of consent* (1938) and *Rooms and houses* (1968). In spite of their verbal defiance and physical efforts to elude the horrors of petticoat government, though, Lindsay's male characters are shown repeating (and thereby endorsing) the experience of their elders. He seldom shows a successful 'escapee'.

In like manner, Lennie Lower's *Here's luck* (1930) employs Bohemia as one possible escape route among many – yet Lower effectively describes an escapade, rather than liberation. In Lower's tale, it is the wife who leaves home, to shelter with her mother from the uncaring husband, while the husband and son wreak havoc on the house through their stereotypical domestic incompetence and the staging of wild parties. Lower, like Lindsay, distinguishes gender types by a shorthand assignation of gender roles, and the novel is structured around the hilarious efforts of the father and son to feed and clothe themselves. Jack Gudgeon's son Stan brings home a girlfriend to cook and clean the house, and his treatment of the girl compels Gudgeon to see his behaviour as monstrous. At the novel's end, Gudgeon and his wife effect a reconciliation during a turbulent party while their now ramshackle house burns down around them. The destruction of the house is a device that lets Lower have a final sentimental fling: with banishment of the sister-in-law – a 'parrot-brained Gorgon'[14] – finally revealed as the enemy of the couple's felicity, and with the symbol of their previous life in ruins about them, love can start afresh.

Considered as realism, it's not entirely satisfactory, but realism is not what Lower is about. This is not the world of Louis Stone's slum-dwellers, nor of Katharine Susannah Prichard's opal miners, timber-getters or circus folk. Lower's novel continually signals its intention to entertain rather than to instruct: in its farrago of comic vernacular, its serial knockabout action and its overarching assumption that nothing can be done to break out of the fate dictated by society and biology. Twenty-first century readers, more preoccupied than Lower's contemporaries with delineating refinements of gender politics, may find his comedy of manners a lamentable lapse of etiquette, or inadvertently take his fiction to be a mirror of an age, rather than a sideshow's magic mirror maze.

In three of the novels of WS (William Stewart) Howard, a Sydney journalist who flourished in the 1930s and 1940s, suburban males leave home.
In *Forty-six* (1934) the trigger for doing so is the frustration of male desire
by a socially ambitious wife; in *Ah there, Ffyshe* (1937) it is a wife who has
nothing but contempt for the man's sexual or other abilities; and in *Uncle
Aethelred* (1944) the man is thwarted by the stratagems of a social-climbing
mother.[15] In each case the man repudiates the career path his wife supposes
is the conventional masculine obligation.

In *Ah there, Ffyshe*, Launcelot Ffyshe one day walks out of his home to
perform an errand and simply proceeds to the city, with no other aim than
to distance himself from the scene of his frustration. Breaking with a lifetime's temperance, he gets drunk, meets two disreputable journalists, and
is introduced through them to a 'man's' world. Ffyshe is ultimately engaged
by a circus, and at the novel's conclusion he has a fresh identity and a new
partner: an exotic and adoring younger woman who has seen him battle
with criminal types and 'prove himself' as a man who can look after himself
and, of course, her.

In *Uncle Aethelred*, Charles Lippincott-Smythe and Louise Chislehurst,
both scions of respectable families, react to efforts to dragoon them into
conformism. Lippincott-Smythe, heir to a tallow fortune, and Louise,
daughter of the Bishop of Oceania, detest the idea of the marriage that has
been arranged to advance the fortunes of their houses. They find freedom
in the wild company of an unorthodox menagerie of social types headed by
Charles's Uncle Aethelred, a renowned author, Falstaffian lecher and boozer.
At the end of the novel, Charles and Louise, having survived various tests of
their strength of purpose in avoiding conventional trammels, are meet for
the altar. As the narrator observes, 'young Mr Lippincott-Smythe and even
younger Miss Louise Chislehurst played out for the billionth time one act
of a comedy that has been performed ever since men and women became
men and women'.[16]

In a later novel, *Mid-Pacific* (1942), Howard's hero is an undercover
police agent working with a beautiful blonde to uncover an opium ring in

Fiji and the Pacific Islands. After chastely sharing accommodation with her for some weeks, and breaking up the smuggling ring, Howard's hero takes the step foreshadowed throughout the book.

Howard paints himself into a corner: what can the once-adventurous male, preoccupied by unfulfilled diurnal routines and a savourless marriage, do but succumb, or escape, find an exotic partner and start all over again? In *Forty-six* the hero, Richard Westring, feeling himself 'chained' to women, dreams of returning to the Pacific Islands where he had sailed as a youth. At the age of forty-six, he recollects the adventurous life that first drew him to his wife, and breaking the 'chains' signs aboard a windjammer, resolving that he will not succumb again to the 'opiate' of long engagement with women, but will 'take them' when and if he needs them.[17] Westring's fantasy might set up readerly anticipation that he will effectually pursue a libertine course, except that Howard throws in a complicating factor. Westring's ambition to recapture the 'zest' that once provoked him to write fiction, before he lapsed into a bank managing career, points to the limitations of conceiving male contentment as the product of only sexual fulfilment.

This element – the unsatisfying nature of professional life, as much as that of the domestic engagement – is characteristic of Howard's fiction, and sets it apart from that of Lennie Lower and others, who depict escape as evanescent. In all his novels, Howard dwells on the debilitating effects of domesticity on creative spirits, and it is hardly surprising that *Forty-six* is dedicated to Norman Lindsay.

Lindsay's younger rebels owe as much to the appeal of scallywags in literature like Lazarillo de Tormes, Tom Sawyer and the scapegraces of the *Pickwick papers*, in that their actions constitute escapades rather than a scission that has life-altering consequences. Howard's characters, in a significant variation on the theme of family oppression, are presented at the point of crisis in middle age, when they are well established in a career. Education, class aspirations and lifelong experience determine their projections of alternative lives. Lindsay's satires on smug or pretentious denizens of country towns and suburbs offer contrasting bohemian characters who enact the artist's life as an alternative – one that will not suit every temperament, as Howard's comedies indicate.

Howard's fiction reveals the forces of conformity and reaction as more malign. In his Australian polis, the representatives of social order – the termagant wife, hideous in-laws, voyeuristic neighbours, supine fellow wage slaves – appear to be under a hypnotic spell. Urban peons keep nit on each other, pulling back into line those less self-serving, less bigoted, or more educated and reflective than themselves. Ignorance is worn like a badge; alien ideas – any ideas – are to be rejected by such exemplars of 'normality'. Socialites are vapid inhabitants of a world remote from the producers of labour; the professional classes police unquestioned orderliness. A modest competence is the outward sign of the efficacy of worshipping mediocre idols. For these secure, smug agents of social control, foreigners exist as typological curiosities. They are the Australian equivalent of what HL Mencken called the 'boobocracy'. Judged as fiction representing actual conditions, Howard maintains a cartoonish political reading of an Australian society that DH Lawrence, a decade before, found stiflingly complaisant. In Lindsay's fiction, for all the ostensible celebration of rebelliousness, the slapstick action and signposted typecasting of oddballs mask a disdain for those who do not share the narrator's creative vision: society is fodder for the Olympian artist. Lindsay's artistic 'solution' does not threaten the foundations of society; Howard's solution, by contrast, reveals the frustrations of everyman (or every man), an artistically challenged Australian Mr Polly type.

By the time Howard wrote *Forty-six*, Australian men and women writers had long rung the tragic or comic changes on the outcome of efforts to escape conjugal or parental tyranny, so that what began as earnest or entertaining exploration of the possibilities of escape inexorably lent itself to ironic and humorously resigned restatement.

None of the novels overtly criticise the status quo: all assume that the bourgeois state is insuperable. Convention will never be overturned by the heroes' activities: society is a hypocrite. Politicians, lawyers, the media, bureaucracy, police and other monitors of convention are bolstered in their

efforts to control and standardise the citizenry with the complicity of the
citizenry itself. The police are complaisant, as are the leading lights of the
community, so, with an abundance of pubs, sly-grog shops, the races, gambling dives, Bohemian parties and bordellos, Sydney is a speakeasy. If the
official guardians and moral exemplars turn a blind eye to misconduct in
these fictions, we can presume that such occurrences have nothing to do with
'real life', but everything to do with conventions of comic and picaresque
exaggeration as old as Cervantes and Lesage. Children and adolescents in
the Antipodean comedies nurse their frustrations only until they can strike
out and play their part in the grown-up pursuit of self-gratification. At that
stage, they will discover more subtle forms of coercion and, in the most
highly wrought variations on the theme, will confront their own odious
traits and console themselves that, if one cannot be perfect, one can at least
tolerate one's flaws.

Australian life in the popular comedies is thus settled, predictable and only
equivocally comfortable. Where a catalytic event permits temporary – rarely
permanent – flight to an unfamiliar place (Fiji, the Gilbert Islands, or a
country town just beyond the last suburb), regular society is missed, and
the fugitive sets about making a 'home' in every sense. Yet the dream of
flight, for the male in particular, remains: a sort of nostalgia for the future.
Things of beauty resolve into fleeting glimpses of an accommodating 'girl',
a bottle of beer, a financial windfall. Possession of any of these comes about
through an irruption of magic that grants a holiday from the world of rent
collectors, cadgers, bailiffs, doorknocking evangelists, prying neighbours,
officious public servants, stingy publicans, the 'barnacle' uncle or other
close relations. The benighted heroes can only dream of a less complicated,
more carefree time based on their pre-marriage memories. But nostalgia is
a cheap nostrum, without efficacy to relieve the burdens of the intolerable
present. Just as in women's fiction dealing with escape the father, husband
or brother are agents of domestic tyranny, Ma, 'the wife', or their surrogates
are figures of oppression in the masculine comedies.

Perhaps much of the social and specifically family welfare legislation produced during the period 1900–1950 lent this type of fiction some nostalgic piquancy for contemporary male readers. Like contemporary women's fictions of the period, the male comedies demonstrate the impossibility, whatever the desirability, of altering the bourgeois nature of society. For the male characters, escape is limited: after the binge, sobriety. As well, many of the fictions satirically qualify their definitions of manly character by clear reference to the frustrations of both sexes (I leave aside that category of stories which predominantly addressed male adventures in which women had little if any part to play).[18] In effect, they endorse the less comical interpretations of marital discord written by female authors, wherein certain women dream of separation, or actually flee from dull or tyrannical partners.

At the beginning of the period, Mary Gaunt's 1897 novel *Kirkham's find* and Miles Franklin's *My brilliant career* (1901) are landmark warnings of the woe that marriage represents for creative women; Phoebe Marsden and Sybylla Melvyn both resort to flight at the prospect of ceding control of their lives. Women's fiction that deals directly with marital dissatisfaction and women's fantasies of or actual escape throughout the first half-century is so copious as to constitute a genre. Examples include Ethel Stonehouse's *Earthware* (1918) and Jean Devanny's *The butcher shop* (1926). *The butcher shop*, although written and published before Devanny migrated from New Zealand to Australia, reveals the class constraints as well as the patriarchal constraints on a sensitive woman yearning for expression. Devanny's grimly naturalistic portrayal of a sophisticated woman's dilemma when she is subjected to a domineering and possessive male has something of a precursor in Vera Baker's novel *Equality road* (1922), which depicts the awakening of Val Amory to her husband's true nature when floods and other catastrophes bring financial ruin to their Victorian farm. Val's husband, Guy Amory, whom she has married for want of better choice in the agrarian remoteness of north-western Victoria, reverts to type and horsewhips her. Val flees to Melbourne, where, in the lower echelons of society, she encounters a larrikin-like male protector with whom she ultimately shares a happier life. Throughout the 1930s and 1940s, Christina Stead (*The house of all nations*, 1938), Myra Morris (*Dark tumult*, 1939) and Eleanor Dark (*The little company*, 1945) and others revealed in their fictions the class and educational restraints that compounded the relational exigencies of their female characters.[19]

One final question: given the popularity of the 'escapist' male fictions (publication statistics indicate large print runs of cheap editions and, in the case of Lindsay and Lower, numerous reprints), why have they been critically neglected?

Australian publishing thrives on the production of work by glamorous new writers; out-of-print comic writing, however appealing the opportunities to profit by lapse of copyright, is less likely to attract publishers' attention. Cultural amnesia is induced by the effort required to keep pace with contemporary writing. As well, contingent mythologies are still associated, by the ill-read, with earlier writing that is assumed to enshrine values and strategies that we have outgrown. Women's choices during the period of composition of these fictions may be seen as being limited to marriage and motherhood, religion or seclusion. But this is to impose later twentieth-century notions on earlier productions. 'Religion' in Lindsay's usage is represented by near-travesties: wowserish attitudes to pleasure at one extreme and, at another, sarcasm relating to hypocritical sentimentality and formalism in carrying out social obligations. The concern to be seen doing the right thing amounts to frightened or unthinking conformity to conventions which Lindsay's fiction is at pains to undermine and explode. These are contentious explanations. One overriding reason for the comic novels' invisibility in contemporary literary discussions has to do with the prevalent low opinion in which, for all the focus of literary theoreticians on playful texts and interpretations, comic writing is held. Why such prevalence? Perhaps it does not help one's career as literary middle-manager to be caught in the act of seriously writing about a body of work that parodies the very enterprise of criticism.

Some readers may be embarrassed to find themselves enjoyably regaled by the roles these masculinist fictions assigned to women. At the same time,

a preliminary glance at the comic (and realist) fiction by women writers of
the period and later – such as Margaret Fane, Kylie Tennant and Margaret
Trist – suggests that no act of reversal served to stem the flow of comedy.
Quite the opposite: the comedy might be said to have resided in part in the
exaggerated imbalance of roles. The masculine comedies bring into relief
the pretensions of their self-obsessed heroes, but it would be an inattentive
reader who would identify with the male leading characters, or who might
assume that the writers endorsed the behaviour they displayed. The male
protagonists, no less than their wives, mothers, fiancées and landladies, are
creatures of comic, not tragic, imagination. If we can withhold a propensity
to see the world of those comedies as a sombre Manichean dispensation
wherein men are always demons and women the betrayed angels still loyal to
an idea of marital rights (including protection) and obligations, we will better see that the writers were not entirely the mere entertainers we take them
to be. If we reflect on the lineaments of the 'normal' society from which the
masculine figures wish to fly, we will find the soul of fictive suburbia figured
forth in a narrow-minded, thought-policed security state remarkably like
the one we inhabit.

In such a state as the fictions portray, the very notion of individuality
is scoffed at or denounced by family and neighbourhood quislings, and by
every municipal, borough, state and federal functionary with whom the
hapless protagonist comes into contact. The strategy for survival in such
a world is mute conformity or escape to an alien culture, or a bohemian,
criminal or demimondaine subculture wherein one might gain respite from
coercive bureaucracy and the self-hypnotic brainwashing of one's 'regular'
peers. In such an otherworld, where nothing is as straight as it seems, one
behaves like Gil Blas, getting in first, conning others before one is conned
oneself, even denouncing others before one is denounced. The alternative,
to willingly embrace the secure world where freedom and individuality are
illusions and thereby refuse to break out, however briefly, is to throw in
one's lot with hell's imperialism and acknowledge defeat.

Seriously funny: Happy returns of humour in Australian short fiction

Bruce Bennett

The excuse might be that we're not in the mood any more in the early twenty-first century. That the alleged paradigm shift that occurred with 9/11 and led us into a war and then a Free Trade Agreement with the powerful country that felt terrorised has left us bereft of laughs. A sense perhaps that the laughs are on us. But this bad mood existed to a degree too after the Second World War and induced a boisterous, bolshie response from Miles Franklin, who yelled from the page, 'Let laughter return!':

> A trenchant sense of humour could aid in disinfecting unholy depths, prosaic common sense could encourage sanity, gaiety disperse gloom and restore hope: even flippancy is more curative than despair. Solemnity is oftener symptomatic of a stupidity than profundity.[1]

Her book about Australian writers and writing in which she expressed these sentiments, *Laughter, not for a cage*, is dedicated to a group of male 'literary friends' with whom she felt she could share a laugh and some serious views – TJ Hebblethwaite, Henry Lawson, AG Stephens and Joseph Furphy.

Can we still find the threads back to the laughter of these 'bush realists'? (Hebblethwaite, a clerical scholar and lyric poet, seems a little out of their company.) Ken Stewart makes an interesting attempt to take us back there in his 1983 essay in celebration of Lawson's story 'The Loaded Dog'. In Stewart's reading, two general characteristics of Lawson's work are evident in the story: his emphasis on gregariousness and his assumption of the essential 'hardness of things'. Lawson's recurrent expression 'Ah, well', Stewart explains, is a statement of his 'felt resignation . . . a kind of sad moan'. Countering this moan – and preventing Lawson from becoming a boring whinger (though Stewart does not put it as strongly as that) – is his examination of 'perspectives on a seeming innocence or state of grace, a condition in which the Hardness of Things dissolves or loses its oppressiveness . . .' Stewart's intuitive logic takes us suddenly to the heart of the matter: 'The Loaded Dog' is an inversion or softening of Lawson's characteristic 'hard reality' of loneliness and despair. Having gained the reader's trust and confidence, by putting his case in a lively and convincing way, Stewart proceeds with relish to show how 'The Loaded Dog' moves to its big bang and beyond, and why it deserves the 'serious compliment' of being 'Australia's greatest bush nursery yarn'.[2]

Taking a leaf from Ken Stewart's essay, I will try to spotlight some examples of seriously funny Australian stories and their authors with an eye to the traditions they represent and the literary friendships or partnerships they have developed across generations.

A mateship across generations that appeals to me because of its apparent incongruity is that between Steele Rudd and Frank Moorhouse. Before Moorhouse, Miles Franklin regarded *On our selection* as Australia's only major 'tale', in which the burlesque element was complemented by an 'underlying pathos [which] moved those who knew and loved Australia . . . to sigh as often as they laughed'.[3] In his review of Richard Fotheringham's biography *In search of Steele Rudd*, Ken Stewart highlights the remark reportedly made by Rudd that 'If I let myself go I'd be gloomier than Lawson'.[4] Thus, for Stewart, Rudd's humour is dependent on his capacity for melancholy, perhaps even despair. Rudd, like Lawson, was a serious drinker for whom a chemically reinforced loneliness strengthened an inbuilt sense of isolation.

It is easy to see why a later critic, AD Hope, who appreciated the Lawson of the Joe Wilson stories, and also enjoyed Rudd, should nevertheless have found Rudd's 'slapstick' humour one-dimensional and overdone.[5] Yet, as Bob White observed, danger is 'detonated in slapstick' in Rudd's stories about the daily perils of the battler on his bush block situated on the margins of civilisation.[6] ('Detonation' is, of course, a word that applies more directly to 'The Loaded Dog'.)

It is worth noting how Frank Moorhouse registers his latter-day appreciation of Steele Rudd. In 1986, when *A Steele Rudd selection* was selected and introduced by Moorhouse, he predicted a 'post-multicultural' identity in which second- and third-generation immigrants would move towards an 'Australian' identity informed in large part by settlers' tales: 'The special and peculiar trials and hazards of those days in the bush, with all its infinite metaphorical variations, will continue to seep into our heads'.[7] As if to reinforce this prediction, Moorhouse produced a number of humorous fictional encounters with and retreats from the bush and country towns by his own metropolitan Australians. Moorhouse's metropolitans, who often have country-town backgrounds, are not at home in the bush any more than are Rudd's. But some of them, reflecting Moorhouse himself, are attracted to the freedoms it seems to offer. In 'Going into the heartlands with the wrong person at Christmas',[8] Moorhouse questions what is 'natural' or 'unnatural' when humans enter the wilderness outside cities. While we are not invited to guffaw at Moorhouse's man and woman 'outside town' as we are sometimes invited to do at Dad and Dave and their family group, we are wryly shown the oddity of individuals 'out of place', or discovering where they belong.

Moorhouse's 'sex on the rock' scene in his story is a half-century in time and attitudes from Rudd's jokes about Dave's sexual urges. In their *Penguin book of Australian jokes*, Phillip Adams and Patrice Newell devote their opening section to 'Dad 'n' Dave in the bush'. They reveal how tastes and expectations of humour change, as in the following anecdote about preparations for Dave and Mabel's wedding night:

Dave was going to marry Mabel, so he went down to Melbourne to book a room for the wedding night. He found a pub he liked, in he went, in high spirits, very jaunty. 'Gidday. I'd like to book a room for me honeymoon night, luv'.

'Yes', said the female receptionist, 'bridal suite?'

'Ahh, no thanks, dear. I'll just hang on to her ears.'[9]

The joke here is surely on Dave, though his guffawing male companions in the pub may also have been excoriating their own awkwardness about sexual relations. But these friends of Rudd at the bar were not on a different planet from Moorhouse's narrator telling about how he and his sexual friend Belle tried out their rock in the bush for discomfort. The storyteller's setting may have changed from pub to boutique wine bar, but in both cases a man's exposure of sexual taboos and difficulties is at its core.

The Aussie male anecdote that has its roots in the Dad 'n' Dave tales was transported most notably into mid-twentieth-century Australia by Frank Hardy in his Billy Borker yarns. Hardy's pub audience was enlarged considerably by Clement Semmler's championing of Hardy as a raconteur on ABC television in the 1960s and 1970s and by his assistance in publishing *The yarns of Billy Borker* and other examples of Hardy's anecdotal humour. In Semmler's view, the figure of Billy Borker is a 'dinkum Aussie' who is 'the stuff of legend [. . .] in the same bracket as Paterson's Saltbush Bill and John Manifold's Bogong Jack'.[10]

Hardy's stories of the racetrack jostle with those of waterfront workers, butchers, taxi-drivers and other working men. They have an inbuilt repartee that continually favours the point of view of the 'ordinary bloke' and the larrikin over the rich and powerful. Their generic form is often that of the 'shaggy dog' or 'tall tale' laced with Hardy's characteristically iconoclastic irony. In one story he tells of the Yank who has never heard of Sydney until Australia is mentioned: 'Ah yeah, that's where we sell all our old films to the television stations'. Hardy seldom treads the sexual territory of Rudd or Moorhouse, but in 'A shaggy billiard table story' Borker tells his interlocutor of a millionaire who orders a mink-covered billiard table with one leg for 'a hundred thousand nicker' before he goes to the Gold Coast for his honeymoon:

> Well, away he choofs on his honeymoon to Surfers Paradise in his luxury yacht. And he lies in the sun with his beautiful young bride while the tradesmen knock together this special billiard table.
>
> That's the way of the world.
>
> Yeh, and on his way back the yacht ran into a great storm and it sunk. Lost all hands.
>
> You're pulling my leg again. Whew, look at the time. I've got to be going.
>
> Hooroo. If you hear of anyone who wants a good billiard table I know where they can get one cheap.

Here, as elsewhere, the humour resides in part in the storyteller's jocular attempts to convince a listener of the truthfulness of a patent 'porky'. The tall or shaggy tale, he suggests, has a truth beyond facts.[11]

The humour of Australian women who sit on verandahs of country houses and yarn has been less investigated than the 'masculine tradition'. Fiona Giles's anthology represents a tradition of nineteenth-century romance writing by women. Here, from time to time, we find a quieter, less assertive but no less engaging capacity to find cause to laugh at the various adversities of bush living. For example, in Rosa Praed's story 'Old Shilling's bush wedding' – which takes place at a hotel called 'Coffin Lid' in North Queensland – we are told a version of the Beauty and the Beast tale. The princess is a poor but beautiful young Scandinavian emigrant who can't speak English and the beast is a clapped-out, ugly old alcoholic farmer called Shilling. The narrator relates her sense of the incongruity of the wedding:

> It was the oddest wedding I ever witnessed. I don't think any of us felt quite comfortable about the proceedings, and I agreed with the postman,

who came in and stood by the fireplace while his fresh horse was being saddled, that 'it was a d——d shame to let a fine young woman be tied up to that dirty old hunchback'.

The narrator hints that the young woman may have her own reasons for desiring this new life in Coffin Lid (she already has a wedding ring). But the marriage is apparently a success and Praed shows how accommodating Australian bush life can sometimes be to the most apparently absurd situations and unions. This is the other face of that exclusionary humour which reinforces prejudice and is a feature of tales by both women and men of this time.[12]

Another form of women's humour from the verandah is the ghost story. Ellen August Chads' 'The ghost of Wanganilla: Founded on fact', for example, writes back to its parent form of the English ghost story and develops its humour from ironic contrast between forms of ghostliness in Britain and Australia. The ghostly vision of a woman with outstretched arms in the moonlight is revealed in daylight to be a dead gumtree apparently struck by lightning. In this case, the anti-climactic humour of a 'real' source of ghostly visions leads to romance. The ghost is laughed out of court (and off the verandah) but has created opportunities for a young man and a young woman to get together.[13] More broadly, it can be said that Australian ghost stories, often by women, express an ironic sense of humorous contrast between English and Australian conditions while confronting the anxieties and fears of the new place. In the introduction to his *Oxford book of Australian ghost stories*, Ken Gelder wonders whether Australians 'have a closer relationship to ghosts than we might have first imagined'.[14]

How did humour reassert itself in Australian short fiction by women in the mid-to-late twentieth century? Two distinctive modes are evident in stories by Elizabeth Jolley and Thea Astley. Jolley's early volumes of stories *Five acre virgin* (1976) and *The travelling entertainer* (1979) suggest links with the humorous dimensions of stories by colonial women writers in Australia. The chief difference is Jolley's lack of moralistic intent as she tracks the emotional lives of a new generation of European immigrants in Australia. The sadness that Jolley discerns at the heart of the emigrant/immigrant experience is countered from time to time by witty and humorous interludes. Ambiguity is often at the source of such humour, as in her title story 'Five acre virgin', which plays on the virginity of land and the inexperience of new settlers, to reveal a comedy of settlement dramatically different from heroic sagas such as Mary Durack's *Kings in grass castles*.

Amongst the apparent trivia of domestic situations, in shops or hospitals or on weekend farms, Jolley recurrently lightens an encompassing sadness. A vignette from *Five acre virgin* indicates Jolley's comic versatility as she presents the narrator and her mother waiting at their small rented farm cottage for their recalcitrant son and brother:

'If only he'd be early!' Mother stood up beside the logs where we'd been sitting waiting all the afternoon. There was a pile of them up a bit from the weatherboard house, they must have been pushed there years ago. From these logs we could see the road. She shaded her eyes with her hand.

'Nature has her own ways', Mother always tried to comfort my brother as everything filled in so quickly when he cleared. Mother worked hard even though the place was not hers and she was only on it by this gentleman's agreement. She stood by when the owner, Dr Harvey, was having trouble with the bore he had put down. The engineer had come and Mother was out there right on top of them telling them what to do. You could see the doctor felt uneasy to be on his land with us being there, and though he was quiet and very polite while the engineer was trying to get the siphon going, it was clear he was wishing Mother miles away. There was a great long black plastic pipe all down the slope to the small three-cornered water hole we called the dam, its banks were muddy and trodden down by the few cows left behind from Grandpa's time.

'It's like a stomick wash out', Mother explained at the top of her voice. 'You must get the whole hose full of water before you let it start to run. Fill the hose, pinch it while it fills and then let it go into the dam and it'll start the siphon. Just imagine!' she shouted at them, 'water coming up from all that way down under the earth, no trouble at all!'[15]

Jolley's experience as a nurse continually bursts forth in dialogue or situations that reveal a down-to-earth appreciation of Lawson's 'hardness of things' and ways in which the pressure of this knowledge may be alleviated. The comedy of bodily functions is set against the ineffability of music, literature and the knowledge of death. In *Mr Scobie's riddle*, two lesbian nurses engage in repartee, one asking the other if she smokes after sex, to which her partner answers, 'I don't know, I've never looked'. The pathos occasionally evoked by a hospice of dying people is enlivened by reminders of the energy and irreverence of youth and night sisters' reports such as the following:

November 4. Night Sister's Report
Room 3. Mother vioded room three sponged slept well 4 am kitchen floor washed as request sweet potatoes prepared also pumpkin please matron can I have a knife for the veggies. Nothing abnormal to report. Signed Night Sister M. Shady[16]

Thea Astley's satiric portraits are generally guided by a more moralistic outlook than Jolley's. Her Mango-dwellers are from North Queensland as surely as Jolley's hills dwellers are from Western Australia. In the title story of Astley's *Hunting the wild pineapple* volume, she presents her male narrator in this ironic self-description:

I am bearded now (arty or distinguished according to company), wooden-legged (the limp is captivating), and with a fringe of hang-ups, monstrous puritan-liberal growths like gall-wasp. No nodes on the skin, mark you: merely a flicker of epidermic sun-spotting – I call it bagassing – where the north has bitten me.

Through this somewhat jaundiced figure, Astley presents her denizens of
the 'parish' of North Queensland, including long-time locals, dropouts from
the south and con-men and -women of the tourist trail. She also dramatises
the painful farce of religious clashes and difference.[17] As in Graham Greene's
work, Astley's Catholic conscience mediates human dramas that can never
be simply funny and sometimes exude a sense of bitter disappointment.
Somewhere behind them lies a notion of paradise from which Australia's
north-east has become estranged. Physically beautiful and entrancing to
the senses, Queensland's tropical rainforests emblematise Astley's Paradise
Lost.

Thea Astley's Paradise Lost is nevertheless one where laughter is both
natural and necessary. Her 'middle-class bums from the south' who hitch to
Queensland for their bit of pot and Paradise encounter a stubbornly resistant culture. The clash of cultures offers a comedy of 'manners' that Astley
exploits to the full:

> The town was crawling with Kombi vans that lurched in from unsur-
> faced roads to the north, and out of them the kids would saunter to
> sprawl about the road-house tables. Sometimes one would mooch across
> unslinging his guitar.
>
> 'Can I rip you off for a fag, man?' he asks, the hand already half-way
> to my pack. 'I'll give you a rain-forest song.'
>
> 'I'll give you one not to play', I say, but he doesn't hear me and he
> plays six choruses of melancholy while the tourist straights come in for
> milk or hamburgers and grin at my plight.

Characteristically for Astley, this humorous scene is followed by a longer,
more reflective view that both undercuts the humour and gives it extra
resonance:

> I wonder sometimes what will happen to these kids at forty, fifty. Already
> a few of the trendier, middle-aged straights around town have made

palliative gestures by adopting the patois if not the dress. It's sad watching them jostle the ranks of the ear-ringed lotus-eaters. Lotus-eaters land was certainly what it was in the northern mornings with light hachured between forest and road, a land in which it always certainly seemed afternoon for those casual pilgrimages from one shack to the next, one joint to the next, with the occasional water sounds of plucked strings while the weeds lushed up and over and no one turned a sod. They had had enough of acting and of motion, they.

The longer view edges back into the comedy here, acting as its necessary complement in Astley's work. It complicates any simply comic world-view, lending it an air of opportunities lost.[18]

The problematic comic outlooks of Astley and Jolley are further complicated when we consider the short fiction of Lily Brett. Brett's stories of the Jewish diaspora in Melbourne in *Things could be worse* (1990), *What God wants* (1991) and her *Collected stories* (1999) reveal a different kind of inherited burden from Astley's Catholicism. Brett's narrator and alter ego Lola Bensky owns 'a library of one thousand books on the Holocaust' and has 'woven many of her own fantasies into the fabric of her parents' past'.[19]

The dark humour of Brett's stories derives largely from this 'double vision' of a daughter who lives through her parents' suffering and survival at Auschwitz and thus sees the absurdity of people's behaviour in contemporary Jewish society in Australia. Ghosts emerge from the past and enter Lola's thoughts and feelings. At the same time, she observes with piquant curiosity the way Jewish-Australians manage to live with that past and make some kind of life in the present.

Lily Brett's privileged insight as a woman into family and social relations among Melbourne Jewry provides the opening for narratives that build on older traditions of storytelling. When Lola meets Mrs Kopper at Polonsky's kosher butcher shop, she and another woman, Mrs Singer, are regaled with Mrs Kopper's telling of an old Sholem Aleichem tale:

There was a village where many people had troubles. They came to the rabbi and said 'Rabbi, why do I have to have so much trouble? My neighbour doesn't have such troubles. Why was I chosen to have this trouble?' The rabbi heard these complaints many times. One day the rabbi said that everyone who had troubles should put their troubles in a bag, and bring the bag to the market place. The people of the village did this. Then the rabbi said that everyone should choose someone else's bag to take home. When the people got home and saw what was in the bag of troubles that they had chosen, they said, 'Oh God, please give me my own troubles back. My own troubles were not so bad'. The next day everyone returned to the market place to get back his own bag of troubles.

'Excuse me', said Mrs Singer: 'I know that you are telling this story, Mrs Kopper, but it is important to tell it right. I don't think that Sholem Aleichem said that many people in the village had trouble, just a few people.'

'All right, all right, Mrs Singer', said Mrs Kopper. 'What does it matter? That is not so important. What is important is what I was trying to tell Lola. And that is that things can always be worse.'

'I can tell you straightaway about two sisters who are worse', said Mrs Singer.[20]

The 'value added' to Aleichem's tale is the humorous interchange between these women in the butcher shop vying for the most terrible thing that has happened to them or to people they know. Lying behind many such interchanges are the horrors that family or friends have experienced at Auschwitz or other concentration camps, for which such conversations are a displacement or substitute.

Brett's short fiction also shows a capacity to humorously reveal the anxieties of an increasingly multicultural Australian population in the 1980s and 1990s. In 'Moishe Zimmerman's wife', Ruth is worried about her widower father Moishe being lonely, when he makes a surprising request:

Ruthie, Eddie and Moishe were eating at Scheherezade. They ate at Scheherezade every Sunday night.

'Ruthie, do you have any old clothes?' Moishe asked.

'Of course I've got old clothes. What do you want old clothes for?'

'For Esmeralda, the Chinese girl from the flats', said Moishe.

'A Chinese girl called Esmeralda? That's an unusual name for a Chinese', said Eddie.

'Yes', said Moishe. 'She's very poor. She's got only two skirts and two tops. She was brought to Australia by a terrible man. She was a post office bride.'

'Do you mean a mail-order bride?' said Ruthie.

'I think she's probably Filipino, not Chinese. Esmeralda is definitely not a Chinese name', said Eddie.

'Chinese, Filipino, what difference does it make? She is very poor', said Moishe.

'OK, Dad', said Ruthie. 'I'll put together a bag of clothes for her.'[21]

Moishe's more startling announcement, a little later, is that he intends to marry Esmeralda. Remarkably, it is the father rather than his daughter who adjusts to the New World, suggesting also a continuing rapport with his dead wife and Jewish tradition:

'Jewish, not Jewish', said Moishe. 'What does it matter? I lived all my life as a Jew. Now, I'll see what it is like not to be so Jewish. Ruthie, Esmeralda is not taking the place of your mother. If I had married Renia or Sofia or Rivka your mother, wherever she is, God rest her soul, would have been uncomfortable. But Bluma will be happy to see me married to Esmeralda. Bluma always liked me to look nice. You didn't even notice, my dear daughter, that I have got new clothes.'[22]

Sophisticated Jewish humour with its powerful literary tradition may seem at arm's length from Aboriginal storytelling. However, the writing of Kim

Scott and Herb Wharton shows a similar capacity to create humour from
adversity while building on oral traditions of storytelling rich in dialogue.

Indigenous Australian humour receives a late apotheosis in the short
stories of Herb Wharton, which tap the traditions of campfire yarn and
country and western music, as well as the colloquial language of Murri
stockmen and drovers. The question with which I began this essay, whether
we can still find threads back to the kinds of humour shared by Lawson,
Stephens, Furphy and Franklin, seems to be answered in the affirmative
by Wharton. In 'Waltzing Matilda', for example, Wharton writes back to
Paterson's song and the nationalistic mythology that has accreted around
it, in a spirit which celebrates the land and its stimulus to storytelling, for
Murri people as well as whites. Wharton's 'Waltzing Matilda' is a genial
parody in the sense that it celebrates Paterson's poem by imitating and
drawing on its narrative and imagery; but it also changes the original by
adding an Aboriginal experiential dimension that can now be seen to have
been lacking.

The two Murri stockmen around whom Wharton's story revolves,
Knughy and Bunji, create their own drama from Paterson's song as they
camp by the same Combo waterhole where Paterson had set his poem.
Wharton's story modulates from humour of situation to the wary humour
of a ghost story. The core of the narrative is approached through the old
man Knughy's recollections:

> I can tell you that long time before all that happen [Paterson's story of
> the Jolly Swagman] people still came walking here. This waterhole was
> proper sit-down place then, with plenty yudie, plenty fish, sugar-bag
> [honey] too. These people, they all belonga this land and they say – if
> you want 'em tucker you take 'em yudie. There weren't no branded and
> earmarked animals in them days. The laws said you could take 'em yudie
> if you was hungry. And it might be, like that swagman, after they sitting
> down a while, they move on to hunt another place.[23]

Then, 'might be', says Knughy, that the hungry swagman comes along, 'belly pinching and feet aching', when 'them thum-bas [sheep] come down to water while he's sitting under his coolabah tree with his billy on the boil':

> Well, he grabs one, butchers it up and has a big feed. He real Jolly Swagman then, belly bulging, tuckerbag full. He sits there singing, no worries – and that's when them Ghungies come riding silently along. They seen that thum-ba's fresh skin, no meat in it, in the creekbed. 'Hey, that's strange', they think. Might be someone been steal thum-ba belonging to big fella boss owns country, owns animals – might be his own Ghungies too.[24]

The pleasure of such passages occurs at several levels. First, there's the fellow-feeling of an Aboriginal stockman for the imagined swagman of the underclass ruled over by the bosses of the land. Second, this fellow-feeling leads to humorous variations on the widely known words of Paterson's 'Waltzing Matilda' – 'thum-ba' for jumbuck, 'Ghungies' for policemen – which show how he enters into the spirit of the song. Third is the sheer pleasure of the fresh colloquial rendering of the tale.

In keeping with many Aboriginal and white tales, Wharton's 'moral' or 'message' is kept till last. Although ghostly presences are evoked earlier, the story's expressed meaning is fresh, practical and down-to-earth and emerges through dialogue, with the old man Knughy having the final say:

> 'What can I learn?' asked Bunji. 'Don't steal sheep, be careful where I light a fire, don't try to escape from lawful custody – is that all, old man?'
>
> Knughy shook his head emphatically. 'The point is this: under no circumstances should you dive into deep water with a full belly. That's what killed that Jolly Swagman, my boy – going for a swim on a full belly.'[25]

The anti-climactic humour here can be shared by white and black listeners alike, but Wharton adds a layer of reflection at the end by his younger stockman Bunji's questioning of myth, history and fiction as the old man snores away by the campfire.

Herb Wharton's moral tales are characterised by an inclusive humour that takes a dig at human frailties shared by blacks and whites. His story 'Dreamtime future: Bungo the money god' blends fantasy and Dreamtime conventions to show how the worship of material wealth can infect all cultures.[26] When Knughy and his family visit the city (Brisbane) they seek out its sacred sites, the principal one being the Casino, whose guide thinks how he can describe what it stands for, its values:

> Their guide . . . looked around in awe; for the first time it came to him that there was a true Dreamtime story behind all that glitter. As he watched the multi-racial mix of people come and go, he thought that these people too had a Dreaming. He recalled the past history of this building and the people's desire for wealth. In money terms, this was indeed the Dreaming Place of many tribes. But how, he wondered, could he put into words the long, almost forgotten history of this place – the sleeping place of Bungo the great Money God?[27]

Stimulated by his Aboriginal visitors, the guide waxes lyrical about the Bungo creation myth and the happiness he spreads. But there is friction with the original tribal people of the country who worship another god called Mother Earth. Bungo's people get richer and want to get richer still and chant their tribal need and creed: 'Bungo, bungo, bungo – more bungo, more, more more!'[28] Their unfulfilled desire culminates in the construction of the Casino, which, however, leads many to despair, drugs and prostitution.

The deftness in Wharton's satire of Western values is evident in his lightness of touch. Instead of extending the joke, he switches time and place to the desert homeland of Knughy and Nulla. Here they are prevailed on to tell of their visit to the city, which they do in the Corroboree of the Money God Bungo, showing that they too have been infected, in a small way, by Bungo's spell:

> In outback Australia, as the sunset fades and the moon rises around the campfire, while didjeridoos wail and clap sticks rattle and the red dust rises from barefoot dancers, the Dreamtime story of Bungo is enacted. The flickering flames from the fire illuminate a large sign: ADMITTANCE TO ENCLOSED AREA – FEE $2.[29]

At a time in Australia when laughing clubs are proposed for individual therapy, the healing power of humour and laughter for a national culture has been little explored. Literature has a part to play in this enterprise, especially the short story. Writers must never shrink from exploring and expressing 'the hardness of things'. But Miles Franklin was surely right, and Ken Stewart too, in showing that solemnity can betoken stupidity and that laughter can restore sanity in the darkest of times.

Parody

'To write or not to write': Some Australian literary parodies 1820–1850

Elizabeth Webby

For many years the Association for the Study of Australian Literature (ASAL) featured a 'parody night' as part of its annual conference, where conference-goers produced satirical versions of their favourite – and not-so-favourite – authors and works. One of the masters of the ASAL parody nights was Ken Stewart, whose parodies of Christopher Brennan, AD Hope and other Australian authors remain treasured memories for all who heard them. The practice has now fallen away, but it was a recognition that there were very few contemporary outlets for literary parody, and so it could be said to have met an unspoken need.

In nineteenth-century Australia there were many more outlets, although the works parodied were, of course, mainly English, with a couple of exceptions. Shakespeare was, as he has no doubt remained, the author most parodied, because the best known. And the most parodied passage was of course Hamlet's 'To be or not to be' speech. As well as including some examples of parodies of this and other passages from Shakespeare, I will look at several satirical rewritings of Thomas Hood's well-known poem 'The song of the shirt' (1843), as well as some parodies of other authors.

In the first half of the nineteenth century, most Australian news-papers and magazines were not illustrated, since woodcuts, expensive and time-consuming to produce, were the most readily available technology.

So political and other cartoons did not begin appearing until the second half of the 1840s, apart from some very crude woodcut cartoons and line engravings occasionally published in Launceston's *Cornwall Chronicle* from 1836 to 1838.[1] This did not mean that Australian newspapers were lacking in comic and satirical commentary on local affairs. The satirical 'pipe', rolled-up sheets of libellous verses attacking government officials that were dropped in public places, had become a feature of political life in New South Wales soon after the colony's foundation. This tradition soon transferred itself to newspapers once a free press was established with the issuing of *The Australian* by WC Wentworth and Robert Wardell in 1824. Even when illustrations became more widespread in the second half of the nineteenth century, satirical magazines such as *Melbourne Punch* still often published a poem as well as a cartoon on a particular topic.

A favourite method used by those in the nineteenth century when writing comic or satiric verse was to make 'A new song on an old tune'. Sometimes the lack of fit between the original words and the new ones was part of the fun, as with the Irish servant Lanty O'Liffey's song in Edward Geoghegan's musical play *The currency lass*, first performed in Sydney in 1844. His 'The raal ould Irish rollicker', a song in praise of the Irishman, gets added points by being set to the tune of the well-known song 'Fine old English gentleman'.[2] This song was quite a favourite with parodists. Although unknown today, it clearly remained popular into the 1870s, since Marcus Clarke draws on it to make ironic comment on Maurice Frere and his attitudes in the opening chapter of the original serial version of *His natural life*.[3] To write a parody of a passage from Shakespeare, or of a poem by Hood or Byron, was then an extension of this practice of writing new words to well-known tunes, one still employed by writers of university revues today. As an example of this practice, here is 'The monstrous boy', a parody of the popular Thomas Moore ballad 'The minstrel boy', from the *Hunter River Gazette* of 12 March 1842. This paper, published in Maitland, was the first in New South Wales to appear outside Sydney.

1.

The monstrous boy to the Plains* is gone,
  On the Gwyder's banks you'll find him;
His father's sword he has girded on –
  His double-barrel slung behind him.

2.

'Land of Beef!' said the Squatter bold,
  'Though all the blacks betray'd me,
A stockyard shall my cattle hold –
  My pistols, too, shall aid me.'

3.

The Squatter fled! For bohea and spleen
  Soon brought his gaunt form under;
The hut he built ne'er stood again,
  For he tore the slabs asunder.

4.

And said, 'No more of this for me –
  Damper, and beef, and misery!
To the Hunter settlers I will flee
  For peach preserves† and gaiety.'

* Liverpool Plains.
† The Monstrous Boy had a penchant for peaches.

Unlike several of the other parodies discussed here which also deal with the problems of squatting, this charming little piece does not seem to have much of a political axe to grind. Perhaps it can be read as a caution to young men about going off into the wilds in pursuit of fortune rather than staying safely at home. Given its place and time of publication, it would be tempting to attribute it to Charles Harpur, though his parodies of squatters are usually much more savage, as we will see. In its use of the grotesque and mock-heroic, and its comic undercutting of the noble sentiments and pathos of the original ballad, however, 'The monstrous boy' is very characteristic of colonial parodies.

As more newspapers representing different political positions began to be published in Australia, the rivalry between them was often reflected in their satirical and comic verse. One of the earliest Australian parodies of 'To be or not to be', 'The Monitor's soliloquy', was supposedly spoken by the editor of the radical *Sydney Monitor*, and appeared in its more conservative rival, the *Sydney Gazette*, on 13 January 1829:

> To write, or not to write, that is the question;
> Whether 'tis better for my purse, to suffer
> The fines and censures of a Court of Justice,
> Or cease to flounder in a sea of libels,
> And, by my silence, end them . . .

> . . . Get thee to a grog-shop; why wouldst thou be a seizer of Patriots? I am myself not very peccant; but yet I could accuse me of such things, that it were better the Colony had not known me: I am very proud, malicious, jacobinical; with more black libels in my head, than I have quills to write them with, printers to give them shape, or folk to sell them to: – What would such fellows as I do scribbling in New South Wales? We are arrant deceivers all; believe none of us; – Go thy ways to a grog-shop . . .

Another parody of Hamlet's speech, by one 'X.X.X.', appeared in the *Sydney Times* on 23 September 1837, though seemingly without any political intent. Again, however, alcohol was prominent. Here are the opening lines:

> To drink, or not to drink, that is the question.
> Whether 'tis nobler for a man to rove
> From inn to inn mad with the fumes of rum;
> Or take up arms against such beastly habits,
> And, by opposing, end them? grow sober – rich –

No more! – and by this change to say we end
The headache, heart-burn, and a thousand ills
That drunkards suffer! 'tis a consummation
Devoutly to be wish'd. To pray – to drink –
To drink – perchance get drunk – ay, there's the rub –
For, in a deep debauch what deeds are done,
When man has shuffled off fair reason,
Must give us pause. – There's the respect
That makes good natured man drink all his days:
For who would bear the gripe of want and misery –
The spurn of vintners, when his money's gone,
The dun of creditors; the bailiffs chase,
The fears of Jail, and all the insults rude
That canting swaddlers of the drunkard take –
When he himself might save his reputation
By turning Methodist? Who would drink rum,
To groan and spew before an ale-house door
But that the dread of conquering rooted habit
(That powerful tyrant, from whose grasp
Few tipplers e'er escape) puzzles the will,
And bids us rather take another 'ball,'
Than grope our homeward way to cheerless hearths?

The author of 'Incantation scene', published in John Dunmore Lang's *The Colonist* on 2 January 1839, was rather more original in writing a parody of the witches' scene from *Macbeth* to contribute to the controversy surrounding the trial and execution of seven stockmen for their part in the Myall Creek massacre of Indigenous Australians the previous year. While this parody includes some graphic description of the murders, its main target was the *Sydney Herald*, which had throughout their trials and eventual conviction been strongly supportive of the stockmen and published much racist material attacking Indigenous Australians and their supporters.

INCANTATION SCENE

Scene – A Plain – a spot slightly cleared from the surrounding Forest – and a smouldering Fire. The mangled remains of murdered Blacks
are lying half consumed.

WEIRD SISTERS

First Witch

O They were a gallant crew!

Heads and arms the ground bestrew –

Women, children, infants too;

But their deed they soon shall rue.

Second Witch

Native dog his bay begins –

Wakeful vultures flap their wings:

Hark! the creep of crawling things;

For this deed the culprit swings.

Third Witch

Let us sing in under tone,

Hark, again! the dying groan;

Keep each large and little bone –

Hemp for noble necks is sown.

Chorus

There will be trouble for little and great,

For villain in bondage, and man of estate.

  First Witch

  Prepare then the charm,

    That we may speed well:

  Second Witch

  Fill earth with alarm –

    Forecast and foretell.

  Third Witch

  Extend each right arm,

    And mutter the spell.

Chorus
Our cauldron is here, a fire is found –
Children of Fear, dance blythely around.
First Witch
O'er the fumes of roasting men,
    As the bloody vapours rise;
While muscles quiver, now and then
    We snuff the sacrifice.
Second Witch
See the cauldron's ample rim;
    Cast in the head, cast in the limb;
Sprinkle blood upon the brim,
    And feast your gloating eyes.
Third Witch
Now, to make the charm secure,
    Add a written brazen lure,
A smooth word, and a look so pure;
    Then stir the broth so nice.
First Witch
Now it boils – the visions come;
    Blow with breath the rising scum;
Read, O read the guilt of some!
    Revenge will soon arise.
Second Witch
Ingratitude uprises grim,
    Bids the leaden bullets swim.
What strange vapours floateth dim?
    The Prince of Treacheries –
Third Witch
Lo! POISON comes – for crafty head
    And coward heart distributes bread –
He feeds his guests – he drugs them dead,

And murmurs fill the skies.

Chorus

Sighs and tears, we hear you well;

Revenge is yours – we work the spell –

But need a higher spice of hell.

First Witch

Sisters, mix up perjury –

Second Witch

Give an Editorial lie –

Third Witch

A Correspondent's ribaldry.

Chorus

Last, the bounce and sophistry

Of ------ and O'Felonry;

If these succeed not, naught will do:

These embrute and poison too.

Hubble bubble! toil and trouble!

Hell-broth boil, and cauldron bubble.

See, it works! the spell is true, (*With glee*)

And the awful vengeance due.

Revenge for men of sable line

Shall fall upon a bloody crew.

Hubble-bubble! toil and trouble!

Hell-broth boil, and cauldron bubble.

Revenge for men of sable line

Shall visit yet a bloody crew.

In this last section of the poem, 'O'Felonry' is a reference to Edward O'Shaugnessy, an ex-convict who wrote for the *Sydney Herald*; JD Lang and *The Colonist* had been carrying on a feud with him for several years. The 'Editorial lie' may refer to the *Herald's* claim on 14 December 1838 that three of the stockmen sentenced to death had been wrongly identified. When asked to provide evidence for this, the editor had hastily backed down, saying it was not his business to do so. There are several possibilities for 'A Correspondent's ribaldry' as many anti-Aboriginal letters were published in the *Herald* over this period. The most infamous, by 'Anti-Hypocrite', appeared on 19 September 1838 and attacked the use of government funds for the benefit of 'cannibals, to whom the veriest reptile that crawls the earth holds out matter for emulation . . . the most degenerate, despicable and brutal race of beings in existence'. 'Anti-Hypocrite' was supposedly a grazier on the Murrumbidgee, but it was not unknown at the time for editors to write letters to themselves. Certainly, his sentiments were endorsed in a *Herald* editorial on 8 October 1838, which referred to Indigenous Australians as 'black animals' and 'murderous wretches'.

If WA Duncan had been publishing his radical journal, the *Weekly Register of Politics, Facts, and General Literature*, in 1838–39, it would certainly have joined in the controversy over the Myall Creek massacre. As its full title suggests, the *Weekly Register* took a lively interest in local politics, being firmly on the side of the lower orders against the growing power of the squatters, and published much satirical verse, including many parodies. 'The "Association" in Council', a parody of Byron's 'The destruction of the Sennacherib', appeared on 19 October 1844 under the pseudonym 'Byron Junior'. It may have been by Charles Harpur, who was contributing much satiric and other verse to this journal at the time, though Elizabeth Perkins does not include it in her *Poetical works of Charles Harpur* and some of the versification is rather poor. Here are the first three stanzas:

The big Squatter stood up, like a jack in the box,
And his chummies were kindling with thoughts of their flocks;
And the show of their souls was like sheep in the sun,
When the blue skies seem spanning some New England run.

Like a flight of macaws, when the maize is in cob,
The Council were seen at their favourite job;

Like a flight of macaws, which the settler has shot at,
They soon will be driven from the work they're so hot at.

For the murmurs of Hate fill the homes of the poor,
And doom the 'sheep-Counts' to be Solons no more;
And the ears of the senators tingle and burn,
And they hope there'll be gullibles still to 'return!'

Although the author uses the non-Australian term 'macaw' to describe a
flock of parrots, cockatoos or perhaps galahs in the corn, the picture given
here is still very vivid. It is characteristic of Harpur's satirical poetry that he
uses local imagery just as plentifully as in his better-known serious poems.
This is seen particularly strongly in 'The patriot of Australia', published in
the *Weekly Register* on 22 November 1845 and definitely by Harpur. What
is being parodied here is not so much a specific author as the classical heroic
poem. The target of Harpur's scorn is William Charles Wentworth, once
a democrat and himself in 1816 the author of satirical pipes attacking the
government[4] but now a leader of the squattocracy, or the 'sheep counts'
as Harpur describes them. Again, local fauna are brought in to add to the
fun, and some wonderful pictures of life in colonial Australia are created as
an incidental to the attack on Wentworth. Harpur also shows his mastery
of generic and formal conventions, necessary if this type of parody is to be
successful.

THE PATRIOT OF AUSTRALIA
A Heroic Poem in Ten Cantos

Invocation
O for a Muse as fervent as the steam
That noseward rises from the golden heart
Of a maize doughboy, newly from the pot,
And deftly quartered by the trenchant knife

Of hungry settler clad in dungaree!
So might I soar into the highest heaven
Of Poesie, as surely as a 'Possum
Can skither up a gum tree, whilst I sing
Of Wentworth, our great Patriot! But his name
Alone is Inspiration! From the runs
Beyond the boundaries, hark! and ghostly wise,
From all the boiling down establishments,
A multitudinous bellowing, bleating sound,
Mixt with the roar of out-at-elbow sheep counts,
And oath-clencht plaudits from the 'Forty Thieves',
Even as I write it, gathers o'er, to swell
The heroic syllable, and hearten me
To cut this Invocation and begin.

Canto First

When the great Mantuan Bard first saw the light,
'Tis said that bees did swarm about his mouth,
To signify that thence mellifluous streams
Of honeyed song should flow; and when Glendower,
Old Cambria's 'learned Theban', with the squall
Of his Nativity did scare the mice
From dining on a vast and moon like cheese
That graced his mother's chamber, Heaven, 'tis said,
Was filled with fiery shapes, and the old earth
Griped full as much as though she had swallowed whole,
And raw, the cheese just mentioned; all, no doubt,
To certify that to his race was born
No common child: So in the infant days
Of this young World, when on that fertile Isle
Since desecrated by the tears and blood
Of exiled Toil, the Hero of my song

Came bounce into this breathing life, our wilds
Laboured with Signs and Tokens – most of which
Are now forgotten, but what yet remain
Within the failing memories of the past,
The Muse shall chronicle. The Hostess then
Of Sydney's only Tap, on whose pert nose
Prophetic ardours burn'd, gan all at once
To scream – 'a Patriot is born!' but like
Cassandra's rage of old, her pious words
Were then unheeded, for the sneering rogues
Who heard them, only at each other winked,
And swore the jade was drunk. Also that day,
As certain 'lags' that in the Bush stript bark
Did afterwards report, great Kangaroos,
Not christened yet 'old men', did round them dance
The Blacks' carobbora; whilst Bandicoots
In the broad sunlight ran about and squeaked;
And from the hollows of the ironbarks,
Ram 'Possums poked their fearless heads, and jabbered
To Mocking-birds that in the brakes about
Kept shouting 'Billy's born!'

The squatters, of course, were not without their own poetical supporters. Harpur's 'Squatter songs', of which the best known now is 'The beautiful squatter', whose protagonist is 'waddied to death' for his sexual mistreatment of Indigenous women,[5] were a response of a series of pro-squatter poems by Robert Lowe, which appeared in his paper *The Atlas*. My favourite account of the squatter's dismal lot, however, was published, appropriately enough, in a country newspaper, the *Geelong Advertiser*. Printed on 6 May 1846, 'The song of the bush' by H.B. was a parody of Hood's 'The song of the shirt'. Its replacement of the original chorus of 'sew, sew, sew' with 'squat, squat, squat' is one of the features that turns this parody of a serious poem in support of the poor into a comic masterpiece lamenting the squatter's woeful life. Here are the first two of its nine stanzas.

> By the side of a dried-up creek,
> In the glare of the scorching sun,
> A squatter was squatting upon a log,
> Surveying his parched-up run –
> Squat – squat – squat!
> With visage grizzly and gaunt,
> With a rueful look at his wretched hut,
> He sang this dolorous chaunt.
>
> Squat – squat – squat!
> From weary year to year;
> And squat – squat – squat!
> In continual dread and fear.
> It's O to be a rock,
> And an oyster attached to that;
> For a tenure fixed I then would have,
> But now I can only squat![6]

Many other parodies of Hood's poem were published in Australia, including several by GF Pickering, the editor of *Bell's Life in Sydney*, a newspaper that like its model, *Bell's Life in London*, stressed the lighter things of life, such as sporting news and comic verses, and was one of the earliest Australian papers to regularly feature cartoons. Pickering's 'The song of the gold', published on 17 February 1849, was one of several comic poems of the period which cautioned people against rushing off to California by portraying a digger's life as just as unrewarding as a squatter's. And his 'The song of the pen', 3 March 1849, was one of a number that bemoaned the lot of the editor. Two years earlier, indeed, another parody of 'The song of the shirt' dealing with the same topic had been published in *Bell's Life* on

27 February 1847. Entitled 'Song of the editor', it had originally appeared
in the Adelaide paper the *South Australian*. While not as funny a parody as
'The song of the bush', these two stanzas provide an appropriate conclusion
to a study of some of the ways in which politics, newspapers and parody
interacted in colonial Australia:

> Write! Write! Write!
> Tho' fancy soar on a tired wing,
> She must still her tribute celestial bring,
>   Nor own a weary flight!
> And Reason's power, and Mem'ry's store,
> Must prove their strength, and bring the lore
>   Antique, and sage, and mystic: –
> For these, to the uttermost thought and particle
> Must go in to-morrow's 'leading article' –
>   Of argument – wit – statistic!

> Lie! Lie! Lie!
> If he happens to be a party hack,
> He must echo the yell of the greedy pack,
>   And shout the demon cry!
> To Honor's appeal he must never hark,
> But aim like Death at a shining mark,
>   As he speeds the poison dart!
> And then, when the battle so fierce is o'er,
> And the victors apportion the captur'd store,
>   Their 'thanks' shall be his part!

No one ever got rich writing parodies, nor are they remembered in the
canon of Australian poetry. But many of these parodies can still be appreciated for their wit and humour, as well as for the glimpses they give us of life
in Australia in the first decades of the nineteenth century.

'Our serious frolic':
Ern Malley's postwar trip to England

Virginia Blain

Harold Stewart is often remembered, as he feared, and perhaps unfairly, one suspects, merely as the 'back legs' of the Ern Malley 'hobbyhorse', which was essentially animated by his friend James McAuley. He once remarked that the success of the hoax showed 'that not only could people not tell the difference between sense and nonsense but they had lost their sense of humour . . . One of the great brain-washing effects of modern civilisation is the corruption of the sense of beauty and the sense of humour which often go together'.[1] This is an intriguing conjunction not immediately enlarged upon by Stewart, but certainly epitomising his conservative standpoint. It would be true to say that both the senses of beauty and the humour in Ern Malley were simultaneously initiated and stifled by the satiric agenda of the two authors. However, while beauty was purposely turned on its head by various disjunctive techniques, humour was apparently courted. Wisps of each remain, tantalisingly fragmentary. As Michael Heyward has noted, free association and conscious interruption were the key principles in the improvisation.[2] This means that Stewart may have been right to link beauty and humour, but not perhaps fully intending the result that ensued. Just as any vestiges of beauty in image or melodic effects are always jarringly disrupted in order to satirise modernist poetics, sadly the jokes also are often strangled at birth by being firmly hauled into line with a rigidly didactic purpose. The overall 'joke' of the hoax remains – but it is a practical joke, and was only ever truly funny to the perpetrators and their cronies, and to the generally philistine audience who enjoyed Max Harris's public discomfiture at the time. Of course, a number of respected critics and fellow poets have since gone on record in praise of the poems and in defence of the notion that McAuley and Stewart had unwittingly produced work of a far higher calibre than they intended. This is usually argued along the lines that unexpected epiphanies were achieved by dint of the two poets letting the preconscious imagination (normally rigorously censored by both) run loose among their minds' admittedly rich and sophisticated intellectual and poetic furnishings.

The two 'Sonnets for the Novachord' from *The darkening ecliptic* seem to encapsulate the strange disappearing trick of the comic spirit from the fabric of the collection. The title is funny when you know what a Novachord is, or was. The Hammond Novachord was the first polyphonic synthesiser ever produced; first marketed in the United States in 1939, over 1000 were created before World War II finished off production in 1942. It evidently produced sleazy, creepy, synthesised sound, eminently suitable for use in sci-fi or horror movies. 'Sonnets' for such an instrument is a good absurdist joke. But in practice it is not so funny; in the second sonnet, the sestet runs thus:

> If this be the norm
> Of our serious frolic
> There's no remorse:
> Our magical force
> Cleaves the ignorant storm
> On the hyperbolic.[3]

Here 'the hyperbolic' could stand for the exaggerated verbal effects that so often steer the verses into bathos, while the triumphant hoaxers certainly saw themselves as somehow destroying the ignorant storm with their magical force ('Cleaves' is a deliberately ill-fitting verb, while the preposition 'on' renders the image virtually meaningless, a common strategy throughout Malley's oeuvre). The deliberate jettisoning of syntactical logic mimics effects achieved with rather more subtlety in Dylan Thomas (a now completely unfashionable poet, interestingly: maybe he could be hoisted aloft again on Malley's back!). But while Thomas's imagery, at least in his best poems, responds beautifully to an intricate close reading, Malley's does not. Flashes of suggestiveness fizzle out all the time. The frolic is serious in one sense – it has a didactic purpose – but not in another; it has no deep engagement with a lived reality, as true humour has. Is mockery comic? It has to depend on the positioning of the mocked and the mocker. Mockery is a weapon: 'Is it useful?' asks French philosopher André Comte-Sponville in his recent meditation on humour as a virtue. He answers himself:

> Of course, and sometimes necessary. What weapon is not? But no weapon is peaceful, and no irony humorous . . . [I]rony is . . . a laughter that takes itself seriously, excludes itself from its mockery of others, and is always at someone else's expense . . . Irony scorns, disparages, censures. It takes itself seriously and questions only *other people's* seriousness . . . [T]o mock others one must take oneself very seriously indeed . . . Irony laughs at others . . . humor laughs at the self, or at another as though it were the self; it always includes the self in the nonsense it brings about or exposes.[4]

If we agree with these statements, it is easy to see why there is so little humour in Ern Malley.

However, we should not forget that the case is complicated by the purposeful humourlessness of the Malley figure himself. His deathly earnestness, his and his sister's stereotypical names, his doggedly maudlin Preface and Statement about his own writings, his absolute seriousness about himself, would lead one to expect poems far more boring than they actually are. The figure of Malley, with his invented biography, performs an intercessionary role with the reader. He – the Malley figure – both absorbs and deflects much of the ironic intent, allowing measured glimpses of a genuine humour to accumulate. Malley can in no sense be read as a caricature of Max Harris; he has none of Harris's overflowing wordy ebullience. His melancholic, almost bitter, gracelessness is in fact the saving grace of the whole performance, as Sidney Nolan's well-known representation makes clear: he is a down-at-heel clown with tragic overtones. There is a sense of compassion residing somewhere in the construction of this scarecrow sad-sack caricature of a doomed poet:

> . . . Hawk at the wraith
> Of remembered emotions.[5]

I recall a student lecture given by Jim McAuley in the mid-1960s where he followed what I later learned was FR Leavis's line in a ruthless demolition of Shelley's 'To a Skylark' – or was it 'Ode to the West Wind'? When subjected to logical analysis, free association is easy to ridicule.

James McAuley had initially hoped to get Ern Malley to England via the good offices of Herbert Read, well-known essayist, critic and fervid supporter of modernism, later awarded a knighthood. McAuley deeply disliked Read and all that he stood for. A memory shared by Annette Stewart and myself from 1963 is of a lecture given by Sir Herbert Read one dark winter's evening in a dimly lit and thickly curtained lecture room in the University of Tasmania Union building. McAuley had the knack of persuading every UK visitor of note who came to Australia to include Tasmania on their itinerary, whether it be Robert Graves, Iris Murdoch or, on this occasion, his old bête noir. One wonders at his personal agenda in such an invitation, but Read succumbed to the soft soap and flew in one evening from Melbourne. Annette remembers a small grey-haired figure with a neat moustache. I cannot recall his looks, but there was an electricity in the air during his talk, which sparked off in a slightly barbed debate between him and a well-oiled McAuley in the aftermath of question time, and the name of Ern Malley was certainly raised, followed by some rallying remarks on both sides. Of course, we did not know then that one of McAuley's pet ambitions with the Malley hoax twenty years earlier had been to have Ern travel overseas and catch bigger fish than Max Harris, nor that he had felt sure that Read would take the bait. Time had muffled many things, but evidently not his dim view of Read's critical acumen. Many years earlier, he was reportedly furious with Tess van Sommers, junior reporter with Sydney's *Sunday Sun*, for blowing the story of the Malley hoax prematurely. She recalled years later to Michael Heyward how McAuley had exploded at her down the line from the directorate where he worked, 'We won't get Read now!' Heyward reports that:

In November 1944 McAuley admitted, 'It was the egregious Herbert that we set as our mark, hoping to keep the thing going long enough to reach him, and knowing he would be a dead sucker for any gross rubbish that came his way. He is, at least in the publicity sense, "bigger" than the locals, and would give the thing less of an air of taking lollies from children.'[6]

Herbert Read had been an early supporter of Max Harris and the Angry Penguins, and certainly he took their side in the affair:

My opinion was that [the poems] had poetic quality and that the hoaxer, if he was a hoaxer, had got so worked up in the process of imitating certain types of modern poetry that he had become a genuine poet. I was at that time of the opinion that there was sufficient poetic quality in the work of Ern Malley to justify the editor accepting it as genuine literature.[7]

But this is tame stuff, spoken from a safe standpoint by a man knighted for his services to literature, years after the event; and nothing like the pratfall McAuley was so avidly hoping to induce.

Yet Ern Malley *did* travel to England in his full disguise just a few years after his Australian debut, thereby proving that he had the ability to hold his own with panache in wider fields than the local. Although the story of the successfully accomplished hoax had achieved widespread international coverage in 1944, including in London newspapers, nobody in England at the time had had the opportunity to be taken in by it because it had been exposed so early, long before the poems had a chance to be published locally. But in 1949 Ern Malley was to be beheld risen again, holding pride of place once more in a magazine put out by enthusiastic undergraduates, this time at Oxford University. I have not seen any previous reference in print to this English excursion, although Heyward devotes a substantial part of his final chapter to describing Malley's impact on a number of poets in America.

As an undergraduate at St John's College, Oxford, in the dark war years of the mid-1940s, an aspiring young writer named John Wain – later to become extremely influential and well known – gathered some friends and supporters together and started up a new literary magazine, with an emphasis on poetry. The first issue of *Mandrake* appeared in May 1945, priced at two shillings. It was designed like a simple pamphlet clothed in plain blue paper covers with the magazine title overprinted on a running definition of the mandrake plant complete with poetic quotes about it. Its editor was then aged only twenty. Wain signed his first editorial, which kept a modest tone, laying claim only to a freshness of variety and a certain representativeness. This it achieved in some unexpected ways: given the Oxford of those days it is surprising to find that four of twelve contributors were women. Wain wrote in his editorial: 'Amid the exhaustion, the uproar, and the uneasiness of the sixth year of destruction, University students (a class of beings curiously unrecognised and intangible) are not digging holes to hide themselves, but working, thinking, living, recording their impressions'.[8]

This first issue was evidently successful, as Wain's editorial in the magazine's second issue sounds buoyant in its thanks to its supporters and contributors. The second issue has essays and short stories as well as poetry, and a female co-editor, Valmai Adams. Arthur Boyars' name is listed among the contributors of poems: he was later to take over as editor. The ambitious enterprise of a wartime student-run literary magazine evidently paid off, as it continued with irregular issues for more than a decade, finally folding in 1957. It was broader in scope than a typical university student magazine, in that it aimed to publish exciting new work by a wide range of avant-garde writers in and beyond the university. Wolf Mankowitz, Roy Campbell and CM Bowra were among the names published. By 1949 (issue 6), Boyars, himself a poet, was listed as sole editor. He had replaced John Wain, who took up a lectureship at Reading University in that year at the age of twenty-four, though he stayed a frequent contributor, mainly of poems but also of editorial advice. It was in this year also – 1949 – that *Mandrake* published a selection of new poetry from Australia, including works by that rare genius, Ern Malley.

Wain and Boyars both went on to achieve wider recognition as individuals: Boyars made a career as a poet, translator, musicologist and critic, while his name became associated with the publishing house of Calder and Boyars. John Wain had begun his writing success as a radical novelist, one of a small group dubbed by reviewers the Angry Young Men, that included writers such as John Braine, Kingsley Amis, Alan Sillitoe and John Osborne. Somewhat in contrast to this allegiance, he was also a member of The Inklings, a radically conservative Oxford literary group united by a love of literature and traditional values. Other members included CS Lewis and JRR Tolkien. Wain was also associated with 'The Movement', a group composed mainly of postwar British poets such as DJ Enright, Thom Gunn, Elizabeth Jennings and Philip Larkin. Later in life Wain achieved eminent respectability on his appointment to the prestigious Oxford Professorship of Poetry, a position he held from 1973 until 1978. Sadly, his reputation appears to have declined steadily since his death in 1994.

In the summer of 1967 I was a graduate student at Oxford University, having arrived the previous September on a scholarship from the University of Tasmania, where I had studied English under McAuley. My first year at

Tasmania had been his also. Like so many of his students, I had found his teaching of poetry to be an inspiration, but I had never expected to become an academic myself. During that first summer in Oxford I had a visit from Jim and his wife, Norma, probably to check up on how his protégé was getting on. Not particularly well, as it happened – I was just twenty-two and had found the transition from Hobart to Oxford by no means easy. Being both a colonial and a female were major handicaps in the snobbish and heavily male-dominated Oxford of those years. I was feeling quite adrift and was staunchly refusing to admit it. McAuley invited me to lunch with him and his wife at The Mitre, a venerable and rather grand hostelry in the High Street, where they were staying overnight. McAuley was essentially a kind man, but he presented with a worldly wise, rather forbidding exterior. Although I had been his student for four years, I remember I still felt somewhat intimidated both by him and by our surroundings. He questioned me closely about my progress, my choice of thesis topic, my supervisor, and no doubt made some pretty shrewd judgements from my hesitant answers. I felt I had in some way let him down – I should have been writing on Shakespeare or Milton, not an obscure Victorian novelist. However, I also had a question for him: Would he meet with John Wain?

As Jim's student, I had known of the Ern Malley affair. It was intermittently a subject of gossip among us. But when we plucked up our courage and asked him about it, he was cagey and wouldn't be drawn. He insisted that the poems were tosh, and at that time most people agreed with him. He and Stewart had made them up one humid afternoon, bored in a military outpost in Melbourne. Actually, I am sure he told us they were composed in New Guinea, but that is probably a false memory. As he said, they had used whatever bizarre combination of materials came to hand, including a textbook on the breeding habits of mosquitoes. According to Jim, anyone who read the results as constituting serious poetry was a fool. He did, however, change his views on poetry during those years when he was first at Tasmania – in large part, I believe, owing to the influence of the much younger Vivian Smith, a very gifted poet who challenged his inflexible thinking about prosody, among other things. As a result, his own poetry style underwent a radical change, culminating in some very fine late poems that entered a personal realm he had previously striven to avoid. But his style did remain traditional, and he never softened in his attitude to Ern Malley. Or so it is generally assumed.

In my second term at Oxford I had come across the eccentric figure of John Wain. I had attended an evening lecture he gave on TS Eliot, and afterwards we happened to walk the same way and he overtook me and we got talking. He had not only heard of Tasmania but showed an unusual interest in it, and it turned out he had known someone I knew slightly, Lee Cataldi (or Lee Sonnino as she then was), a brilliant student of Renaissance rhetoric who had grown up in Hobart and had travelled to Oxford for graduate study a few years earlier. Wain himself lived with his family on the northern outskirts of Oxford in a vestigial village called Wolvercote Green. Here he and his wife gave memorable parties where they prided themselves on bringing together an extraordinarily eclectic mix of people. I was invited to one of these marvellous gatherings, full of literary people of all ages: writers, critics, teachers, students. It was all very exciting. I had read Wain's best-known novel, *Hurry on down* (1953), but not his poetry, to which he had always felt more deeply committed. I remember he told me he was one of only forty-five writers in Britain who were able to earn their living as freelancers, and that it had not been easy. Subsequently, he was appointed to the prestigious Oxford Poetry Professorship, which not only pleased him enormously but seemed to vindicate his chosen path.

The John Wain I knew seemed in his own way just as eccentric as James McAuley. Both had strong views about literature that might have been labelled radically conservative. Both cared intensely about poetry. Neither cared how he dressed or looked. McAuley was noted for appearing in the lecture hall on occasion quite oblivious of his mismatched socks, for example, or constantly hitching up trousers he had forgotten to belt. Wain went further, cultivating a kind of down-at-heel tramp look: ancient saggy tweed jacket,

ditto hat or workman's cap, pulled low over his brow, scraggy hair poking
out, rough boots stumping along the street, usually heading for the nearest
pub for a pint. He saw his writing vocation as placing him among the workers. One of his eyes was a glass one, he said, but if so it was good enough to
fool most observers. Perhaps he saw himself as a kind of Arnoldian Scholar
Gypsy. One might come across him on the river, making his way upstream
in his old canoe, lost in thought, scorning the elegant punts favoured by the
fashionable, which could navigate only the more inhabited reaches of the
river. He would have loved to canoe some of the wild rivers in Tasmania, he
used to say, wanting me to tell him about them. But, like McAuley, he was
a wonderful talker about poetry and the art of reading it: a great critic, in
fact, in the special way that only practising poets can be – from the inside.
When he heard that McAuley was planning a visit to Oxford, he asked me
to arrange an introduction. I was taken aback to find he had even heard of a
minor Australian poet, so inured had I become to insular British attitudes.
But one of the traits I admired in John was his openness to new ideas and
other cultures. This must be part of it, I thought.

As it turned out, it was – but in a way far more extraordinary than I had
imagined. I mainly recall his extreme curiosity about McAuley, wanting to
know everything about him. He was inordinately keen to meet him, but did
not initially let on to me that he was one of those who had been taken in
by the Malley hoax. However, when I questioned him more closely as to his
interest, he confessed. He wanted to meet McAuley out of sheer curiosity,
it seemed. What was the man like who had invented Ern Malley and pulled
off the hoax with so much success?

Somewhat apprehensively and looking very out of place, John Wain
slouched shyly into the back lounge of The Mitre, where we three (Norma,
Jim and myself) were perched awkwardly on lounge chairs holding deco-
rous cups of coffee after lunch. In his tweed cap and shapeless jacket of the
nondescript ilk he favoured, John was ostentatiously shabby. Perhaps it was
his defence against meeting someone who had had the better of him in the
past. His usual haunt was more likely to be the tiny smoke-filled, raftered

pub on St Giles called the Eagle and Child, known locally as the Bird and Baby. He seemed relieved to find McAuley looking equally ill-at-ease in the plush surroundings of The Mitre, although Jim was much more carefully dressed than usual. Norma soon excused herself to go shopping for some items she tactfully said she needed. Pleasantries were exchanged, then the conversation seemed to falter. I remember feeling a sudden disappointment. Surely they were not going to pretend Ern Malley never happened?

Before I could stop myself, I blurted it out: 'What about Ern Malley?' Both men laughed in some embarrassment. Wain took the plunge. 'It was a brilliant hoax', he said. 'An experiment', corrected McAuley.

> Wain: Well it certainly gathered me in; Arthur asked my view and I said
>   Yes!
> McAuley: Pardon?
> Wain: Arthur Boyars. He was editing *Mandrake* then, and he asked my
>   views on the Australian section he was planning.

It then emerged that Jim had no idea that Malley had visited England at that time. Nor had he heard of the existence of the little magazine called *Mandrake*, or of Arthur Boyars, minor English poet and *Mandrake*'s second editor. He was intrigued and clearly rather flattered. But he couldn't resist some sly jabs, either. He expressed incredulity that Wain or anybody else with half a brain could have been taken in for a moment by Malley, and delivered himself of a back-handed compliment.

> McAuley: But you've written some decent stuff yourself!
> Wain (*wryly*): Thank you, so have you. But Ern Malley had talent too.
> McAuley: Humph! People say that, to justify themselves. Carefully
>   crafted rubbish. Did you lift it from *Angry Penguins*?
> Wain: No, no. We published later – second round, as it were. Geoff
>   Dutton at Magdalen [an Oxford college attended by Dutton as
>   an ex-serviceman mature student] got Max Harris to send it to

us, along with other pieces, by himself, Donald Kerr and others.
Harris wanting a fresh field, I guess.[9]

McAuley: Poor old Kerr! His stuff was dreadful, poor fellow. Nearly
as much drivel as Ern's. I suppose the whole thing kept pretty
quiet over here, not much fuss about it, so you didn't know about
Ern . . . But that was naughty of Maxie . . . and Dutton too.

Wain: In 1944 Art and I were nineteen, we were students, we hadn't
heard of *Angry Penguins* – or any Australian verse for that matter.
We didn't see the London papers; no, we knew nothing about it
at all. Babes in the wood, we were, in those days. But when we
met him five years later we both liked Malley – and I still do.
That poetry holds a real erotic charge, I reckon.

He smiled reminiscently.

McAuley laughed, and said that perhaps he should read him again, as
he hadn't looked at him for twenty years, but a parody of eroticism couldn't
be erotic – the obscenity trial was utterly absurd and absurdist. He did feel
sorry for Max about that, he said. It turned out Wain knew nothing of
the obscenity trial, and he professed himself gobsmacked. 'Perhaps I won't
visit Australia after all', he said. 'Oh yes, you must come to Tasmania, the
university, give a talk. We'll show you around, get you other gigs as well',
countered McAuley, in his usual form. After this, the two began to ask
politely about each other's current work, and then, perhaps for my benefit,
about the perils of mixing teaching with writing. McAuley denied there was
any conflict, but Wain was strongly of the view that teaching sapped energies better expended in writing. That is why he threw in his teaching post
after only five years, he said. Both agreed, however, that practising poets
wrote the only criticism worth reading. After this exchange, helped materi-
ally by a fair number of drinks, they parted the best of friends. As for me,
I determined to seek out copies of *Mandrake* in the Bodleian the very next
day and carefully appraise what had been printed in the Ern Malley issue.

It never happened. Well, I did take a quick look, but in 1967 Ern Malley seemed remote and old hat and nothing to do with me. After a cursory glance at some of the twenty-year-old pamphlets labelled *Mandrake* that I called up in the Library, printed on thin wartime paper, I felt unexcited. I had a thesis to write, classes to attend, a new love affair to pursue. I still ran into John from time to time and he was always charming, but he never thanked me for the meeting with McAuley, and he never visited Tasmania.

It was only when I came to prepare this essay that I turned once again to the *Mandrake* archive in the Bodleian Library at Oxford.[10] I discovered that it was really only the first three (wartime) issues that looked so amateurish. Once Boyars took over the editorial role and the war had ended, the technical side of things looked up considerably: glossy covers, better paper, much more professional presentation altogether. The issue for 1949 containing the Malley poems is a stylish seventy-five pages. The section titled 'New Verse from Australia' runs for sixteen pages, and includes poems by Ern Malley, Donald Bevis Kerr, Max Harris, Alister Kershaw and Geoffrey Dutton. It is prefaced by some brief 'Notes on contributors'. Donald Kerr is listed as a '23-year-old airman killed in operation near Buna in 1942', and the founder of *Angry Penguins*. Max Harris is billed as its editor and 'one of the first to recognize the merit of Ern Malley to whom he devoted an issue of his review'. Kershaw: 'an Australian heretic who now divides his time between France and England – accent on France'. Dutton 'served during the war as an F/O in the RAAF and is at present reading for a degree in English at Magdalen'. However, pride of place is given to Ern Malley who, we learn, came to Australia after the last war, and worked as a mechanic, an insurance pedlar and a watch repairer. 'Little is known of this period of his life and he showed no special feeling for literature. He died in his early twenties leaving the manuscript of The Darkening Ecliptic.'[11] Six of his poems are included. These are: 'Durer: Innsbruck 1495', 'Sweet William', 'Boult to Marina', 'Palinode', 'Perspective Lovesong' and 'Petit Testament'. As a balance, Kershaw has five poems, the other Australians four each. Perhaps Dutton was the conduit for the poems, including those of Malley: but whether he alerted Boyars to this second run of the hoax is unclear. I would guess that he did not, since John Wain indicated that he and Boyars had been equally duped. Other contributions to the issue include critical essays on Eugene O'Neill and on James Joyce, as well as a piece titled 'Arrangement of Pindar' by CS Lewis and a symposium on 'Drama in the universities'.

Over the years many people may have forgotten the Ern Malley affair, or at least may be content for it to sink into mythology, but somehow the myth itself remains evergreen. The host of articles and even books written about it, and the numerous reprintings of the poems, seem set to ensure Ern's immortality and, with it, that of James McAuley and his 'back legs', Harold Stewart. History shows that the thirst to pull off a clever hoax just never dies, and events certainly conspired to ensure the ultimate widespread success of this one. A success of a kind very far from that envisaged by its perpetrators, and perhaps more undermined than underwritten by humour. Latter-day believers in Malley's essential poetic integrity – and they far out-number his detractors – appear to have discarded the nexus of humour in their readings of the poems. It is as though any notions of comedy or even satire would hinder any fully appreciative recognition of Malley's power as a modernist poet. Yet even modernists could be funny, and if, as seems most likely, it was indeed Dutton who persuaded the *Mandrake* editors to give Ern Malley another run, then Malley himself may have had his last laugh in England.

What Inigo had built I perceived
In a dream of recognition,
And for nights afterwards struggled
Helpless against the choking
Sands of time in my throat.[12]

Writing humour

Michael Wilding

They laughed when I said I was going to be a comedian . . . they're not
laughing now. (Bob Monkhouse)[1]

For a while as a child I wanted to be a radio comedian. But in those days
comedians had their four or five minutes of fame and then they sang a song
to end their set. And that was the impossibility. I would happily tell jokes.
But standing up and singing, that was unthinkable. I had had to do it in
school and found it terrifying, blushing and croaking in front of a knowing, derisive class. No way could I sing a song in public, not even to be a
comedian. So that left the possibility of reading the news. You didn't have to
sing a song to end the news. Not in those days. The delivery had to be a bit
more deadpan than that of most comedians, but the material had its risible
side. But I don't think I thought that then. Or did I always think that? Was
that the origin of my later conflation of comedy and politics? Whatever,
recognising the lack of openings for a seven-year-old newsreader, I turned
to writing fiction.

In a collection of essays focused on humour, I would have liked to have
been able to say that the very first story I wrote was comic. No doubt I could
still say it, but the truth is it was a serious piece called 'The old, old man'.
Or maybe 'The old, old, old man'. I followed that reduplicative practice for
emphasis in those days, as in Wagga Wagga or Mooney Mooney. The old,

old man was, as far as I can remember, a snowman who beats up the bad boys who have been tormenting the protagonist. A satisfying though simple narrative line. I wrote it when I was seven and preserved it carefully in a spiral-bound notebook. Fifty years later I presented it to Mitchell Library with the rest of my manuscripts and papers.

After that there is a break of seven years. And then there was the Physics class at school. I was gazing out of the window or into space, gazing anyway away from the theorem on the board. The Physics master seized on my abstraction. 'What are you thinking about?' he asked. 'Nothing,' I replied, the normal reply to such demands. 'Then write me an essay about it,' said the master.

And that was the next initiating moment. Making something out of nothing. I launched into the task with delight. Hours of day-dreaming had provided me with lots of practice. I used all the resources of wit, paradox and irony that I could command. Growing up in a small, landlocked country town, creating something out of nothing seemed the only thing to do. In the desperate, stretching emptiness of those days, or what I perceived of as emptiness, it was the way to keep yourself amused, diverted, hopeful.

Creation out of nothing, ex nihilo, has its metaphysical tradition. I have never been much of a metaphysician, and it worried me, later, when I began to feel that writing should draw on observation and experience of reality, that nothingness should have been that initiating subject that persuaded me I could become a writer.

But it was not, of course, simply nothing. There was that sense of harassment by authority. Persecution, victimisation would be to express it too strongly. But it was a conflict with forces more powerful than myself, and I chose to deal with the conflict by humour. Humour was a way of defusing the confrontation. A way, even, of appeasing the authority. And at the same time a way of laughing at it, subverting it. A contradictory and rather doomed enterprise, perhaps. But a way of reconstituting the conflict into something I could find more acceptable to live with. A re-aspirated example of what Stephen Knight, discussing the *Carry on* movies, called 'the Ealing power of comedy'.

This, I think, was also the origin of the first story that I sold commercially. Or one of the origins. A coffee bar had opened up in town, something new and cosmopolitan and exotic. We flocked to it. The waitresses were entrancing, or one of them was. As I remember it, we went for coffee in pursuit of the waitress and ended up being lured into ordering a meal we could ill afford, and the waitress was off duty. Sexual fantasy, financial catastrophe, humiliation and embarrassment: potent sources for fiction. I exorcised the embarrassment by treating the episode with humour and recouped the financial loss by selling the piece to radio and having my humiliation broadcast nationally. I never got to hear it because I was working as a breadroundsman at the time and in those days delivery vehicles were not fitted with radios. The vans we drove were electric-powered, and sometimes the batteries ran out before we got back to the depot. There was no way they could have powered a radio as well. And I could not afford a portable transistor. All I heard was the closing announcement at someone's back door and the typescript has now been lost.

It wasn't, however, the first piece of writing I sold commercially. Five months earlier I had begun writing for the local paper on the literary associations of the region I lived in. My very first article was called 'Miserrimus'. It was about the gravestone of an unhappy man, celebrated in a poem by Wordsworth. It was not at all humorous in content, though it appeared auspiciously on April Fools' Day, 1960. Often, as I hung onto my day job in the ensuing years, I reflected on the significance of such a start to a literary career.

I would have liked to have been able to say that my first volume of fiction was humorous. But its title, *Aspects of the dying process*, suggests otherwise. It was published towards the end of the era of portentously lugubrious titles. I made a dialectical reversal for my next book, a determined bid for the positive, and called it *Living together*. It was a novel in the tradition of the comedy of embarrassment. I suspect this is more of an English tradition than an Australian or European or American. The English are much better at it, both at feeling embarrassment and at inducing it in others. Indeed, it is so much a part of the English way of life that I was not consciously aware of it as a theme while writing the book. My focus was on the replication of parent–children relationships by supposed adults. My experience of parental intrusion was still vivid, and I had observed it in house-sharing situations in which I had participated. A part of myself was there in both the parentally oppressive Martin and the filially oppressed Paul. Bruce Clunies Ross has indicated the other sources.[2]

Relationships of power, of dominance and submission, are always open to a comic interpretation. It is one way of defusing the brutality of the oppression, which is always there. There are elements of cruelty in this sort of comedy that have their distasteful aspect. I had already explored them in a long story, 'Hector and Freddie', which I wrote in the mid-1960s about two Oxford contemporaries.[3] The original of Hector went on to become a quite well-known journalist and speech-writer to the royal family. Brian Kiernan has indicated how the thematic structure of 'dominant and recessive male personalities who compete in many of the earlier stories' recurs through my fiction.[4]

Yet even as I completed *Living together* I felt that it belonged formally to a passing era. Formally it was a consciously structured, patterned novel, and I felt that the days of such novels were over. They weren't, of course, and it proved very popular. Frank Kermode wrote to me that it was the funniest book he had read since Kingsley Amis's *Girl, 20* (1971). But at that point in time I no longer read Amis and was yet to rediscover him. 'So you think you're some sort of Balmain Barry Oakley', John Forbes remarked; one of the more offensive things Forbes ever said to me, as I told Barry one time we were discussing the young Forbes' characteristic offensiveness.

By the mid-1970s I had committed myself to exploring a more open-ended, spontaneous form, to moving on from the aesthetic of Henry James into the spontaneity of Jack Kerouac, Leonard Cohen, Richard Brautigan. *The short story embassy* was the breakthrough. Yet, as Carl Harrison-Ford gleefully pointed out, the spirit of Henry James was still there; what was the title *The short story embassy* but another formulation of James' House of Fiction?

There are other continuities. There was still the comedy of embarrassment in the sufferings of Laszlo and Tichborne. There was still the pattern of dominance and submission. But the theme I now began to pursue was the comedy of paranoia. Laszlo's tortured imaginings are in part a serious exploration of sexual jealousy; but they are also the basis for the comedy of over-interpretation, of the excess of the paranoid imagination.

Again, there was a powerful tradition on which to draw. As William Burroughs remarked somewhere of paranoia, 'when you know that you know all the news'. Its material base is undoubtedly to be found in the very fabric of our social order; but it requires an awareness of the truth, or the lies, of the social order to perceive it. The British, with their self-satisfaction in the British way of life, freedom, parliamentary democracy, justice, all the great sonorities, are exceptionally blinkered, and Australia in this remains in the British tradition. The Europeans, with their centuries of experience of undisguisedly authoritarian regimes, are much more open to admitting the existence of controls and conspiracies into their world view: these are part of the fundamental vision of Stendhal, Balzac and Conrad. American writers are similarly more attuned to a vision of conspiracy, seeing the social order as based on hidden forces and dark manipulations: I think especially of Norman Mailer, Don de Lillo, Robert Stone and William Burroughs.

It is a well-established tradition. But I suspect it was the widespread use of drugs in the 1960s and 1970s, especially cannabis, that revived paranoia as a way of seeing the social order. For the nineteenth century, cannabis was thought of as 'the drug of travel'. Hashish, taken in quite considerable doses, offered psychedelic visions of other realms. It was also known for producing what was referred to as 'the dual vision', a sense of being oneself and also standing beside oneself. Both of these experiences can be found in Marcus Clarke's stories.[5] But it is the drug's capacity for making new connections, for revealing overreaching patterns and exposing hidden conspiracies, that appealed to mid and late twentieth-century writers. And insofar as these connections could be excessive, the imaginative leaps often as absurd as revelatory, then it provided the possibilities of humour. It is quite often a deadpan humour. It was not until I heard a recording of William Burroughs reading from his work that I could catch onto his sardonic wit. And it is a humour that is often self-deprecating, that often cancels itself out.

In *The short story embassy*, like *Living together*, the focus is on personal relationships. The comedy arises from the appalling exercise of power. But through the 1970s I had been trying to imbue my writing with a stronger political content. The tradition of the Anglo-Saxon novel, and of its associated literary criticism, had been to exclude the political. In the universities this had pretty well been achieved – in the critical methodology and in the selection of the canon. But there was a strong countervailing movement through the 1960s and 1970s, and I drew what I could from that. I tried to draw on my experience of the ferment in the universities at that time to write a novel drawing on some of the politics; but somehow I could not bring the political into focus, and in the end I cut it all away and was left with a long story, 'Campus novel', which focused on the comedy of the material.[6] With *The Paraguayan experiment*, however, the political was uppermost, and humour not a feature.

But there were precedents for politically engaged comedy. Hašek's *The good soldier Schweik* brilliantly captures the comedy of survival within an authoritarian society, the transparent police informer in every café, the petty abuses of power, the ruses of evasion. Ken Stewart has written most engagingly in this book of the humour of Henry Lawson's 'The Loaded Dog'. Yet even this masterpiece of comedy carries its political freight. The good dog is coloured the red and black of the anarchists when it bears its terrorist bomb, and at the story's triumphant, positive end is shown 'smiling his broadest, longest and reddest smile of amiability', the red of revolutionary socialism, whereas the bad dog is coloured the yellow of a yellow-dog contract, a non-union contract.[7] The phrase is no longer current in Australia, but it survives in the United States, from blues lyrics to Ross Thomas's political thriller, *Yellow-dog contract* (1976).

I mention these as precedents, though I do not think they directly influenced my specific practice. I did, however, learn a lot from the English television series by Antony Jay and Jonathan Lynn, *Yes, Minister* and *Yes, Prime Minister*. Here the comedy was classically designed to instruct with delight, radically demystifying the manipulations of the political establishment. Who could ever again believe that a commission of inquiry was designed to do other than provide a whitewash? Who could ever expect ministers and prime ministers to do other than lie? Who could ever again believe that principles and policies took anything but second place to political survival? When I came to write *Academia nuts*, I consciously attempted to inform the humour with a similar didactic purpose. I chose archetypal episodes and situations that would reveal the reality of university life. Nonetheless, I would not want to minimise the pleasure I have experienced from reading the non-didactic humour of such great masters as PG Wodehouse, Evelyn Waugh and Kingsley Amis, though in what specific ways they have influenced me, it is hard for me to assess.

A visit to the United States in 1978 fuelled me with a new enthusiasm for an alternative view of the public world. Conspiracy theories were rife there. They were extreme and exciting and they made great plots; and plots were what the etiolated Anglo-Saxon novel had for too long been lacking. I rehearsed them endlessly in the Indian summer of the late 1970s. Geoff Gold suggested I write them in a column for *Nation Review*, which he had just bought. In keeping with the apocalyptic mood of the times, I wanted to call the column 'Last Days'. But Don'o Kim told me that that was the title of a novel he was writing, and begged me not to use it. I surrendered it to him. As it happened, apocalypse was deferred yet once more, and so was Kim's novel. A quarter of a century passed and the new millennium dawned before he finished it in 2003, and by then he had decided to call it something else. So it was that *Nation Review* came up with its own title for the column, 'Wilding's paranoia', and the damage was done. I was labelled.

It was a light-hearted column. The excitement of making connections, of drawing parallels, was the stimulus. The comedy of over-interpretation, the outrageousness of the plots, provided the edge. Unfortunately, one by one the extreme speculations proved to be true. I would imagine the worst conspiracies I could think of, and over the years they were pretty well all revealed as reality. Or as what passes for reality in the political world. This was not a matter of comedy any more. 'We have a machine on the phone that flashes a red light if the line is being tapped', Geoff Gold phoned me up to tell me. 'And it's flashing now.'

I gave up the column, *Nation Review* died, but, as dear old Henry James put it, things were never again as they were. And all for the sake of those magnificent articles, as Marcus Clarke once reflected. The material, the world view, the consciousness, now fed into my fiction, and the edgy comedy of paranoia and conspiracy informed the stories of *Reading the signs*, *Under Saturn* and *This is for you*, and the novels *Wildest dreams*[8] and *Wild amazement*. From a concern with social justice and a preoccupation with class discriminations, colonial oppressions and economic exploitation, I had slid into explorations of the slippery world of control and surveillance and the suppression of dissidence, the fringes of the secret state.

It is tricky writing about humour, particularly your own. You run the continual risk of a stony-faced reception, the glazed look, an absolute lack of response. Often the things I found funny to write have not been perceived as at all comic. Often in the process of writing, the humour lies in the language, in the allusions, in the verbal excess, in the play of the written against the unwritten. I found 'The phallic forest'[9] comic in the excess of its imagery. I found 'Beach report'[10] comic in the narrator's bland acceptance of appalling authoritarian conformity, in the eager search for any sign to follow. But not everything I wrote was imbued with the political. The comic horror of 'This is for you' was purely personal; bad behaviour provided the humour of 'I am monarch of all I survey' and 'The imagination'; 'The beauties of Sydney' recalled an episode that could have been tragic but remained in the realms of slapstick, when Rudi Krausmann offered to take the visiting English poet Jon Silkin sailing on Pittwater, and the dinghy sank before reaching the yacht.[11]

It was Elsie Duncan-Jones, a colleague of mine when I taught at the University of Birmingham, who once said to me, 'Dear Michael, I do wish you would write your campus farce, rather than living it all the time'. In the end I did. Having taught in universities for thirty-five years, I made another attempt at writing about them. Endlessly people had been inciting me to do this. But it had not seemed a terribly good idea while still working in the system. Once I could see early retirement beckoning, however, what was there to stop me? Very little. And farce, indeed, had established itself as one way of writing about universities. Bold, broad comedy, extreme situations, the comedy of excess and exaggeration. So *Academia nuts* has its generic farcical note. Inevitably it occasionally touches on the no less generic, politically incorrect sex comedy, replete with *double entendre*, that has been a feature of campus novels.

And necessarily, as it charts the destruction of the universities, it has its serious note. Many of my fellow academics are among those not laughing now. John Lucas and Carole Ferrier both told me how painful they found it. Brian Kiernan remarked sadly that the *Southerly* reviewer of the novel seemed to find our wretched last years the subject of mirth.[12] The English columnist Laurie Taylor expressed his doubts that campus novels could any longer be comic: 'A witty campus novel? In 2004? It seemed as likely as a holiday romance set amid the tropical delights of Guantanamo Bay. Where in the technological, bureaucratic confines of the modern university was there room for the happy academic indulgences and airy pretensions and self-conscious posturings that were once juicy fodder for Bradbury and Lodge and Amis?' But in the end he laughed.

> It is politically incorrect. Appallingly so. But it is also very funny. So funny that I had to stop reading it in bed in case my roars of laughter were disturbing the neighbours: so funny that it deserves to be the final great campus novel. It is unlikely to be challenged. For what Wilding's aged unreconstructed dons are playing with such absurd brio is unmistakably the last waltz.[13]

I forget which president of the United States it was who particularly upset novelists. I think it was Nixon but it could have been any of them. The

enormity of his behaviour, his lies and deceptions and plots and fabrica-
tions were so extreme that novelists began to complain that his behaviour
far exceeded anything that the fictional imagination could ever put into a
novel. No one would believe in a character like that. Readers would reject
the book in disbelief. Reality, as it was so called, had superseded fiction. It
was putting novelists out of business. In the course of writing *Academia nuts*
I began to feel much the same way about the universities. Events began to
outstrip my imagination. The unthinkable, the unimaginable, continually
exceeded the most extreme imaginings I could come up with.

I had already completed the novel when it was reported that the vice-
chancellor of one of the bigger Australian universities had resigned because
of allegations of plagiarism. This was far more extraordinary than anything
I had invented. Would anyone have believed such an incident? They would
have said it was excessive, absurd, unrealistic. But I incorporated it into the
second edition.

I must say I found the story hard to believe myself. I have few illusions
about management, as university administrators now like to call themselves.
I taught for a while on a campus where the president or vice-chancellor or
CEO was under investigation for allegedly receiving kickbacks on plumb-
ing contracts. The campus novelists there were vastly amused and we shared
many a joke about it. But plagiarism. I suppose what amazed me was that
senior management ever claimed to have written or published anything,
plagiarised or not. In *Academia nuts* I have one of my characters deliver a
tirade about such people:

> What sort of academic would become a Dean, a Pro-Vice-Chancellor, a
> Vice-Chancellor? Only one who was no longer concerned to teach, only
> one who was no longer concerned to research. The people who occupy
> these administrative roles are self-selected failures from the academy
> they presume to control. They are people whose teaching skills were so
> derisory that they avoided teaching by getting teaching relief for admin-
> istrative duties, whose ability to write or research was so inadequate that

they avoided research by hiring research assistants to do their research
and write their publications for them.[14]

It is a tirade and I felt it sounded excessive. It was meant to sound excessive. Indeed, I felt the situation had become excessive. *Academia nuts* has
characters getting their research assistants to write their work for them. It
has academics, or one academic, considering hiring a ghost-writer to write
a book, as JF Kennedy and J Edgar Hoover are said to have done. But
plagiarism. I never thought of inventing that. Reality had gone beyond the
imagination. And yet it was not the first time. Writing about *Academia nuts*,
Don Graham recalled:

> Well, at a university in Texas where I was teaching in the late 1960s, the
> university president was discovered to have plagiarised his dissertation
> and was, after much storm und drang, dismissed and the degree stripped
> from him. At the time he held a post as Under-Secretary in the Depart-
> ment of Health, Education, and Welfare under Lyndon B. Johnson. In
> fact, when this episode played out, he was the only 'intellectual' left in
> the Johnson administration. Vowing to clear his name, the ex-university
> president instead entered into real estate, selling properties in rural Texas,
> and became a multi-millionaire. Such is life.[15]

Much of *Academia nuts* consists of dialogue. Academics sit around in the
common room or the faculty club and talk. In a sense, I suppose, I wanted
to create some sort of surprise, some gentle shock effect. The comedy was
to lie in the discrepancy between the expected and the actual. Instead of
discussing abstruse scholarly issues, the minutiae of textual scholarship, the
nature of truth and so on, the academics in *Academia nuts* mainly discuss,
and indeed embody, the degeneration of the university. Instead of collegiality they demonstrate a deep dislike and suspicion of their fellow academics.
This, after all, is the tradition of the campus novel. These are the expectations of the genre.

Not any more. Or at least, not at the University of Sydney, where I taught for so many years. The staff club, the university club as it was officially known, was closed down by senior management in the year *Academia nuts* appeared. No longer is there a site for conversations. No longer is there a focus for dialogue and discussion. No longer is there a staff club. The characters in *Academia nuts* eventually ceased going to their faculty club because their colleagues upset their digestion, the barman seemed like an informer, and they suspected the place was bugged. These were consciously extreme imaginings. But I never imagined the utter extremity of a university administration actually closing down its staff club.

I should have known, though. I had taught in the United States and been amazed to find that academics there were not in the habit of having lunch together in the club or morning tea in the common room. There were no staff clubs, no common rooms. It was the model of control. There was nowhere for people to sit around and compare notes, to contrast different practices in different departments, to exchange information, to discuss change, to foment resistance, to tell jokes. Removing any focus for academics to meet is a basic way of keeping the staff separate and alienated, a basic way of preventing any cooperation, collegiality or rebellion. I knew things were bad but I failed to imagine how bad. The novelist outstripped by contemporary reality again. Inevitably I have come to speculate whether there is any future for the campus novel. As the universities crumble by the minute, will there be anything left to write about? As they become unimaginable, who will ever write about them any more?

But there will always be a future for comedy. No matter how bad things become, comedy will continue to provide a positive note. I hope. But who will publish it? As I reflected on the grim state of publishing, I began to formulate a black comedy about the world of writing.

More years ago than I care to remember, let alone admit to, a friend assured me, 'Film's about film, Michael, you know that'. It was kind of him to concede my knowledge, but I didn't know that. I used to think that films were, like novels, about social reality, about the illusory real world. But Pete, who was adept with the hand-held camera – these were the days of Godard and Truffaut, when we were still learning to call films 'movies' – had introduced me to the world of postmodernism. Way, way before we knew it was called that.

If film was about film, then writing was about writing. Self-referentialism, we learned to call it. Narcissism, the unfriendly conservatives would snarl. Though they should have embraced the concept, and indeed they soon did as it became the favoured aesthetic of modern times. Self-referentialism was the ideal opposition to realism, from their point of view. Keep out any troubling social observation, any political critique, any commitment or engagement – to employ a couple of terms then fast fading from the acceptable agenda of artistic production.

I mention all this from a certain embarrassment at admitting that my latest novel, *National treasure*, is about the world of books. And yes, so was the previous one, *Wild amazement*. And yes, *Wild amazement* was a companion to my earlier *Wildest dreams*, which was also a book about books, a novel about a novelist. But there is a difference. History repeats itself, as one of the great grand narrators of the past put it, first time tragedy, second time farce.

I had written enough tragedy about writing. 'You must be a very unhappy man', Bob Ellis said to me after reading *Wildest dreams*. I hadn't thought of it like that. I had simply tried to chart the age-old story of literary hopes and resistant reality, a modern *Lost illusions*. As long as the literary world was there, and there were some kindred spirits around to have a long literary lunch with, I felt quite happy.

But I didn't want to write another sad story. I didn't want people going around thinking I was sad. 'Always smile when you go into university,' my one-time colleague Stephen Knight advised me, 'it makes them anxious to think you're happy.' I decided to write a comedy, indeed a farce.

The germ, the idea, of *National treasure* came to me at one of those spirit-raising literary lunches. It was a birthday celebration for my colleague Brian Kiernan. Brian had written the biography of David Williamson, and

David was one of those present. At some point he began telling the story of a writer he knew who was using a research assistant.

The universities are notorious for the research assistant racket. The aesthete Villiers de l'Isle-Adam famously remarked, 'As for living, our servants will do that for us'. Academics rapidly adapted his aperçu: as for writing, our research assistants will do that for us. In *National treasure* the novelist protagonist Scobie Spruce is assured by the poet Prickett: 'Politicians don't write their own speeches. Academics don't write their own articles. Why should novelists write their own novels or poets their own poems? The best ones don't, not the successful ones'.[16]

Having seen the comic potential of the novelist who doesn't write his own novels, I began to consider other flagrant inauthenticities of the literary world. Plagiarism was an obvious theme. Lots of precedents for that. Then there was the practice of providing handwritten original manuscripts to order for the rare-book trade and institutional library collections. More than one writer has told me about how they've copied out the odd poem or novel for that market. Then there were other atrocities, like the book launch with no beer (or wine or spirits) I once went to – a high-profile media event, but distinctly un-Australian, I felt. Once I'd started, all the dodgy stories of the writing scene flooded before my eyes.

The characters are all fictional, as the disclaimer at the front of every novel assures suspicious readers. But many of the events have their archetypal reality. There was the shameful awards-night dinner where Morris West got shouted down in his speech and bread rolls shot round the room like rockets in today's Baghdad. And it was Allen Ginsberg who regularly stripped naked at readings when challenged about the truth. 'I'll show you the naked truth.' Scobie Spruce's disastrous public appearance draws on these events.

Yet reality always outstrips fiction. As a culminating episode, Scobie discovers what he claims is his Aboriginality. (Wise career move, as someone cruelly remarked of Jack Kerouac's early death.) The novel was written and well into production when Les Murray announced to the press that he was thinking of having a DNA test to discover whether he had Aboriginal ancestry. No, Les, I was not alluding to you, truly.

The common reader scanning over these reflections might wonder about the propriety of the novelist writing about his own novels. Is this not going beyond self-referentialism and into the world of self-promotion? It probably is. But is there any difference in this age of self-advertisement? After all, writing about how I wrote my novel has now become a genre of its own. More than a genre, it's a way of getting space in the weekend papers to publicise your latest book. Well, nothing wrong with that. Nice work if you can get it. And a practical application of literary criticism, after all.

Performance

'The rude rudiments of satire': Barry Humphries' humour

Anne Pender

Barry Humphries' extraordinary career in theatre began in the early 1950s. In this decade Humphries experimented with straight acting roles, intimate revue, pantomime, radio, film and television, performance art and street theatre. Humphries' early career as an actor was a series of stops and starts, in which the characters that now define his humour were almost incidental to his developing repertoire. Between 1952 and 1959 Humphries devised strange street-theatre spectacles and Dadaist 'events'. He appeared in *Hamlet, Love's labour's lost* and *Twelfth night* and acted in plays by Molière, Shaw, Saroyan and Beckett; he moved to Sydney in order to perform in intimate revue and he did one performance at an RSL club. Moreover, it was in this period that he invented two of his enduring characters, Edna Everage and Sandy Stone.

In this formative period of his acting career, Humphries also began to develop his comic persona as a visual and performing artist. This comic persona is often difficult to disentangle from his performance life. During the 1950s Humphries' attitude to Melbourne, the city in which he had grown up, inspired his first sketches and monologues. As his career progressed, the city and its suburbs became a paradigmatic place in Humphries' satire.[1] Aware of the indelible mark of Melbourne on him, in 1983 Humphries stated that 'Melbourne is something that never leaves you. It stays in your blood like herpes'.[2]

In order to understand the nature of Barry Humphries' humour, it is helpful to examine the origins of his signature characters, the influences on his performance style and the variety of his activities. Humphries' wide-ranging performance history in the 1950s reveals his idiosyncratic impulses, his struggles as an actor, and a very definite personal mode and style of humour that has shaped his career as an entertainer. It would be fair to call this his 'instinctive' or 'natural' style of humour, which was raw, daring and experimental at the time. At the beginning of his career Humphries' humour was subversive, extreme and shocking. Over the ensuing decades, this provocative element of his humour has never been far from the surface, even in the popular Dame Edna sketches that have brought Humphries to prominence in Britain and the United States.

As with most actors, his early years as a performer were somewhat haphazard, opportunistic, gruelling and difficult. In the early 1950s Humphries' energies were more focused on Dadaist pranks and visual spectacles than on traditional theatrical pursuits. His youthful fascination with the Dadaist artists of the early twentieth century inspired him to put on an art exhibition in the Melbourne University Women's Graduate Lounge, organised by the ALP Club, in 1952. He referred to the meat-pie-inspired exhibits as 'Piescapes'. Standing in the Lounge at the opening, the eighteen-year-old Humphries placed his elbow in a tub of tomato sauce to check its temperature and then proceeded to drink it. After that he tipped the sauce on his head. He gleefully described this act as a tribute to the Australian national drink. Another of his exhibits was called 'I was eating a pie and I coughed'. One of the features of this kind of modern art, he said, was that it only lasts two days.[3] His other exhibits included various strange objects, an old beer bottle with a Melbourne Grammar School tie around its neck, a 'cakescape' consisting of two framed glass sheets with squashed lamingtons, swiss roll and cream cake between them, a 'shoescape' showing several beaten and worn old shoes salvaged from the dump that were nailed to panels of wood; it was called 'My foetus killing me'. Another of his 'works' presented a pair of filthy boots from the tip overflowing with congealed custard, called 'Pus in boots'. There was no doubt about Humphries' intentions with this kind of art work; he set out to disturb, disgust and provoke viewers.

Humphries' taste for the bizarre and the strange was part of his obsession with grotesque parodies of art and his interest in forms of art that challenged the idea of art itself. His attraction to the savage aesthetic critique of the Dadaists of the period after World War I reflects an important dimension of Humphries' artistic sensibility. Dadaism was largely experimental and was based on freedom to play and to take chances. It was risky and confrontational. In his autobiography Humphries confesses to offering lifts to strangers on Melbourne streets and taking them on long car rides in which he sat in the front passenger seat playing a crazed psychopath, shouting at the driver, his friend Robert Nathan, to gun the accelerator harder and harder. After a few minutes in the speeding vehicle with a screaming lunatic in the front, the terrified victims would plead for release, or would leap from the car at the first red light.[4]

At Luna Park, Humphries would don a ghoulish mask with blood dripping from the eye sockets. Just as the Big Dipper was about to drop, he would tap the shoulders of a couple seated in front of him, giving them a terrifying leer as the Dipper made its stomach-turning descent. If the pranks and exhibits were undergraduate in character, they were carried out with dramatic flair and precision. They were part of Humphries' early exhibitionistic repertoire.

Humphries was a schoolboy in the 1940s when Dadaism was being reconsidered and accepted for the first time as a serious precursor to the late modernist and postmodernist art that followed. He was determined to create a spectacle and to witness the effect his antics produced. Provocation was the aim, and the behaviour of people when they experienced disgust or terror was the key to the exercise. Humphries' desire to disturb and confront has informed his comedy throughout his career. His interest in shocking an audience has never waned. However, the nature of his humour has evolved over his career as a performer.

One of the stories that is integral to Humphries' autobiographical reper-toire deals with his first stage show, a kind of Dadaist revue entitled *Call me madman!*, its title parodying the popular musical by Irving Berlin, *Call me madam*. Humphries' revue was staged in the Melbourne University Union Theatre in the days when he was a long-haired student aesthete. It was Sep-tember 1952.

In this sketch Humphries played the wife of a missionary. The mission-ary and his wife were sitting at a table full of raw meat, vegetables and cakes. As the missionary announced a series of shocking statistics detailing a current Indian famine, his wife shrieked in falsetto, 'I don't care . . . I've got plenty of food . . . lots of food . . . and they've got nothing . . . wogs, nigs, yids'. The missionary went on with the awful statistics while the wife laughed more and more hysterically, until finally the couple began to throw the raw chops and then the cream cakes at one another and ultimately at the audience who began to fling the food back at the actors and all around the theatre. The voice continued with the grim statistics over the amplifiers. Incensed, the student audience then stormed the stage, while 'God save the Queen' blared out over a gramophone at various speeds and a woman dressed as a nun stood on the stage swearing and gesticulating at the audi-ence. During the storming of the stage, Humphries is said to have taken refuge in a cupboard. At any rate, the revue gained Humphries notoriety at the university.[5] According to one of Humphries' friends, this 'neo Dadaist folly' also included a provocative joke about the monarchy, which was what had led to the storming of the stage. The 'scurrilous' lines were: 'Why are you kicking that rotten old football about like that?' 'Because it reminds me of Her Royal Maggoty Queen Lizard.'[6]

In fact, it was the complaints of a group of young women that landed Humphries his first paid acting role. John Sumner, a young Englishman newly arrived from London's West End (and later on founder of the Mel-bourne Theatre Company), persuaded the vice-chancellor at the University of Melbourne, George Paton, to fund a professional repertory company to the tune of £1500 on a trial basis. At the time there was no professional repertory company in Melbourne.[7] Sitting in his manager's office one day, Sumner received a 'deputation of ladies' complaining about Humphries' act in a student revue. Sumner went to see the act and promptly offered Humphries a job in the new company – the Union Theatre Repertory Company (UTRC).[8]

In the act that had offended the young women, Humphries played a politician standing on a soapbox waiting to be introduced to an audience; he was wearing a long coat and a battered hat with straw sticking out from under it. He spent the whole act trying to pull off his gloves, fixing his hat and 'chasing the elusive sheets of his speech'. Sumner found this mime compelling. He noted that it was at times suggestive, and he was impressed by the sharpness of the observations that were embodied in the sketch.[9] It was the first in a long series of Humphries' comic works that have aroused indignation and vociferous criticism over five decades. The perceived indecency and vulgarity of Humphries and Nicholas Garland's cartoons published in *The wonderful world of Barry McKenzie* led to the banning of the publication in Australia in 1968.[10] During the 1970s Humphries was savaged for the crudeness and vulgarity of the Barry McKenzie films, in spite of praise garnered from Geoffrey Dutton, Patrick White and Manning Clark.[11]

Humphries' first paid acting role in the fledgling UTRC was in a play directed by Sumner called *The young Elizabeth*, chosen partly because of the new Queen's visit to Australia in 1954. Humphries played a courtier. Zoe Caldwell played the young Elizabeth I. Sumner's company produced a new play every fortnight, with the total rehearsal period for each play lasting only two weeks. The speed with which these productions were worked up meant there was time for only one dress rehearsal. To Sumner's surprise, in the dress rehearsal for *The young Elizabeth* Humphries, who was dressed in Elizabethan hose, altered his moves and seemed to be playing upstage of the furniture, contrary to the blocking that had been agreed. When Sumner asked him why he was hiding behind the furniture, he said he was worried about the appearance of his skinny legs arousing hilarity among the cast.[12]

Sumner also directed Humphries in *His excellency* by Dorothy and

Campbell Christie. Humphries played a chief of police and made a raucous entrance on to the stage at the dress rehearsal wearing a very noisy row of medals. He made all sorts of gestures that drew wild laughter from the cast and the audience, he frequently seemed to be reaching for his forgotten lines, and he received a round of applause when he made his exit from the stage, much to the chagrin of Sumner and his cast who hated to be fully upstaged. In view of his idiosyncratic talents, Sumner advised Humphries that he should perform solo.[13]

During the rehearsals for *The young Elizabeth* Humphries met Peter O'Shaughnessy, a member of John Sumner's new company who had recently returned to Melbourne after spending four years in the English theatre. They became firm friends and their artistic collaboration in several ventures over the next few years influenced Humphries' development as an actor and a scriptwriter. In fact, their shared interests and compatibility as actors led to a series of performances in which Humphries' particular style of acting and his highly original humour flourished.

Humphries initially studied Law at university, then Fine Arts, but in his second year he became less and less interested in study, until finally his scholarship was withdrawn. Eric Humphries, Barry's father, concerned at his son's lack of focus, suggested he take a job at EMI. Humphries' main task turned out to be smashing hundreds of discontinued 78 records in the basement of the Flinders Lane offices, to make way for the new microgroove records. Humphries recalls in his memoirs that he 'sat in that small airless basement room all day for weeks on end pulverizing' records: 'if there was a Dadaist's hell, this was it'.[14]

But Humphries still found time for acting. In his lunchbreaks he would dash across the road to the Assembly Hall to play in Molière's *Le malade imaginaire*. It was an abridged version for the lunch-hour slot and part of a new venture by Peter O'Shaughnessy, who had been encouraged by the actor Noel Ferrier to start up this 'Lunch Hour Theatre'.[15] Barry played Thomas Diafoirus. In the same year (1954) Peter O'Shaughnessy also cast Humphries as Holofernes, the pedantic schoolmaster in *Love's labour's lost*.

In these roles Humphries seemed to find his voice, and he excelled in portraying grotesque and monstrous characters. O'Shaughnessy recalls that it was as if he had discovered the liberating power of the mask.[16] Humphries' Edna Everage, in her later incarnations, reminds us of the humour that surrounds Molière's characters, who are pompous, domineering and full of false, self-devised notions of their own authority.

Prior to this, Humphries had been somewhat tentative and slightly uneasy in his straight roles. At times he experienced difficulties with his voice, which would sound thin, weak, high, even quavering.[17] Like many actors in Melbourne at the time, Humphries had no vocal training. In fact, he had not had any acting training either. He was a novice. The occasional problem that Humphries had with his voice, his tendency for awkward movements on stage and his self-consciousness about his legs did not make him an obvious choice for straight roles. In spite of these problems, he always managed to get a laugh. The humour he exploited in playing straight roles arose from his novel uses of the script and his eccentric interpretations of the characters.

In 1955, just before John Sumner left the UTRC to join the newly established Elizabethan Theatre Trust in Sydney, he and Ray Lawler (the new director) cast a production of *Twelfth night*. Frank Gatliff played Orsino for the Melbourne season. When Gatliff turned down the offer of playing in a country tour, which Sumner had arranged under the auspices of the Council of Adult Education, Humphries was offered the role.

According to Sumner, Humphries kept the cast and audience alert and entertained 'by deliberately misreading Shakespeare' and arousing laughter in the strangest ways.[18] In the line referring to the food of love in the first scene of *Twelfth night*, Humphries' rendering of 'Enough, no more' was extraordinary. He declaimed 'Enough, no *more*!' In his own memoirs Humphries recalls feeling extremely out of place as the duke, convinced that the audience was laughing at his absurd performance and ridiculous legs, once more clad in tights and breeches.[19] When the tour began, Lawler took over from Sumner as director. Lawler also played Feste. In retrospect it would be easy to say that Humphries was miscast as Orsino and would have made a marvellous

Malvolio or Andrew Aguecheek, but at the time Lawler had no experience
of Humphries as an actor. Lawler soon became aware that Humphries felt
uncomfortable in the role of Orsino but believes that he played it well. He
brought an intelligence to it, conveying an 'in love with love' sensibility that
was whimsical and poetic.[20] But he was gawky, and looked 'like a big black
spider in a too-small black velvet suit with little silk tassels hanging around
his lank page-boy bobbed hair'.[21] The strangeness of his appearance was an
important element of his humour throughout this period.

The company toured Victoria in a bus affectionately known as 'the mon-
ster'. The tour was long, the accommodation was very basic and the weather
was freezing. Humphries would entertain the cast on the long bus rides
with improvised and sometimes cruel speeches in parody of the predictable
words of thanks given in every town by ladies of the Country Women's
Association (CWA) or Arts Society in dreary church halls where everyone
was in their best clothes and tables of food 'groan[ed] with asparagus rolls,
party pies and lamingtons'.[22] Humphries' sense of humour manifested itself
most brilliantly in an impulse to laugh at these well-intentioned women.
His mockery was based on a razor-sharp observation of personal speech
habits, mannerisms and a teasing delight in revealing the absurd and banal
comments of those who appreciated the theatre tour most. It marked the
beginning of a talent for parody and a penchant for a tormenting humour
that Humphries has cultivated and honed over the years, in which teasing
of his adoring audience is a hallmark.

Ray Lawler was keen to produce as much Australian material as possible
for his Christmas revue following the country tour. He asked for suggestions and Humphries came forward with a sketch about a woman called
Edna Everage, who was modelled on the women he parodied on the bus
tour. Mrs Norm Everage was offering her home to visiting athletes for the
Olympic Games. The Games were to be staged in Melbourne the following
year and the city was fixated on the problem of housing the many visitors.
In the sketch the government official listed all the nationalities of the potential guests and Edna responded with nasty, bigoted comments about all of

them. The sketch was called 'The Olympic hostess' and Noel Ferrier played the official interviewing Mrs Everage. Humphries had suggested that June Jago play Edna but Lawler insisted that Humphries do it.

Like many satirists, Humphries picked up speech from all around him. One night during the revue season he asked Lawler if he could cut out a bit of the sketch in which Edna is talking to the government official and says she will telephone her home to ask her mother how she feels about something he says. Edna, holding the phone, says, 'Oh, it's you Kenny, dear, what does the dicky bird say, Kenny? Birdie, birdie'; she repeats this ridiculous, patronising routine to the child who was supposedly on the end of the telephone several times. Lawler was reluctant to cut out the routine and Humphries explained: 'Well, the trouble is that I've got my landlady coming to see the show tonight, and this thing with the birdie is what she does with her grandson'.[23]

Thus Edna Mae Everage, the character invented to pass the time on the bus on the *Twelfth night* country tour of Victoria, made her debut in Lawler's show, *Return fare*, on 19 December 1955. The first production of Lawler's *Summer of the seventeenth doll* preceded the Christmas revue by a few weeks. In this premiere of what became one of the most significant plays in Australian theatre history, June Jago played Olive, Noel Ferrier played Roo and Lawler played Barney. The contrast between the two productions was extreme. But both the revue and the straight play portrayed Australians as conservative, comfortable, somewhat infantile city-dwellers unsettled by changes in postwar society.

When the *Doll* was taken up by the Elizabethan Theatre Trust for a tour, Lawler left the UTRC. Around this time he recommended Humphries to the Phillip Street Theatre in Sydney. Bill Orr was looking for talented actors to play in intimate revue and asked Lawler to recommend actors who would be suited to it. Orr particularly wanted a married couple for his next revue, *Mr and Mrs*. Humphries and his very young bride, Brenda Wright, whom he had met and courted during the rehearsals of *Love's labour's lost*, were invited to perform in the show at Phillip Street.

Phillip Street Theatre, under Orr's direction, was one of the first Australian theatres in the 1950s to present intimate revue. The theatre seated
300 and had a small stage and a narrow gallery running around three walls.
It was the parish hall belonging to the gracious St James Church designed
by Francis Greenway.[24] The revues at Phillip Street were original, popular,
fashionable, 'topical, brash, sometimes dishevelled, irreverent, funny and
never coarse'.[25] In one of his revue appearances Humphries sang a duet with
Wendy Blacklock. During the song he changed all the words, ad libbing
comically and skipping around the lyrics, making Blacklock's contribution
difficult and frustrating but very funny.[26]

Humphries also played in *Around the loop*, featuring Max Oldaker, June
Salter, the young English actor Gordon Chater, as well as Humphries and
Blacklock. Chater had recently finished a successful three-year tour with
Seagulls over Sorrento for JC Williamson, or 'the firm' as it was known. Oldaker was a legendary performer, deemed the 'last of the matinee idols' by
actor and theatre critic Charles Osborne.[27] He had sung with Gladys Mon-
crieff and had starred in opera and musical comedy in London. As a child,
Humphries had been taken to see Oldaker perform at Her Majesty's Theatre
in Melbourne in a famous production of *The desert song*, in which Max, 'disguised as the Red Shadow and mounted on a white charger . . . enraptured
the matrons of Melbourne'.[28]

Humphries shared a 'subterranean dressing room' with Max Oldaker
and Gordon Chater. Humphries and Chater would tease Oldaker. ' "Isn't
it funny, Max?" panted Gordon one night as he dashed down the rickety
wooden stairs to execute a lightning costume change, "in a few years time,
Barry will be 30, I'll be 40 and you'll be dead." '[29] The taunt, attributed to
Humphries by Reg Livermore (Chater's understudy), is the kind of remark
Dame Edna might hurl at one of her hapless guests on her television talk
shows.

The daily advertisement for the production of *Two to one*, starring Max
Oldaker, made a gibe at the cringing practice of local theatres and their
obsession with 'imported stars': 'Overseas Importation / Following the

example of other Sydney theatres, Phillip Street proudly announces their overseas star – MAX (Tasmania) OLDAKER in *Two to One*.[30] Oldaker was most 'piquant', according to Humphries, in his own self-send-up. He sang a song about Tasmania called 'I'm just a shadow of my former self', alluding to his role in *The desert song*. Humphries remarked in 1988 that:

> this was in the period when that always intriguing phenomenon,
> Australian Sophistication, was moving, albeit slowly, from primary
> to junior school and we had reached the age of the Send Up.
> Although we lacked, and still lack, any perception of irony, we were
> beginning to grasp the rude rudiments of satire.[31]

Humphries' potent retrospective analysis of the state of Australian humour is indicative of his acute ability to take soundings of Australian society, and turn them into pungent comedy. This gift enabled him to lampoon Australian boorishness in the 1960s and 1970s with remarkable success. Humphries' character Bazza McKenzie and his adventures in the mother country portrayed the dilemma facing Australians and expressed by its leaders: how to throw off the symbols of colonialism. But it took several struggling years in the English theatre and a fruitful association with Peter Cook and other British satirists for Humphries to reach this creative milestone. In actual fact, when Humphries departed for England in 1959 he was grateful for an introduction to the theatre world in London. Max Oldaker wrote to Charles Osborne stating that Humphries 'is inexperienced, but has a devastating sense of quiet comedy and, I think, a touch of genius'.[32]

During Humphries' eighteen-month stint at Phillip Street he wrote a new script in which Edna railed at the design of the Opera House to be built at Bennelong Point and its lack of facilities such as 'comfortable lounges where our kiddies and loved ones could come after school . . . TV facilities and a lovely dining room where we mothers could be sure of getting a good home cooked three course meal, moderately priced'.[33] Peter O'Shaughnessy made suggestions for the sketch for this much bossier Edna, and Humphries tried it out at Phillip Street.[34] But it lasted only a few performances. This newly confident Edna prefigured the brazen, objectionable Edna of the future. The humour embodied in the sketch reflected the comical and philistinish alarm that the designs for Jørn Utzon's Sydney Opera House aroused when they were revealed in 1957.

In the same year Peter O'Shaughnessy asked Humphries if he would like to come back to Melbourne to play Estragon to his Vladimir in his *Waiting for Godot*, the first production of Beckett in Australia. Humphries was desperate to take this opportunity and was very excited to be involved in this extraordinary tragicomedy. He made the set himself, using a tree he had built in one of his earlier art exhibitions.[35]

The critical reception was mixed, with some very positive reviews. The following year O'Shaughnessy presented *Waiting for Godot* in a two-week season at the Independent Theatre in North Sydney. In his view the production of *Godot* was Humphries' first real break in the theatre.[36] The bleak humour that infuses the play seemed to answer, satisfy and relieve Humphries' obsessive interest in Dadaism. His enthralled reverence for Beckett reflected his seriousness and passion as a young actor, his emerging interest in modernist drama and his talent for pathos in comedy.

Before the decade was out, Humphries performed in other revue productions and a pantomime directed by Peter O'Shaughnessy for children in which he featured as a Bunyip. It was at the opposite end of the theatrical spectrum to Beckett's *Godot*. Yet Humphries drew on the same innocent, tender and derelict comic spirit that had made his Estragon so appealing. Inspired by Frank Dalby Davidson's folk tale *The Children of the dark people* and the launch of Sputnik, *The Bunyip and the satellite* was a commercial success, with critics suddenly enthusing about Humphries' odd but unique abilities as a performer. Bruce Grant recognised Humphries' 'shining talent' and the Bunyip as a 'true relation of the great fools and clowns of the stage, a legend with gum leaves in his hair'.[37]

Humphries has become a loved and loathed national clown as his humour has developed over the past fifty-six years. His experiences interpreting

Orsino, Thomas Diafoirus, Holofernes, Estragon, the Bunyip and the various characters he portrayed in intimate revue undoubtedly fed into the enduring Edna and Sandy figures with whom he experimented during the 1950s. Taken as a whole, Humphries' contribution to Australian theatre in the 1950s reveals a native talent for comic performance and a brilliant sense of the 'rude rudiments of satire'.

Now that the pantomime dame is a Broadway star and Humphries a Tony Award winner, his more perverse Dadaist antics have largely been left behind. But they haven't completely disappeared. In his recent television series, *The Dame Edna treatment*, Humphries put some of his celebrity guests through excruciating and humiliating paces. He mocked, derided and parodied many of these famous actors and singers mercilessly. Their reactions to him were ridiculous and very funny. The daring, confrontational element of his original Dadaist follies was evident once more. Clearly, the gall and spirit of the 1950s university student is still present in the 'housewife superstar', and the Dadaist impulse is alive in this great Australian comic actor.

Comedy and constraint: Lenny Bruce, Bernard Manning, Pauline Pantsdown and Bill Hicks

John McCallum

Comedy, by tradition, has a special licence to speak of the unspeakable, to call a spade a spade. From Aristophanes' obscene and scurrilous personal abuse of politicians sitting in the sponsors' box, to the Bakhtinian carnival of the medieval festivals, to the semen and dick jokes that Letterman and Leno told gleefully on television about Bill Clinton, the comedian has been society's sanctioned rule-breaker: unselfconscious, uninhibited, wild, free and unconstrained.

Spaces devoted to performance have also always had a special licence: the Theatre at Dionysus, the city square next to the cathedral during festival time, the late show in its special slot after the kids have gone to bed. Just as there are certain special joking relationships and situations in social and community life, so there are special spaces in performance that are by custom free from the constraints of everyday convention. In theatre, these are the clubs and pubs in which the stand-up comedian holds sway. These spaces are licensed not just legally under the Public Halls and Liquor Licensing Acts but culturally as places for comic transgression. The words 'licence' and 'sanction' are central in the discussion of comedy, and are now one of the chief constraints on comedians, as historical changes in their usage have reflected. Once a guarantee of comic freedom, comic licence has become a form of social control.

Since late Middle English, 'to license' has meant simply 'to allow' or 'to permit'. Now, when we talk of licences we mean official bureaucratic and legislative restrictions on what you are allowed to do. The sense of complete freedom from constraint once implied by the word survives now mainly in derived words such as 'licentious'. In the late eighteenth century, 'to sanction' meant 'to authorise', with loose associated meanings including 'to encourage' and 'to give approval to'. Now, when we talk of sanctions we mean penalties applied to transgressive behaviour, especially that of Arab nations.

A form of genuinely free licence is granted in the United States by a constitutional right to free speech, which is why American tonight-show hosts were allowed to have so much fun with Bill Clinton's sex life, in jokes that could never be made in the United Kingdom or Australia on broadcast television about English or Australian public figures. It is a licence restricted in Australia by defamation laws, in which truth alone is not a defence, and in which 'public interest' is a contested site of institutional and industrial argument.

The comic licence is based on one essential premise: *comedians do not tell the truth*. No matter what they say, they are just joking. It is with this endorsement, or at least on a shared pretence about it, that their licence grants them the right to transgress. It becomes a particularly irksome restriction for comedians who also see themselves as social critics. The resultant conflict produces what Will Kaufman calls 'irony fatigue', a condition characterised by creative exhaustion brought on by the need to keep on the comic mask, to maintain the ironic stance, to continue with the masquerade, when what the comedian really wants to do is tell the truth.[1] In extreme cases, such as that of the first example, the condition can be fatal.

Lenny Bruce

Stand-up comedy in contemporary popular culture has its originating myth in the work of Lenny Bruce, a comedian who is still a reference point for young comedians who like to think of themselves as wild and dangerous. He is still, forty years after his death, the paradigmatic rebellious comic: a product of the beat generation, a Jewish hipster who spent his youth in Negro jazz clubs, a jobbing performer who remodelled himself as an idealistic reformer under the extraordinary pressure of legal and police harassment during the last five years of his life, from 1961 when he was first prosecuted for obscenity until his death from a drug overdose in 1966.

The difficulty of reading him now is that there were many Lenny Bruces, or rather 'Lenny Bruce' now represents a highly complex personal, social, political and mythic construction. Its fields include: the model since the early 1960s of the 'committed' comic who did political material; the 'sick comic' who was rebellious, obscene and angry about society; the horny, self-absorbed, red-blooded young beatnik, kin to Jack Kerouac and Nelson Algren; the hardworking 'jobbing' professional performer who had it tough but who finally achieved success; the victim of society whose career was tragically cut short by police harassment and oppression by 'the system'; and the flawed individual whose career was tragically cut short by self-destructive behaviour and drug abuse. Antonin Artaud wrote of Vincent Van Gogh as 'the artist suicided by society'.[2] Lenny Bruce was, in these romantically rebellious terms, an artist suicided by the establishment. His followers believed, and many still believe, if you ask them in the small anti-establishment clubs and pubs where his legend still lives on, that his comedy was so rebellious that hegemonic control failed and institutional force – in the form of continued police and judicial action – had to be employed to constrain and finally destroy him.

Whatever facts might lie behind this legend (and certainly Bruce's personal behaviour, especially his drug use, gave the establishment plenty of opportunity to harass him), it remains true that Bruce created a style of rebellious comedy, with real substance, that marks him as the most influential figure in modern comedy. There are very few comedians working now who come anywhere near him, a sign perhaps that when the establishment abruptly revoked his comic licence it knew what it was doing.

His material that now reads as 'committed' and idealistic was principally his integrationist stance on 'the Negro question' and his opposition to organised religion, although he had a wide range of 'bits' that were topical and satirical. In his notorious 'Religions Inc.' routine he managed to offend Protestants, Catholics and Jews more or less equally, which was at least evenhanded of him.[3] His first prosecution was for saying the word 'cocksuckers' on stage, perhaps the first and last time that anyone has been taken to court over an eleven-letter word. His sexual frankness and use of what was then considered obscene language was bold and shocking, but from this distance it does not seem to be his strongest material. He earned his reputation as a radical comic, in the press of his time, because of the obscenity charges, and then, as he became more and more embroiled with the police and the law, because of drug charges.[4]

The most famous/notorious part of the Lenny Bruce myth is that he reacted to his own persecution, during the series of arrests for obscenity and drug-taking which filled up the last four years of his life, by reinventing himself, or being reinvented by the press, as an idealist. This is not to suggest that Lenny the man didn't sincerely mean everything he said in those years, but, as Eric Bogosian said in his introduction to the 1992 re-issue of Lenny's autobiography, the 'big kid' (as Bogosian called him) found out, as he developed, 'that full blown idealism in his art was his secret weapon', and he took to it like any big kid takes to the latest online tournament in World of Warcraft.[5] He discovered that he could take onto the stage all the sitting around talking about Life with a capital 'L' that he and his friends had been doing since demob after the war. He scorned jokes and punchlines, and revelled in his freewheeling ability to improvise. He called himself an 'abstractionist'; he was a type of jazz scat-comic. He believed that the whole beat style of hedonism that he and his fellow 'white niggers' had built up during the 1950s could now become both a means of rebellion and an influential part of mainstream public discourse. Like Bill Hicks after him, he thought that he could carry his angry underground style onto national broadcast television. Irony fatigue set in when they revoked his licence. Bruce reacted by disclaiming his role as a comedian. His performances notoriously degenerated, in terms of their comic craft, into tedious public readings of transcripts of his trials.

The process began, both personally and publicly, at about the same time as he began to be called a 'sick comic'. This was a label first given him by *Time* magazine. He always hated it, although his 1959 album was called, with his presumably ironic approval, *The sick humor of Lenny Bruce*.[6] But in his performances he kept asking who was really sick: himself or the mainstream comedians who did harelip and moron jokes. He referred with great scorn to the genealogy of 'She's so ugly . . .' jokes, from Henny Youngman on, and to the 'buck-teeth malocclusion' Japanese stereotypes being performed at the time by Jerry Lewis.[7]

Bruce was no sensitive reconstructed male. The chapter in his autobiography in which he attacks the 'sick comic' issue is just that: an attack. In his performances he did 'chick' jokes, 'wife' jokes and 'faggot' jokes, just as Jack Kerouac did in his writing. In his defence of himself against the attack by the press that he was a 'sick comic', Bruce went to the material he knew best: the horny beatnik stuff.[8] This material sat alongside his now better remembered routines such as 'Religions, Inc.' and his most famous bit, 'Are there any niggers here tonight?', in which he introduced comedically what has become a commonplace strategy of marginal people everywhere, the proud appropriation of the abusive language of the centre: 'nigger', 'queen', 'poof', 'dyke', 'boong', 'wog'.

The point? [he asked] That the word's suppression gives it the power, the violence, the viciousness. If President Kennedy got on television and said, 'Tonight I'd like to introduce all the niggers in my cabinet,' and he yelled 'niggerniggerniggerniggerniggerniggernigger' at every nigger he saw . . . till nigger didn't mean anything anymore, till nigger lost its meaning – you'd never make any four-year-old nigger cry when he came home from school.[9]

Bruce was a naive wild boy. He had a barely articulated anger at public hypocrisy, an anger that found its only real expression when he became so involved in his own arrests and trials. He wanted to do well professionally as much as the next guy, but he was also mostly honest about what he saw, and he was observant. His deep respect for the law as an institution, which underlies his almost neurotic obsession with fighting his charges through the courts, suggests a marginality unconscious of itself.

Perhaps his legend now is based on the fact that he was, in spite of himself, caught up in the socially radical and culturally unstable moment of the invention of modern stand-up comedy. Certainly he rejected the masquerade towards the end of his career, and tried to concentrate on what he called '*truth* truth'. As he said in one of his most famous 'bits': 'I'm not a comedian. And I'm not sick. The world is sick and I'm the doctor . . . I'm a surgeon with a scalpel for false values. I don't have an act. I just talk. I'm just Lenny Bruce'.[10] This, reduced to his often quoted tag-line during his performances towards the end of his life and career – 'I'm not a comedian, I'm Lenny Bruce' – remains the classic statement of the rejection of the comic mask, the tearing up of the comic licence.

Bernard Manning

Bernard Manning came from a completely different tradition, but he also is a reference point for debates about the constraints accepted by or imposed on comedy. To most liberal-minded audiences, even those who are scornful of the constraints of political correctness, Manning's comedy was abhorrent. His home base in Manchester, the Embassy Club, was a bastion of the old working-class racist, sexist comedy of the northern English club tradition: the tradition against which the London-based alternative comedy of the late 1970s reacted so strongly and decisively. There is no doubt that 'alt-com', as it was dubbed in the media at the time, completely reset the agenda for British comedians. It is itself now old hat. A new generation of post-alternative comedians in the 1990s, such as Frank Skinner, David Baddiel and Robert Newman, were pioneers of the 'new laddishness', a type

of ironic postmodern return to the humour of the old lads. This is comedy
that recycles the old line 'It's just a joke', and turns it into an entire comic
aesthetic. It avoids irony fatigue by the simple device of abandoning any
pretence of telling the truth. One of the most reviled comedians in smart
young circles in England then was Ben Elton, the ultimate alternative comedian: non-sexist, non-racist, every routine with a message.

Manning survived in that new world partly because he was a relentless
self-publicist, partly because he was very good at his craft, but also because
he used his licence as a comedian in such provocative ways. He stood at his
microphone and told a string of old in-group/out-group jokes as if they
were classic texts, devoid of context. In a time of political correctness he was,
perhaps, postmodern in spite of himself. He told Jewish jokes, Irish jokes,
women jokes and, more controversially, 'nigger' and 'Paki' jokes, with a style
that implies that they are just texts, not to be taken seriously:

> There was a plane crash in Madrid about six months ago. Two hundred
> Japanese on it. Broke my fuckin' heart – six empty seats.

> 'How do you feel about Pakis?'
> 'Well, I couldn't eat a whole one.'

> What's the difference between a dead rabbit and a dead Paki on the
> motorway? No skid marks by the Paki.

And in 1995 his Rodney King joke:

> [In America] they knock fuck outta them coons. Los Angeles police unit
> kicking that fucking nigger on the floor, I thought, 'fuck me, that's not
> on! Not enough police there!'[11]

These are offensive jokes, but they are also structurally comic and have a
long history. In Australia, the motorway gag is an old Aborigine joke, but

it also has a respectable pedigree as a lawyer joke. It works perfectly well
no matter what comic butt is placed dead on the road with no skid marks.
The problem with Bernard Manning becomes one of context, and perhaps
intent. He was at the centre of two significant court cases in Britain in the
mid-1990s, both of which raised issues about the constraints on comedy.

Burton and Rhule vs De Vere Hotels Ltd was a dispute in the Nottingham
court in which two black waitresses brought a harassment charge against
their employer after Manning had singled them out as comic butts of jokes
delivered to his white audience. The case was an industrial one, involving
harassment by the audience as much as by the comedian; one of the waitresses was groped by an audience member and the other was asked whether
'a black pussy tastes like a white one'. The case went way beyond Manning's performance, clearly, but it involved Manning's comic leadership and
complicity.

In 1995 Manning was again the centre of a controversy when he performed at a private police social function in Liverpool and racially baited
the only black policeman in an audience of three hundred. The media
attention, in a country in which relations between white police and Afri-
can and Pakistani Britons is a highly sensitive issue, was focused on the
enthusiastic response of the police audience to his act. In this case the
'victim', PC Macdonald, made no complaint (and in fact made statements
supportive of Manning in the press) and no charges were laid, but the
public outrage was considerable.

Manning, unconstrained at his own Embassy Club, and performing in
this case at a private function, lost a few bookings and was vilified in the
liberal press, but his work as a comedian continued with scarcely a hiccup
until his death in June 2007.[12] The waitresses working for de Vere hotels
may have been innocent victims, but at the police function in Liverpool
everyone involved, including PC Macdonald, was a willing and enthusiastic
participant. This was surely a licensed comic event. It was recorded secretly.
The public outrage was based partly on the social implications of it being
the police who were laughing at PC Macdonald.

There have been comparable cases in Australia. One was sports bureau-crat Arthur Tunstall's notorious Cathy Freeman/Lionel Rose joke, told to a friend at a private party, overheard and reported in the press. Freeman and Rose are both famous and popular Aboriginal sports stars, and the joke was about Aboriginals being thieves. Another was the private police party in Queensland, videotaped and released to the press, at which two policemen in blackface make-up posed before the camera with a noose around their necks, in a parody of the controversy surrounding black deaths in custody. In all three cases, a joke for limited circulation, in a situation framed and licensed as appropriate for comedy – a quiet moment between friends, a private party – was reframed by the media and the comic licence revoked. It was the attitudes of the laughers as much as the comic material that was the subject of the controversy.

Howard Jacobson wrote a defence of Manning based on two apparently contradictory principles: that comedy is play, and so takes place in a spe-cially licensed discursive space; and that comedy deals with dangerous or offensive material and so has a cathartic function. '[It] lances the boil,' he wrote. 'It enables the pus to run.'[13] There is clearly a distinction to be made between these two arguments, but they are not necessarily contradictory. There is a false dichotomy in a lot of commentary on comedy: that it is either funny and false or serious and true. The difficult area is where it is funny and serious, which both Bruce and Manning, from opposite ends of the political spectrum, are. The idea of serious silliness has legal implica-tions in the third example, the work of the contemporary Australian queer satirist, Pauline Pantsdown.

Pauline Pantsdown

Bernard Manning was a comedian on the right attacked from the centre and the left, and scarcely constrained at all except for the usual call for a boy-cott on his shows – which was unlikely to be successful considering that the centre and the left weren't his target audience. The case of *Burton and Rhule vs De Vere Hotels Ltd* was, as I have said, a harassment case with no legal implications for the practice of comedy. Pauline Pantsdown is a converse case in which comedy from the left was attacked and successfully gagged by forces on the extreme right. The case raises important questions about the licensed masquerade of comedy. In this example, the comedian leaves the licensed stage entirely and enters the mainstream. His performance is a Bakhtinian carnivalisation of politics.

Pantsdown is a drag act by a comic political activist who dogged politician Pauline Hanson, leader of the extreme right-wing One Nation Party, before and during the 1998 election campaign, and attracted – in a way that Jerry Rubin, the original Yippie, would have admired – enormous media attention. The carnival was given a boost when Hanson won a temporary injunction in Queensland in September 1997 against one of Pantsdown's parodic songs, 'Back door man'. Hanson didn't pursue the case, presumably in order to keep the injunction active, and the Australian Broadcasting Corporation (ABC) appealed against it. The appeal was rejected on 28 September, five days before the poll. The court cases were as much part of the carnivalisation as was the media hype that surrounded Pantsdown's campaign as a candidate for the Senate, running against Hanson.[14]

Pantsdown is a character created and performed by Simon Hunt, then a tutor in sound design at the University of New South Wales College of Fine Arts and a drag performer interested in political satire. One of his techniques – that which produced 'Back door man' – is to electronically sample public speeches by the objects of his satire and to break them up and remould the pieces into pastiches in which the satirical objects appear to be saying obscene, outrageous or stupid things. When a comic artist is dealing with ideas that he or she (in this case both) believes to be so extreme as to be beyond the reach of satiric exaggeration, then one solution – for Hunt at least – is to leap sideways and queer the entire discourse, in the way that serious political drag and queer performance artists have been doing for many years. Hunt traced the artistic influences on his work back to the Weimar cabaret of the 1930s, in which the rise of fascism was such an extreme and shocking phenomenon that comic artists found that they could only

respond in a way (popularly celebrated in the musical *Cabaret*) that anticipated the contemporary political sense of 'queer'.[15]

Hunt had already created a work using the speeches of conservative Christian politician Fred Nile before he turned his attention to Pauline Hanson
for 'Back door man', originally made for performance at a dance party. The
second Pantsdown song, 'I don't like it', was commercially released during
the election campaign, with a video clip screened on *Rage*, a popular television music program, and given a great deal of airplay on JJJ, the ABC's
youth-oriented music radio station.[16]

'I don't like it' is a less confronting work at first hearing than 'Back door
man', more wry in its comic style and apparently lighter in tone. The CD
includes a radio mix and a dance mix, with the Hanson vocals a catchy background for those who want to dance and a satirical text for those who care to
listen. Its success, supported by the publicity surrounding Pantsdown's Senate
candidature, was an example of effective political commentary piggy-backing
on a popular form. The procedure for producing such works – whatever one
might think of the result – is technically sophisticated and involves many
hours of serious and creative work in a studio. This was not a simple prank.[17]

In 'Back door man' a voice recognisably that of Hanson claimed to be
homosexual and proud of it. In the Queensland appeal case, Hanson's lawyers
argued, on the basis of the comic text, that Hunt's work alleged that she was,
among other things, an enthusiastic recipient of anal sex. No attempt was
made to investigate whether spectators and auditors of the work would actually be led by it to believe that she was. It seems unlikely that they would:

I'm a backdoor man, I'm very proud of it
I'm a backdoor man, I'm homosexual
I'm a backdoor, yes I am, I'm very proud of it
I'm a backdoor man, I'm homosexual [giggles] . . .

I'm a backdoor man for the Ku Klux Klan
with very horrendous plans

I'm a very caring potato.

We will never have the chance[18]

It was reported widely in the press that 'potato' is a slang word for 'recipient of anal sex', which, even if it were true, would not have been widely known and makes no more sense out of the offending verse. It should be repeated that the effect of these works is in the clever use of sampling: the comic incongruity created by the effect of having the actual voice of a high-profile conservative politician, with a populist image as a simple middle-Australian woman, saying such things.

Hanson's case, as plaintiff, rested solely on the content of the text, and ignored the context of its performance. This context, apart from any broad consideration of comic licence, included the fact that the author of the work and its comic subject were both at the time registered and actively campaigning political candidates in a federal election, and that their audience, therefore, was receiving the work in a highly charged and public political atmosphere.

The appellant's case, in seeking to have the injunction lifted, was based (against his better judgement, according to Hunt, after the decision) on an argument that the jokes and ideas expressed in 'Back door man' were not defamatory because they were expressed comedically. On the face of it, this seems an obvious defence. As Richard Ackland wrote:

The plaintiff's lawyers pleaded that the song, given its ordinary meaning, could be taken by ordinary people to mean: that she is a pedophile, a homosexual, a prostitute, engages in unnatural sexual practices including anal sex, engages in unnatural sexual practices including anal sex with the Ku Klux Klan, she is a member of the Ku Klux Klan, is a potato – which means that she was 'a receiver of anal sex'.

The appeal judges, led by de Jersey CJ, refused to lift the injunction, saying that 'these were grossly offensive imputations relating to the sexual orientation and preference of a federal politician' . . .

With all due respect, as they say, the ABC has a strong legal argument, namely that it is a complete and utter absurdity for any ordinary person to think that the words of the song give rise to the literal meanings contended by Ms Hanson's lawyers.

To think that one would have to believe that Ms Hanson is a male homosexual who indulges in anal sex and is a pedophile. It is all too ridiculous for words.[19]

It is, but such a defence has broader implications: that comedy itself is a ridiculous activity that has earned no right to be taken seriously. This is the crucial issue here, in terms of the constraints on comedy. It implies that comedy is inevitably constrained by its own absurdity and can never operate in the real world of political and intellectual discourse. If this were ever established in a court of law, then many comedians would give up. The comic licence would become like a joke from a novelty shop, like the mock 'Licence to fart' that delights ten-year-old boys. In drama it would be as if the Fool in *King Lear* had a legal injunction out against him preventing him from saying to his master that giving away a kingdom is a stupid thing to do.

The irony is that 'I don't like it', which reached the top twenty during the election campaign, clearly suggests that Hanson is racist:

I don't like it, when you turn my voice about.
I don't like it, when you vote One Nation out . . .

Please explain, why can't my blood be coloured white?
I should talk to some medical doctors, coloured blood, it's just not right.

Hanson's lawyers were unable or unwilling to seek an injunction against the broadcast and commercial release of this song. Apparently the charge of racism is not defamatory whereas the charge of homosexuality is.

Australian libel laws do not allow truth as a sufficient defence, let alone the right of free speech. Yet a possible defence exists, not in arguing that the work is not defamatory because comedy is inherently trivial but in claiming that it *is* defamatory but fair comment. This was the defence used successfully in the case brought by architect Harry Seidler against the *National Times* over Patrick Cook's notorious cover cartoon, 'The Harry Seidler Retirement Home'. The drawing showed a barren field littered with concrete pillar-boxes, each containing a confined old person, and each with an opening at the front for food and an opening at the back for excrement. It was a satiric comment on what Cook saw as the dehumanising effects of Seidler's high modernist architecture. The pillar-boxes in the drawing had the dimensions of the Blues Point Tower, one of Seidler's most notorious buildings, but in the scale of a backyard dunny. The court found that the cartoon was defamatory but dismissed Seidler's suit on the grounds of fair comment.

The defence in the Pantsdown case argued that comedy takes place outside any consideration of the real and the true. This is a most serious denigration of the work of any artist: that it is not measurable against even the most subjective conception of what is important in the lived world. It represents a view that most artists, and most comedians, would strenuously reject. It throws the baby out with the bathwater, challenging such basic principles of comic practice as recognition-humour, identification and comic distance from painful realities.

These three examples represent what we might call judicial endorsements on the comic licence. 'Endorse' is yet another word that has shifted in meaning. Since the late 1400s it has meant to write a comment on an official document, and since the mid-1600s it has also been used to mean 'to approve' or 'to vouch for', but since the early 1900s an 'endorsement' on a licence has increasingly come to mean a record of an offence. In the middle of the last century it also acquired a special meaning in South Africa, where, according to the *New shorter Oxford English dictionary*, 'to be endorsed' meant for a black to 'be moved out of an urban area because of not satisfying the conditions that would qualify him or her to continue living there'.

One could make too much of such etymological considerations, but shifts in language do reflect shifts in belief, and words such as 'licence', 'sanction' and 'endorse' have clearly changed from words of freedom to words of control. Lear's Fool continually speaks truths much more painful than the simple declaration that got Cordelia banished. The mad old king would have had one less companion in his hovel if he had 'endorsed' his Fool's licence in the modern sense.

There are two further constraints on the work of contemporary comedians that also need to be noted. The first is the commercial and industrial conditions under which they work, because, since the nineteenth century at least, successful professional comedians have been able to make big money. This is partly what the politically rebellious comics of the 1960s and 1970s were reacting against, but even Lenny Bruce was not averse to toning down his material for the sake of an appearance on Johnny Carson. Philip Auslander has argued that the rise of the new stand-up in the United States during the 1970s, based in specialist clubs, was partly a result of the gap left by the commodification of rock'n'roll.[20]

After that time, with the rise of the video market, pay TV and large rock venues for comedians, stand-up itself became commodified and moderated by commercial pressures. In Australia, England and the United States bright young comedians were taken up by radio stations and commercial television networks to become announcers, hosts and personalities, and their original comic content was censored and ultimately compromised, leaving only their delivery style, translated out of its formation as a live interactive performance technique into something quite different. In formats such as *That was the week that was* in Britain, and its Australian version, *Good news week*, this transplantation could be very effective, but more often good comedians were given a weak, under-funded revue show or sitcom, lost creative control, and were effectively silenced as creators of original comedy. Cable TV, with its insatiable appetite for cheap product, took up and destroyed the careers of many of the best and brightest comedians of the 1990s. The highly successful public-network Australian satirical team The Chaser parodied this when they responded to rumours that they were about to go commercial by announcing 'We'll only sell out if we are offered enough money'.[21]

The second major constraint arises from the restrictions imposed on behaviour and discourse that come under the popular journalists' heading 'political correctness'. This term masks a complex set of political projects and ideological constructions. Its common currency now results partly from both deliberate and unconscious ideological misrepresentations of the politics of identity-formation arising from the liberation movements of the 1970s, and from certain excesses committed in their name when political theory was translated into public policy, especially in the United States.

Most comedians, not surprisingly, are scornful of the idea, but there is no doubt that the political convictions that imposed 'correctness' in public discourse have already crept into comedy. Probably the best-known example is that of the English alternative comedians such as Ben Elton, already referred to. It is difficult to untangle the reasons for the reviling of Elton by the post-alternative comedians, but they seem to be a combination of jealousy at his success and genuine concern that messages are for Western Union, not for comedians, to deliver.

Bill Hicks

The final example here is that of the American comedian Bill Hicks, whose battle with the commercial networks culminated in 1993 when his appearance on the Dave Letterman show became, as John Lahr first revealed in the *New Yorker*, the first act to be censored at the CBS Ed Sullivan Theatre since Elvis Presley in 1956. As Lahr said, 'Presley was not allowed to be shown from the waist down. Hicks was not allowed to be shown at all'.[22] Hicks was the most serious comic social critic of his time, a savage satirist whose comic mask was that of a seductive and charming wild boy. One of his most famous bits, and most pertinent here for what it reveals about the tension between the comic masquerader and the truth-teller, was one in his advertising routine (available in the video *Bill Hicks live*)[23] in which he refused to make a joke but kept getting laughs.

Hicks had been feted largely by commercial television because Letterman
and his CBS producers were anxious to prove that moving to a prime-time
tonight show had not compromised Letterman's supposedly daring comic
edge: 'Same Dave. Better Time.' was the promo slogan. CBS producers
followed Hicks around for days before his appearance. He agreed to stop
swearing and to tone down his material. He believed that he was being hired
as a comedian who told the truth.

The censored set is reconstructed by Kaufman, and the key elements of
it can be seen on commercially released videos of Hicks's shows. It includes
an attack on the commercialisation of rock music, a bit on the hypocrisy
of public attitudes towards homosexuality, a bit satirising anti-abortionists
for calling themselves 'pro-lifers', and a routine in which he comments on
Christian iconography and speculates on why Jesus has never returned
('Do you think, when Jesus comes back, he's really going to want to look
at a cross? . . . "I'm not going, Dad. No, they're still wearing crosses – they
totally missed the point . . . When they start wearing fishes, I might go back
again"').[24]

It is a prickly routine, in the context of American commercial culture,
but it is difficult to pick what exactly caused it to be cut from the show.
Hicks claimed not to have known, but acknowledged that he might have
upset any of a number of groups. In typical fashion he didn't care. 'We
now live in the "Age of Being Offended",' he said. 'Get over it.' Kaufman
suggests that the reason was that in the week of the banning the Letterman
show was broadcasting lucrative commercials for the anti-abortion lobby.[25]

Whatever the case, Hicks never appeared on network commercial television again, in spite of offers from both Letterman and Leno. He continued
to perform in clubs and on public television until his death from pancreatic
cancer four months later. Kaufman quotes his final recorded performance,
for ACTV (Austin), in which he said:

Folks, here's the deal. I editorialise for 45 minutes. The last 15, I pull
my chute, we all pull our chutes, and float down to Dick Joke Island

together . . . We will rest our weary heads against the big purple-veined trunks of dick jokes, while bouncing on our spongy-scrotum beanbag chairs, and giggle away the night like good American comedy audiences are supposed to, goddammit.[26]

This is a comic riposte in the face of censorship that Lenny Bruce, in his readings of his trial transcripts, couldn't manage.

Bruce was obscene and a drug addict, Bernard Manning was a racist, Pauline Pantsdown was a scurrilous libeller: these are facts established in American, British and Australian courts and the responsible media. On the other hand, Bruce was one of the most innovative and influential comedians of the postwar period, Manning was for many decades one of the most popular comedians in England, and Pantsdown is one of the few political satirists in current Australian politics ever to have influenced an election result.

Bruce was a superlative comic monologist, with a technically skilful beat-jazz style which absorbed his personal attitude and passion and which reflected the social and political preoccupations of his time. Manning was a great joke-teller who disingenuously treated his jokes as texts without political context, and so tried to free his audience from public and social constraints. Pantsdown is a postmodern performer with a subversive, media-savvy style in which a transgressive and ironic form mirrors, rather than represents, oppositional content.

In each case, if the idea of comic licence is to be salvaged from external and internal forms of constraint, it needs to be reconsidered in the light of the different legal, hegemonic and ideological attacks that these performers have faced. When we include the industrial and cultural constraints of late capitalism, in the example of Bill Hicks – constraints of communication and political correctness – the licence appears to be increasingly worthless. Lenny Bruce's comedy, personally and in terms of its public currency and efficacy, was destroyed by his struggle against constraint, but it was taken seriously. Pantsdown's comedy, personally and in terms of its currency and efficacy, lives so far, but not as serious work. This does not necessarily prove a regression towards increasingly restrictive ideas of what comic licence entails, but it does suggest that there is a postmodern tendency not to take it seriously. Comedy now has a licence to fart, but not to transgress.

'Lookatmoiye! Lookatmoiye!': Australian situation comedy and beyond

Susan Lever

Situation comedies – those precisely scripted series about the funny side of domestic life – have formed a mainstay of television broadcasting since its beginnings. While their origins lie in radio, they have become one of the archetypal genres of television. In the United States, they have developed from the comedies written around a star trained on radio or vaudeville – Lucille Ball's *I love Lucy*, the *George Burns and Gracie Allen show*, Jackie Gleason and *The honeymooners* – to a sophisticated genre that can go anywhere from *Everybody loves Raymond* to *Sex in the city*. The genre is so strong that it can be parodied and subverted by *The Simpsons* or *Malcolm in the middle* and it has formed the basis of several studies of the changes in American society. The British, too, have created their own style of situation comedy, so that the shifts in British cultural interests can be mapped through a range of brilliant comedies from *Steptoe and son* to *Absolutely fabulous*.

So it is a matter for lament that the recognised Australian contributions to television situation comedy are sparse: *My name's McGooley, what's yours?* (1967), *Kingswood country* (1980), *Mother and son* (1985), *Hey Dad* (1987), *Acropolis now* (1989), *Frontline* (1993), *The Games* (1998) and *Kath and Kim* (2002). Though we could trace the decline of the archetypal working-class Australian from Dominic McGooley through the middle-class suburban Ted Bullpitt of *Kingswood country* and the first-generation migrants of *Acropolis now* to the aspirational *Kath and Kim*, the evidence for cultural change is a little thin. Such an analysis would need to enlist some of the Australian situation comedies that, for one reason or another, might be called failures, such as *Nice 'n' juicy* (1966), *I've married a bachelor* (1968), *Snake Gully with Dad and Dave* (1972), *And the big men fly* (1974), *Flash Nick from Jindavik* (1974), *The last of the Australians* (1975), *Alvin Purple* (1976), *Bobby Dazzler* (1977), *Home sweet home* (1980), *Dearest enemy* (1989), *Col'n Carpenter* (1990), *All together now* (1991), *Eggshells* (1991), *My two wives* (1992) and *Flat chat* (2001).

Some of these gained an audience of creditable size, managed at least two series and might have been more successful in a less ruthless marketplace. Others, such as *Dog's Head Bay* (1999), provide fascinating models of failure. But popularity does not guarantee quality; Gary Reilly and John Flanagan's long-running series *Hey Dad* purveyed a bland kind of family comedy, while John Clarke and Andrew Knight's two-season wonder *The fast lane* (1985) is my particular all-time favourite Australian television comedy.

Rob Johnson and David Smiedt provide a broad history of Australian television comedy in their *Boom-boom! A century of Australian comedy*, but they do not attempt the kind of cultural analysis found in books on American television by David Marcs or Barry Putterman. Albert Moran's *Guide to Australian TV series* describes the fates of many of these comedy series. *The fast lane*, for example, had scripts that were:

> well paced, intelligent and comic, and narratively elegant in their resolutions. But nobody told the ABC's powers-that-be at Broadcast House in Sydney – the first series was played in a late-night slot where it almost disappeared without a trace.[1]

Most often, Australian television comedy series are produced on a tight budget, programmed out of prime time and prove unable to compete with the audience ratings of imported material. Yet even these difficult conditions cannot account for the variability in the quality of Australian situation comedy, where new attempts often seem to blunder onto air without reference to the lessons of the past.

This history has grown into the received wisdom that Australians can write soap opera but not situation comedy, a wisdom that can become a self-fulfilling prophecy. In 1990 Deborah Klika concluded that one of the major difficulties for Australian television comedy was the lack of diversity in the writers and producers of comedy and hence its range. She noted that only two television networks, the ABC and the Seven Network, had shown any commitment to such comedy.[2] Klika, like other commentators (such as Weis), believed that it is important for Australians to see their lives reflected and analysed through situation comedy; it is a matter for national psychic health.

Such national needs are not usually left to market forces. The ABC has provided a relatively safe starting point for many Australian comedies, but it seems unreasonable to expect commercial television networks to take a risk on them when lifestyle or reality television can draw large audiences with less investment. Fortunately for Australians, comedy based on their lives emerges on television even without a strong tradition of situation comedy. Despite financial constraints and risk-averse networks, Australian writers and performers have found ways to keep mocking Australian society on television.

Before radio and television, Australians had a strong tradition of popular music-hall entertainment, which emerged as vaudeville in the early twentieth century. Theatres such as the Tivoli in Sydney survived by presenting variety entertainments that included comedians, dancers, singers and a range of novelty acts, and troupes of these entertainers would travel around Australia's country towns. The comedians became the most popular drawcards for these entertainments, and several who later became radio stars, such as Roy Rene and George Wallace, brought a following of listeners who had seen them on the vaudeville stage. In its early years, television also relied on the talents of these adaptable show-business personalities, some of whom had begun their careers as dancers or singers before emerging as comedians and radio entertainers.

On television, we can sometimes find comedy in Australia's successful soap operas, and the tradition of sketch comedy fluctuates with fashion and the emergence of new generations of comic talent, but the most consistent Australian television comedy rides on the variety show, itself a continuation of the pre-television traditions of vaudeville and radio. Obviously, such shows are relatively cheap to produce; they need no large casts or range of sets and they can be strung out over an hour or more of Australian television content. But they have a further advantage in that they use the television medium to do what it does best – offer immediate responses to the world. The best television has a degree of improvisation, so that the audience participates in the moment with the performers. These television shows take advantage of their transience. Rather than the polished control of the best situation comedy, they threaten a kind of anarchy.

When Graham Kennedy disrupted his *In Melbourne tonight* television show of the 1960s with anarchic improvised comedy, he was continuing a style familiar from radio, particularly in the shows hosted by Australia's radio star of the 1950s, Jack Davey. Davey could not make the shift to television, and recordings of his famous wit suggest that 'you had to be there', as they say, to appreciate his humour. While the Melburnian Garrie Hutchinson takes it for granted that Kennedy was funny, the Scottish-born Alan McKee, watching the tapes long after the event, assures us that, in retrospect, Kennedy appears 'transgressive but not particularly funny'.[3] This kind of humour works by engaging the audience in the moment, by making them complicit in the transgression of their expectations. It is transient but exciting. Unlike the humour of scripted plays or films, it depends on the sense of shared time between audience and performer that television conveys so well.

While situation comedy has struggled, the old music-hall tradition of the comedian/host has flourished on Australian television with a range of *Tonight* shows and variety shows. It can carry over into other formats such as quiz shows, panel shows (*Good news week*) and even dancing competitions (*Strictly dancing*, though not *Dancing with the stars*). From time to time, it pushes further towards the fictional comedy, when the host becomes a comedy character rather than merely a comedian or joke-telling master of ceremonies. When this occurs, the imaginative possibility for comedy expands exponentially. Barry Humphries developed his original sketch-character Edna Everage into such a character for British television, and there have been other passing successes, such as Libby Gorr's Elle McFeast and Mary Coustas's Effie. But the high points of the form on Australian television remain Norman Gunston's shows of the 1970s and Roy Slaven's and HG Nelson's *Club Buggery* shows of the 1990s.

Garry McDonald's Norman Gunston set a benchmark for risk-taking on television, as his exaggerated comic character encountered real people. McDonald developed the character of Norman Gunston as part of the *Aunty Jack show* sketch comedy of the early 1970s. There, Norman reported on events in Wollongong, mocked in the show as the exemplar of Australian parochialism. By 1975, the ABC had given Norman his own half-hour television show where he sang songs and interviewed guests in a naïve manner. Norman sent up the simplicities of Australia, particularly its satisfaction with its tawdry material creations (the Nite 'n' Day lounge, the pineapple doughnut). He satirised the idea of celebrity by being a television performer, and hence 'celebrity', while being totally talentless and stupid. At the American actor Warren Beatty's press conference, Norman told Beatty that he was a celebrity like Johnny Carson with his own tonight show. Beatty pointed out that a half-hour weekly show could hardly compare with Carson's hour-long shows, five nights a week. The first series of the *Norman Gunston show* was built on the premise that Norman's luck would soon run out and his show would be cancelled. In its final episode the chairman of the ABC stepped in with an announcement that the show had been saved.

From this point, Norman was able to aspire beyond the 'fabulously well-paid series of cigarette commercials' to a Gold Logie, which he won in 1976 after the second series. So the show satirised the way that television created celebrities from nothing, a propensity that has reached even more absurd levels since Norman's day with the boom in reality television. Of course, Norman was not entirely talentless. His renditions of popular torch songs, complete with literal explanatory gestures, demonstrated how ludicrous and meaningless the words of these songs could be. His version of 'Send in the clowns' manages a kind of pathos while turning lines like 'Don't you love farce? My fault I fear' into 'Don't you love farts? My fault I fear' by the simple addition of hand gestures. His physical appearance, with his pale face covered in patched shaving cuts and his hair oiled and combed over a bald patch, and his loose-fitting suits presented him as a contemporary clown. He performed as a clown, too, always literal-minded and innocent in his approach to the people he interviewed.

His unscripted interviews, though, can still create a frisson of horror or embarrassment years later. Norman's appearance among the throng on the steps of Parliament House the day (11 November 1975) that Gough Whitlam was dismissed as prime minister affronts the tragedy that many Labor voters still associate with Whitlam's demise. McDonald remained in character, eavesdropping on Kep Enderby and Bob Hawke who told him: 'It's a bit too serious for that'. Norman, of course, remained serious throughout the incident, but the uncomfortable laughter from his audiences undermined the sense that any aspect of Australian politics could be taken seriously. A month later, voters confirmed Whitlam's dismissal.

Perhaps Norman did represent the oblivious, self-centred Australian voter. Garry McDonald improvised his responses to the moment, no doubt without any particular plan in mind. The resulting laughter comes partly from discomfort that a clown could enter the most serious political crisis in Australia's recent history. Television's relationship with reality continues to be its most fascinating aspect. In this case, it appears to take an amoral, anarchic role.

But the price for such risk-taking is high. Norman moved from the ABC to the Seven Network at the end of the 1970s, and in 1993 McDonald made a short-lived attempt to revive him on Seven before the impersonation took its toll on the actor's mental health.

Roy Slaven and HG Nelson, the characters created and performed by John Doyle and Greig Pickhaver, are too self-aware to take Norman's risks in interviews. Unlike Norman, they do not pretend to innocence or ignorance (rather the opposite) and they express a masculine confidence in their inter-pretation of the world. This may be because they began by parodying the Australian obsession with sport, and took the time on radio to develop their characters, the hyperbolic sports journalist, HG Nelson (Pickhaver), and his comrade the veteran sportsman who knew everything about every sport, Roy Slaven (Doyle). On radio (ABC's Triple J), they spent whole afternoons calling and commenting on real sporting competitions, to a point when many listeners preferred Roy and HG's comic interpretation to the straight (but hardly more moderate) calls by the genuine sports commentators. On television, the ABC tried them out with a weekly thirty-minute slot in 1995 where they performed as talking heads to the camera. They soon realised that television demanded a little more visual interest and moved on to the weekly variety show of 1996, *Club Buggery*. This show, under various titles, lasted for three series, until Doyle and Pickhaver moved to Seven, where their coverage of the Sydney Olympics (*The dream*) was a popular success.

Roy and HG celebrate Australians' obsession with sport, embellishing it to the point where it is sufficiently ridiculous to be called satire. *Club Bug-gery* mimicked the interior of an RSL complete with poker machines and a memorial torch in the background. The singing of the 'Nissan Cedrics' and Ian Turpie, and the dance routines by Jane Scali and the 'Ford V8s', presented a kitsch form of entertainment that was being sent up at the same time that it was being enjoyed. *Club Buggery* was a night at the RSL as it was meant to be – full of fun because of its tawdry simplicities rather than despite them.

Roy and HG revived the tradition of the sports-loving, know-all, yarn-ing Australian bloke. Their version dressed him in a dinner suit, let him sip cocktails and allowed him to expound intelligently on all kinds of sport-ing and cultural absurdities. Good blokes like Roy and HG never made overtly sexist jokes, but they could fall back on a naughty masculine kind of

humour, such as the regular 'date' segment on *Club Buggery* and their calling
of the gymnastics ('Hello, boys', 'flat bag') during the Sydney Olympics.

Where Norman tried to interview celebrities, and pursued political
figures such as Sir John Kerr, Roy and HG performed best with people relatively unused to celebrity treatment – sportspeople and even the Nobel prize
winner Peter Doherty. At times, Roy and HG seemed to be better interview-
ers because their opinionated tirades on trivia touched a responding chord
in their interviewees. The Ironman champion Trevor Hendy responded to
a question about the number of Vita Brits he eats with intricate and almost
obsessive detail about his eating patterns; the jockey Shane Dye talked about
his relationships with particular horses; and so on.

While Norman's humour included both physical clowning and verbal
play, Roy and HG retain their dignity and celebrate words by sheer excess.
Their shows are almost all talk – talk of the most exuberant and extravagant
kind. They represent a version of Australian mateship and the talk about sport
that bonds Australian men. They need each other to keep the talk going. HG
tends to specialise in the tall story, exaggerating the experiences of an ordinary
Australian man; Roy speculates in a more intellectual and abstract way about
the possibilities of words and ideas. HG might begin by asking Australians
to 'own' Greg Norman's failure as a golfer, elaborating on his efforts to help
Norman by undergoing an extensive ritual that includes shooting a rabbit for
each of Norman's strokes. Roy then shifts the pace to speculate about whether
Norman ('The Shark') should 'jettison Australia', getting up to demonstrate
the Shark's manner of addressing the ball ('I must be mad!') and suggests that
the problem is his rootlessness: 'He should root himself somewhere'.

Occasionally, they introduce political comment. For example, in a 1996
Club Buggery show HG feeds Roy the information that the prime minister
has said that mateship is dead in Australia. Roy explodes in outrage, working from sport as mateship to:

> Collective bargaining is mateship, is it not? When people get together
> and say we're going to do this amount of work for this amount of money.

I mean these individual contracts – that's anti-mateship. If anyone is trying to stamp out mateship it's got to be Reith and the prime minister
himself!

HG then tells us 'vis-a-vis mateship' about all the help his mates have given
him around the house, returning the idea to the daily suburban world.

Most of the time, though, it is trivia that excites them, and their excessive reactions to mainly sporting minutiae make us laugh. Roy and HG
invoke the old nationalist tradition of yarning, at the same time that they
perform, in wittier form, the elaborate conversational rituals familiar at any
Australian barbeque. Their riffs on various subjects move from the scripted
and rehearsed exchanges between anchorman (HG) and expert (Roy) to
extended improvisation. The audience senses when Doyle and Pickhaver are
beginning to extemporise, and enjoys the risks they take. Their occasional
slips or aborted ideas only add to the thrill.

Their most successful shows for commercial television have been their
coverage of the Olympics (2000, 2002 and 2004), mainly because of the
opportunities for their improvisatory skills. *The dream* of Sydney 2000
gradually accumulated pace and new audiences as Roy and HG relaxed into
their roles as commentators on the day's events. In these Olympic shows,
part of their success lies in the element of risk involved and the possibilities
of television in picking up on the absurdities of life as it happens. Their
coverage of the 2002 Winter Olympics faced complete boredom (given the
weakness of Australians at snow sports) until the astonishing win of a gold
medal by Stephen Bradbury for speed skating after everyone else in his race
fell over before the finish line. Roy and HG had patiently sat out all the
non-events to be rewarded by being in the right place for this moment.
They were able to express all the bemused pleasure that other Australians
felt watching Bradbury's win. In Athens, they needed to expatiate about the
quality of the official mascots and the lack of toilet paper in Greece until
amusing things began to happen; Doyle and Pickhaver had the sense to
know that they always would.

While Australian situation comedy stumbles along, then, this parallel tradition of the comic character taking over one of the standard formats of television has provided Australians with some opportunity to laugh at themselves. A closer look at two of Australia's successful situation comedies offers further evidence of the way Australian humour negotiates the limitations and possibilities of television.

Geoffrey Atherden's *Mother and son* of 1985–87 remains the most successful situation comedy ever produced in Australia and provides us with some points of comparison. Furthermore, Norman Gunston's creator, Garry McDonald, played one of the main roles in the series, so it displays his different skills as an actor rather than an improviser and writer. Unlike the anarchy of Norman Gunston set loose on the world, *Mother and son* was tightly written and produced like a series of short plays. The producer, Geoff Portmann, explained that the aim was to create a 'dramatically believable' comedy with 'real-life characters' rather than a vehicle for gags, or caricature.[4] The show was filmed in a studio with a live audience adding to its atmosphere of theatrical performance.[5]

Yet the most controversial aspect of the show was its focus on the growing mental frailty of the ageing Maggie Beare (played by Ruth Cracknell) as she battled to control her son and carer, Arthur (played by McDonald). Unlike most of its predecessors, the series made no attempt to analyse or exploit the Australian character, particularly the tradition of the Australian working-class man with his strengths and prejudices. Instead a daffy but manipulative old woman (Maggie) created the mayhem, while Garry McDonald as Arthur provided the central perspective of a tolerant but frustrated middle-aged son. Arthur aligned with his generation of university-educated Australians; his social commitment was evident in his job in the public service as much as his willingness to care for his mother. His brother, Robert (played by Henri Szeps), showed a more acquisitive side; his education made him that hated comic figure, the dentist, and he spent the series fobbing his mother off on the less selfish Arthur.

Bob Weis argued in 1986 that the key to good situation comedy was

close observation of the characters and their context: 'They are not gener-
alised into obscurity but are particularised to the point that the domestic
viewer could pinpoint the neighbourhood, even the street, which the
characters inhabit'.[6] This was true of *Mother and son*, where most of the
action took place in an unrenovated pre-war Sydney suburban house,
and where the characters had quite specific jobs and social circumstances
(Arthur was recently divorced at the beginning of the series, and Maggie
was widowed).

The series was no mere structure for gags; it developed a crisis each
week that created sympathy for Arthur as he negotiated the obligations and
restrictions of family life. This family situation could not be resolved by
parental or authoritative wisdom as in conventional American comedies.
Maggie's condition could only deteriorate, leaving Arthur with the prospect
of imprisonment by his mother or ruthless treatment of her. While hardly
a joyful situation, Arthur's predicament reflected the double bind of family
life where the people you love might also manipulate and restrict you. Most
reviewers of the first series expressed discomfort as well as amusement at
the comedy. In 1985 I had both a brother-in-law and an uncle in Arthur's
position, living with their elderly mothers, and I often found it difficult to
laugh.

Mother and son mocked the benign notion of family purveyed by American comedies. In the episode entitled 'The picnic' Maggie manipulates her
sons into taking her on a picnic, where she hopes to relive the idealised
picnics of their childhood. Maggie unsuccessfully tries to coax her sons and
Robert's children into ball games and hide and seek, while the children sit
bored, asking if they would get home in time to see *The Brady bunch*. They
form a credible picture of a miserable family enduring the obligation of
a traditional Australian picnic. Arthur and Robert stand by the barbeque
with their sausages watching an Asian-looking man cook an array of kebabs,
prawns and fish. Trying to retrieve their sense of superiority, Robert comments, 'Did you know Australians invented the barbeque?', and the man
replies, 'Did we?'

In this episode Maggie gets on a bus with a group of nursing home residents and settles down in the home to chat and drink tea with her new friends, while Arthur worries frantically about her. This provides opportunities for Robert and his wife, Liz, to speculate about the advantages that would follow Maggie's death, though their comments are presented as insensitive expressions of realistic considerations rather than villainous. Arthur, on the other hand, expresses genuine distress at his mother's disappearance. Meanwhile, in the nursing home Maggie appears to be deliberately deceiving the matron, and when Arthur arrives to collect her she pretends not to know him. Arthur, surprised but aware that this might solve his problems, sympathetically asks Maggie if she would really like to stay in a nursing home. The nature of the place she is in comes as a revelation to Maggie, who drops her pretence and insists that Arthur take her home.

This 22-minute play provides enough comic moments to pass as a situation comedy. Robert and Liz maintain an overtly selfish attitude, supported by their children, while Maggie's behaviour in the nursing home brims with childish pleasure at finding new friends. There is no attempt to disguise the difficulties of the underlying situation, though, and Arthur is clearly presented as the victim of his mother's deceptions and his brother's selfishness. Viewers see that Maggie is not the benign innocent she may appear; she is presented as both vulnerable and manipulative. Arthur expresses a genuinely complex range of emotions, as he begins in a state of irritation at being forced on the picnic, then suffers distress at the loss of his mother, finds himself denied by her, briefly sees a way out of his situation, then is resigned to a return to the old life.

In this way, *Mother and son* addresses a range of taboos about ageing and family obligation that many of the audience have experienced in some form. The actors played it straight, never showing an awareness that they were funny, and the production presented the situations directly, without any gimmicks. The studio audience laughed at the situations and children enjoyed Maggie's performance as the grown-up child. Yet *Mother and son* explored the difficult and almost universal underside to family life.

Nearly twenty years after *Mother and son* first made its appearance, we see a successful return to family situation comedy with a mother and daughter show, *Kath and Kim*. This time the single mother, Kath, is burdened by the return of her adult daughter after a few weeks of marriage to Brett. But *Kath and Kim* takes its cue from vaudeville rather than the serious drama that drove *Mother and son*. The show emerged from a sketch on the show *Big girl's blouse* (1994), and two comedians, Jane Turner and Gina Riley, write and play the main parts, supported by fellow comedian Magda Zsubanski 'creating' and playing Kim's friend, Sharon. The show is populated by other familiar figures from sketch comedy – Glenn Robbins plays Kel, Marg Downie the New Age therapist and marriage counsellor, with guest appearances from a range of others.

The most infectious aspect of the show's humour may be its verbal comedy, with malapropisms ('pacific' for 'specific') and mangling of metaphor and meaning ('gropable', 'body English', 'cardonnay'), as well as a series of catch-phrases ('lookatmoiye, lookatmoiye', 'It's noice, unusual, different', 'I am high maintenance, you've gotta be'). The two main characters adopt broad Australian accents with wavering vowels, then contrast them with the closed voices of the snobbish shop assistants Trude and Prue (also played by Turner and Riley) in the lifestyle shop in the Fountain Lakes mall.

There is also plenty of physical clowning: Sharon enters each episode with an obvious physical ailment (a skin rash, a neck brace, a bandaged nose) that the other characters accept without comment; both Kath and Kim appear in an array of ludicrous clothing, from Kath's pink lycra tights and wardrobe of Australiana to Kim's tiny skirts and low-slung pants exposing her 'muffin top'. Kim often appears in a pair of clawed animal slippers and Kath's hair and make-up are not far from that of the traditional circus clown. Even Kel sports Norman Gunston's favoured comb-over hairstyle.

Furthermore, the narrative of each episode frequently encounters a physical problem: Kath and Kel's wedding is disrupted by the coach-horse's attraction to Kim's horse hairpiece that has become attached to her bottom; Kath's lack of sexual interest is solved when she and Kel go naked; Kath and Kel frequently find themselves working on gym equipment or dancing absurd dances or even boxing. Bodies are grotesquely displayed, twisted or broken. There are plenty of fart jokes and fat jokes, and the show has few pretensions to high comedy.

At the same time, *Kath and Kim* satirises contemporary popular culture, particularly the 'home beautiful' and the obsession with the lives of celebrities ('I want to be a foxymoron like Rachel Hunter'). Kath pursues fashionable fads with characteristic energy, while her daughter loafs around, demanding attention from her mother, friend and husband. Already they are seen as representing a new class of Australians, the residents of the outer-city suburbs in their new project homes, to the extent that commentary on the 2004 election referred to these people as 'Kath and Kim' voters. Living a life confined to the home, the mall and the hospital, Kath and Kim aspire to the world of the celebrity magazine and feel that they can have at least part of it by wearing the clothes, buying the goods, and keeping themselves 'noice'.

So this comedy follows the broader comic styles of Edna Everage and Norman Gunston rather than the more naturalist traditions of *Mother and son*. This allows it to incorporate some of the elements of sketch comedy with its observations of contemporary absurdity and its mockery of television culture. Indeed, each episode functions like an extended sketch. Despite the limitations of such broad comedy, an occasional moment of genuine pathos intrudes when the actors appear to be developing their characters beyond their cartoon origins. In the third series, Kath discovered that her divorce was invalid, and so her subsequent marriage to Kel was also invalid. When her ex-husband (Mick Molloy) arrived to claim his rights, there were scenes where Jane Turner expressed credible anguish about the demise of her 'noice' life with her 'hunk of spunk', Kel.

One of the signs of the writers' confidence that they could take *Kath and Kim* wherever they pleased was an episode in the third series that satirised the Nicole Kidman movie *The hours*. Though Kidman won an Academy Award for her role as Virginia Woolf in this film, it was hardly likely to be familiar to *Kath and Kim*'s popular audience. The show seized on the best-known element in the film – the prosthetic Kidman wore to disguise her retrousse nose – and mocked it mercilessly. In the episode, the Fountain Lakes Dramatic Society produces a musical version of *The hours* starring Kath as Virginia Woolf and Kel as a tap-dancing Leonard. In one scene, a pair of dancing noses hovers in the background, and Kim reinforces the joke by falling over while jogging so that Gina Riley appears with a grotesque prosthetic nose as a result. The episode combined the well-deserved mockery of a pretentious film with fart jokes as Kim's cabbage diet took effect.

In this way, *Kath and Kim* offers the structure for a kind of comedy that can move in a range of directions from word-play, social comedy and physical humour to a more intellectual and knowing satire. Most of these are within the range of sketch comedy, and it is only in passing moments that the acting suggests the possibilities for any complexity of character. This is much closer to Norman Gunston's kind of humour than that of *Mother and son*. Its physical clowning is also distant from the knowing and more inventively verbal Roy and HG.

The success of *Kath and Kim* suggests that the opportunity for the well-made situation comedy has passed forever in Australia. As time passes, *Mother and son* looks more and more like an exceptional achievement. Even the Atherden/Portmann team could not repeat their *Mother and son* triumph; their *Eggshells* (also starring Garry McDonald) lasted for two series, but it could not build up the audience following of the earlier comedy.

Situation comedy, essentially, is writers' comedy, while the broader vaudeville style belongs to performers and writer/performers. Most of the great British situation comedies began with scripts that follow the traditions of stage drama and can stand up to production without their original casts; in Canberra, a local theatre group regularly produces *Fawlty Towers* scripts as short plays. In the United States most successful situation comedies derive from a writer-centred production system where writers are in control of all aspects of their work. As a result, shows like *The golden girls*, *Family ties*, *Frasier* and *Sex and the city* have the well-made qualities of good stage drama. *The Simpsons*, of course, takes this tradition one stage further by parodying the family sitcom and making it the vehicle for broad-ranging satire of American cultural and political life through a cartoon, where the writing team can control both the dialogue and the visuals in a cartoon show.

Only on rare occasions has Australia managed such conditions for situation comedy writing, and most Australian situation comedy successes have derived from groups of sketch comedy performers (*Acropolis now*, *Frontline*) or comedians (*The Games*) writing their own material. This kind of extended sketch writing may be the only future for Australian situation comedy. Certainly, the British situation comedy has also moved in this direction, with the broad clowning of *The young ones*, *Men behaving badly* or *Absolutely fabulous* replacing the writers' tradition that produced *Yes, Minister*, *The good life*, *Dad's army* or *To the manor born*.

The polished and tightly written American situation comedy seems to suit the needs of Australian commercial television better than British comedy or the local product. The vaudevillean styles of comedy that have survived on Australian television require a tolerance of failure and the time to explore possibilities – qualities at a premium on commercial networks. At the same time, their rough and ready, ephemeral nature expresses the essence of television where performer and viewer share the moment.

Nevertheless, the Australian well-made comedy has not disappeared from television and Australian writers now work more often with production companies rather than television networks. In 1998 Andrew Knight and Deb Cox worked with Artists Services to create a series that combined elements of situation comedy with a strong dramatic storyline: each episode of *SeaChange* took sixty minutes to follow a comic and serious plot, and each series (like a soap opera) developed an overarching plotline. It was an overwhelming success on the ABC, running to three series. In 2003, Knight and Cox went on to experiment on Channel 10 with the split narrative of *Crashburn*, playing with the different perspectives of a separating couple and their past and present relationship. It had more claim to drama than comedy, and reviewers worried that it was too clever for commercial television.[7] It did not survive beyond a first series against the obstacles of late night programming and ratings demands.

In the late 1990s the persistent Geoffrey Atherden began work on a new situation comedy about local government. Changes in financing meant that *Grass roots* (2000) became a miniseries rather than a sitcom.[8] Like *SeaChange* and *Crashburn*, *Grass roots* mixed the serious and the comic, and developed a single storyline as well as discrete episode plots. It went even further in changing the time span for different episodes, so that their narratives might cover a week, several months, the whole year, or just one evening. Scenes from one episode reappeared in another, as the series offered new perspectives on the same event. The casual viewer may have found this difficult to follow, but fortunately the ABC screened it for the second time soon after the first. The main difficulty, as I have argued elsewhere, was the balance between comedy and seriousness; *Grass roots* was presented as a comedy, but its implications about local government corruption were a little too serious for laughter.[9] Nevertheless, *Grass roots* was an ABC success, and it received five AFI awards, a sign of its considerable critical success.

In 2004, John Clarke adapted Shane Maloney's Murray Whelan novels *The stiff* and *The brush off*, about a hapless Labor Party functionary constantly involved in crime, into a series of telemovies that recall the sardonic humour and milieu of *The fast lane*. With *SeaChange* and *Grass roots*, this suggests that Australia's comedy writers are finding more scope in the miniseries or telemovie format than in the situation comedy series. All of these have been produced by outside production companies or as co-productions with the networks, rather than by the networks in-house, and it may be that writers find greater creative freedom and control over the final product under these arrangements. This draws closer to the American model of television comedy production.

The record of Australian television situation comedy, then, may not be as pitiful as it first appears. On the one hand, we have a seemingly irrepressible tradition of comic characters taking over the variety formats, exemplified by

Norman Gunston and Roy and HG. On the other hand, we have a small
band of comedy writers ready to experiment with well-made drama on
television, and the production companies to support them. As well, sketch
comedy expands from time to time into genuinely popular comedies such as
Kath and Kim. While these can only loosely be described as 'situation comedy', they demonstrate that the Australian taste for comedy remains firmly
on the side of vaudeville.

Notes

Introduction

1   Phillip Adams & Patrice Newell, *The Penguin book of Australian jokes*, Penguin, Melbourne, 1994, p. 3.

2   A significant exception is *The Australian Journal of Comedy*, first published in 1995 by the Visual and Performing Arts Department at the Australian Catholic University's Christ Campus in Melbourne, which represented a major breakthrough. It ceased in 2002, however.

3   Adams & Newell, *Penguin book of Australian jokes*, p. 6.

4   ibid. p. 10.

5   Peter Coleman from the conservative side of politics, however, has included an interesting essay on Australian humour by Max Harris in his book *Australian civilization: a symposium*, Cheshire, Melbourne, 1963.

6   Dorothy Jones and Barry Andrews, 'Australian humour', in Laurie Hergenhan (ed.), *The Penguin new literary history of Australia*, Penguin, Ringwood, 1988, p. 60.

7   ibid. p. 60.

8   Henry Lawson, 'In a dry season', *Prose works of Henry Lawson*, Angus & Robertson, Sydney, 1948, p. 50.

9   Lawson, 'Water them geraniums', *Prose works*, p. 375.

10   Xavier Herbert, *Capricornia*, 1938, Angus & Robertson, 1971, pp. 117–18.

11   AG Stephens, 'Henry Lawson: Australian humorist', in Leon Cantrell (ed.), *A.G. Stephens: Selected writings*, Angus & Robertson, Sydney, 1973, p. 245.

12   ibid., p. 249.

13 'Crooked Mick', in Gwenda Beed Davey and Graham Seal (eds), *The Oxford companion to Australian folklore*, Oxford University Press, Melbourne, 1993, p. 91.

14 Ian Mudie, 'They'll tell you about me', *Bulletin*, 15 October 1952, p. 12.

15 Ron Edwards, *The Australian yarn: The definitive collection*, 2nd edn, University of Queensland Press, St Lucia, 1996, p. 269.

16 Adams & Newell, *Penguin book of Australian jokes*, pp. 21, 29, 24.

17 George Blaikie, *Remember Smith's Weekly?: A biography of an uninhibited Australian newspaper*, Rigby, Adelaide, 1965, pp. 64–6.

18 Masumi Muramatsu, 'Barbs across the sea', no. 9, in series 'You can say that again', *Nikkei Weekly*, 22 September 2003, n.p.

19 Jessica Davis, '"Taking the mickey": A brave Australian tradition', *The Fine Print* 4, August 2007, pp. 20–7, http://www.emendediting.com/html/ezine/index.html.

20 Keith Willey, *You might as well laugh, mate: Australian humour in hard times*, Sun Books, Melbourne, 1984, p. xi.

21 Edwards, *The Australian yarn*, pp. 269–70.

22 Frank the Poet [Francis MacNamara], 'A convict's tour of Hell', in John Meredith and Rex Whelan (eds), *Frank the poet: The life and works of Francis MacNamara*, Red Rooster, Melbourne, 1975, p. 46.

23 Russel Ward, *The Australian legend*, 1958, 2nd edn, Oxford University Press, Melbourne, 1965, pp. 1–2.

24 Robert Hughes, *The shock of the new: Art and the century of change*, rev. edn, Thames & Hudson, London, 1991, p. 211.

25 Axel Clark, introduction, in Christopher Brennan, *Musicopoematographoscope & Pocket Musicopoematographoscope*, Hale & Iremonger, Sydney, 1982, pp. 4–5.

26 Warwick Hadfield, *The Sports Factor*, ABC Radio National, 1 August 2003, http://www.ausport.gov.au/fulltext/2003/sportsf/s913359.asp.

'The Loaded Dog'

1   CMH Clark, *A history of Australia, vol. 4: The earth abideth forever 1851–1888*, Melbourne University Press, Carlton, 1979, p. 336.

2   Henry Lawson, 'The bush and the ideal', *Bulletin*, 27 February 1897, p. 2 (Red Page).

3   Lawson, 'Andy's gone with cattle', in Brian Kiernan (ed.), *Henry Lawson: Stories, poems, sketches and autobiography*, University of Queensland Press, St Lucia, 1976, p. 73.

4   Lawson, 'That pretty girl in the Army', *Prose Works of Henry Lawson*, Angus & Robertson, Sydney, 1948, p. 640.

5   Lawson, 'Send round the hat', *Prose Works*, p. 627.

6   Lawson, 'The shearing of the cook's dog', *Prose Works*, p. 75.

7   Lawson, 'Two dogs and a fence', *Prose Works*, p. 136.

8   Lawson, 'The Loaded Dog', *Prose Works*, p. 405.

9   ibid., p. 407.

10   ibid., p. 410.

11   Lawson, 'Rats', in Kiernan, *Henry Lawson*, p. 138. See also Kiernan, *Studies in Australian literary history*, Sydney Association for Studies in Society and Culture, Sydney, 1997, pp. 93–4.

12   Kiernan, *Henry Lawson*, p. 118.

13   Lawson, 'The Loaded Dog', p. 405.

14   ibid., p. 406.

15   ibid., p. 406. For a political reading, see Michael Wilding, 'Henry Lawson's socialist vision', *Studies in classic Australian fiction*, Sydney Association for Studies in Society and Culture, Sydney, 1997, pp. 69–71.

16   ibid., p. 407.

17   ibid., p. 409. 'Yellow dog' or 'yellow cur' was a common expression of contempt in the 1890s, and it is used frequently elsewhere in the *Bulletin*. There is little doubt that it was often used with a racist implication, but its origins and its employment here by Lawson are not necessarily racist, and may refer, as 'yellow' traditionally has, to cowardice, or to the dingo, or in cattle dogs to a discolouration in the best bred 'blue' dog.

18   ibid., p. 409.

19   ibid., p. 410.

'Compounded of incompatibles'

1   Ian McLaren, *Talking about C.J. Dennis*, English Department, Monash
     University, Melbourne, 1982, p. 14.

2   CJ Dennis, 'The righteous man', *Gadfly*, 12 September 1906, p. 640.

3   Dennis, *A book for kids*, Angus & Robertson, Sydney, 1921, p. 50.

4   Joan Beaumont, 'The politics of a divided society', in Joan Beaumont (ed.),
     Australia's War, 1914–1918, Allen & Unwin, St Leonards, 1995, p. 44.

5   Dennis, letter to Henry Lawson, 30 June 1915, 'Dennis, Clarence James,
     Songs of a Sentimental Bloke', Mitchell Library, ML MSS A1920.

6   Dennis, 'A Spring song', *The songs of a Sentimental Bloke*, Angus &
     Robertson, Sydney, 1915, p. 13.

7   HM Green, *A history of Australian literature: Pure and applied*, 2 vols, rev.
     edn, Angus & Robertson, London and Sydney, 1984–85, pp. 438, 443.

8   Ina Bertrand, '*The Sentimental Bloke*: Realism and romance', in Bert
     Hogenkamp (ed.), *Film and the First World War*, Amsterdam University
     Press, Amsterdam, 1995, p. 132.

9   Green, p. 444.

10   Dennis, letter to George Robertson, 8 April 1915, Angus & Robertson
     papers, Mitchell Library, ML MSS 314/24.

11   Dennis, 'The play', *Sentimental Bloke*, p. 42.

12   Cited in Les Murray, 'Filming a poem', *Blocks and tackles: Articles and essays
     1982–1990*, Angus & Robertson, North Ryde, 1990, p. 98.

13   William D Routt, 'Me cobber, Ginger Mick: Stephano's story and resistance
     to Empire in early Australian film', in Deb Verhoeven (ed.), *Twin peeks:
     Australian and New Zealand feature films*, Damned, Melbourne, 1999, p. 29.

14   'The play', p. 40.

15   'A Spring song', p. 15.

16   Ina Bertrand, '*The Sentimental Bloke*: narrative and social consensus', in Ken
     Berryman (ed.), *Screening the past: Aspects of early Australian film*, National
     Film & Sound Archive, Canberra, 1995, pp. 101, 105.

17   Dennis, 'Uncle Jim', *Sentimental Bloke*, p. 97.

18   Dennis, 'The kid', *Sentimental Bloke*, p. 107.

19 Dennis, 'Mar', *Sentimental Bloke*, pp. 64, 66–7. Bertrand, 'Narrative and social consensus', pp. 102–3.

20 Dennis, 'Pilot cove', 'The mooch o' life', *Sentimental Bloke*, pp. 72, 114.

21 Dennis, 'Doreen', *Sentimental Bloke*, p. 35.

22 'Uncle Jim', pp. 93, 95.

23 Murray, p. 105.

24 AH Chisholm, *The making of a Sentimental Bloke: A sketch of the remarkable career of C.J. Dennis*, Georgian House, Melbourne, 1946, p. 64.

25 Ian McLaren, *C.J. Dennis: A comprehensive bibliography based on the collection of the compiler*, Libraries Board of South Australia, Adelaide, 1979, p. 114.

26 Dennis, 'The Push', 'Sari Bair', 'The straight griffin', *The moods of Ginger Mick*, pp. 37, 47, 79.

27 Hal Gye, 'The story of C.J. Dennis', papers of CJ Dennis and Hal Gye, National Library of Australia, MS 6480/100, p. 62.

28 Routt, p. 22.

29 Beaumont, p. 35.

30 Dennis, letter to Fred Shenstone, 20 September 1916, Angus & Robertson papers, Mitchell Library, ML MSS 314/24.

31 Dennis, 'War', 'The call of stoush', *Ginger Mick*, pp. 23, 25, 31.

32 Dennis, 'The singing soldiers', *Ginger Mick*, p. 62.

33 'The call of stoush', p. 37.

34 Dennis, 'A gallant gentleman', *Ginger Mick*, p. 119.

35 'Sari Bair', p. 46.

36 The piece is published in Chisholm, pp. 129–34.

37 Benedict Anderson, *Imagined communities: Reflections on the origin and spread of nationalism*, Verso, London, 1983, p. 16.

38 Dennis, preface, *Songs of a Sentimental Bloke* (1915), Angus & Robertson, Sydney, 1916, n.p.

'Aussie' humour and laughter

1 Gerry Turcotte, 'The alternative traditions: An introduction to Australian humour', *Thalia: Studies in literary humour* 10.2, 1989, pp. 3–6. Quoted

material is from pp. 3 and 3–4 respectively.

2   Keith Willey records as 'most representatively Australian' a joke originally
     selected by RF Brissenden (as chairman of the Australian Literature Board).
     It runs:

> A swagman is tramping along an outback road, passing through pad-
> docks, each with a gate which must be opened by anyone going through
> and closed after him so as not to let the sheep out. The plain extends
> endlessly ahead. A heat haze shimmers on the horizon. There is not a
> building, not a tree in sight. Along comes a grazier driving a big Cadil-
> lac. He stops beside the swagman. 'Hop in,' he says. 'I'll give you a lift.'
> 'No thanks,' says the swagman, trudging along. The grazier scratches
> his head over this, wondering what is wrong with the fellow. Then he
> lets out the clutch and drives slowly abreast of him. 'Come on, hop in
> and I'll give you a lift.' The swagman shakes his head, still walking. The
> grazier sits for a moment . . . He drives up again, stops . . . and opens
> the passenger door. 'Come on,' he says, 'don't be a bloody fool. Hop
> in and I'll give you a lift.' The swagman shakes his head. 'No thanks,
> mate,' he says grimly. 'You can open your own bloody gates!' (*You
> might as well laugh, mate: Australian humour in hard times*, Sun Books,
> South Melbourne, 1984, p. 13)

See also 'The great Australian joke (GAJ)', selected as such by Bill Wannan.
While, like the former, unquestionably Australian in locale (the bush) and
characters (two swagmen and their laconic style of interaction), neither in
structural terms nor in theme is the joke unique to Australia. Structurally
it is an incongruity resolution joke with reversed expectations. Its theme is
a conflation of meiosis and exaggeration also found in other cultures, such
as witty sayings about Japanese samurai who laugh too much (a 'dimple in
one cheek every three years' is said to be enough for them: see Jessica Milner
Davis (ed.), *Understanding humor in Japan*, Wayne State University Press,
Detroit, 2006, p. 190).

The GAJ runs:

Two swagmen who had been mates for a long time were tramping out west in the wheat country. There were good young crops on either side of them. Harry took his pipe from his mouth and pointed to one of the paddocks. 'Nice crop of wheat,' he grunted. Five hours later, when they were seated by their campfire, Bill broke the silence. 'Wasn't wheat. 'Twas oats.' Then he rolled up in his blanket and went to sleep. The sun was well up when he woke the next morning. Harry and his swag were gone. Bill found a roughly scribbled note under a stone at the foot of the nearest tree. 'Too much b— argyment in this here camp', it said. (Bill Wannan (ed.), *The Australian: Yarns, ballads, legends, traditions of the Australian people*, illus. Ron Edwards, Currey O'Neil, South Yarra, 1954, p. 47)

Willey's variant of this GAJ in *You might as well laugh, mate: Australian humour in hard times*, p. 121, has the 'argyment' taking place over a desiccated carcase (horse or bullock).

3   Phillip Adams & Patrice Newell (eds), *The Penguin book of Australian jokes*, Penguin, Ringwood, 1994, p. 8.

4   For example, Allan Cornwell, *The unofficial Australian office humour book: Including the office astrologer*, illus. Dennis Miller, Peter Antill-Rose & Associates, NSW, 1989.

5   Adams & Newell, *The Penguin book of Australian jokes*, p. 8.

6   Hyram Davis & Peter Crofts, 'Humor in Australia', in Avner Ziv (ed.), *National styles of humor*, Greenwood, New York, 1988, pp. 1–30.

7   Christie Davies, *The mirth of nations*, Transaction, New Brunswick, NJ, 2002, pp. 92–100. See especially p. 92. The impact of relaxed censorship was first noted by Davis & Crofts, 'Humor in Australia', p. 8.

8   Both are now BBC TV shows. *Little Britain* began on BBC Radio 4 in 2001 and transferred to BBC 3 in 2003. *Men behaving badly* screened originally on ITV (Hartswood Films for Thames) in 1992, starring Martin Clunes, Harry Enfield and Neil Morrissey. Briefly remade for the US market, it aired with even more controversy on NBC from 1996 to 1997, set in Indianapolis, Indiana. For alternative Scottish comedians, see the website www.vomit scotland.com.

9   See Phil Berger, *The last laugh: The world of stand-up comics*, Cooper Square, New York, 2000.

10   *South Park* was created by Trey Parker and Matt Stone for Comedy Central and premiered in 1997. Comedy Central is a highly successful American network broadband channel, launched on 1 November 2005, to screen both premières and reruns of American comedies and comics: www. comedycentral.com/motherload.

11   Christie Davies, 'The progress of Australian humour in Britain', Gerard Matte & Jessica Milner Davis (eds), *Readings from international conference on humour: Australian Journal of Comedy* 3.1, 1997, Sydney, University of New South Wales Press, pp. 15–32, especially p. 30.

12   Jessica Milner Davis, 'Introduction', J Milner Davis (ed.), *Understanding humor in Japan*, Wayne State University Press, Detroit, 2006, pp. 1–14, 9.

13   See Christie Davies, 'Ethnic jokes, moral values and social boundaries', *British Journal of Sociology* 33, 1982, pp. 383–403; *Jokes and their relation to society*, Mouton de Gruyter, Berlin & New York, 1998; and *Ethnic humour around the world: A comparative analysis*, Indiana University Press, Bloomington, 1990. For a summary of methodological issues in cross-cultural studies of the forms and social meaning of jokes, see Davies, *The mirth of nations*, pp. 3–7.

14   Davies makes an extended comparison of Australian jokes told by and against men with the similar category appearing in Irish collections: ibid., pp. 89–107.

15   *The Penguin book of Australian jokes*, 1994, pp. 28–29.

16   For example: 'A New Zealand couple had been living in a *ménage à trois* but it was creating serious tensions. So they ate the sheep.' Adams & Newell (eds), *The Penguin book of more Australian jokes*, Penguin, Ringwood, 1996, p. 339.

17   The punning title of Alex Buzo's book cleverly illustrates both the sheep-theme and the accent: *Kiwese: a guide, a ductionary, a shearing of unsights*, Mandarin, Port Melbourne, 1994.

18   For example: Bill Wannan (ed.), *The Australian: yarns, ballads, legends,*

traditions, 1954 and reprints; *Bill Wannan's classics of Australian humour*, Currey O'Neil, South Yarra, 1982; *Dictionary of humorous Australian quotations and anecdotes*, Melbourne, Sun Books, 1974 and other editions; *Bill Wannan's treasury of Australian humour 1796–1950*, Currey O'Neil, South Yarra, 1960 and other versions; and *Modern Australian humour*, Lansdowne Press, Melbourne, 1962. The same eclectic approach to collation is taken by Tom Hayllar & Rex Sadler (eds), *Aussie humour: Classic Australian humour – from Henry Lawson to Dame Edna Everage*, Macmillan Australia, Sydney, 1988; and Jo Eastwood (ed.), *100% Australian*, illus. Tony Husband, Penguin, Ringwood, 1990.

19   See, for example, the contents of Bill Wannan's various collections, and even that of Roger Fair (ed.), *A treasury of Anzac humour*, Jacaranda Press, Brisbane, [1965]. For the same phenomenon in so-called 'bush humour', see Warren Fahey (ed.), *Classic bush yarns: Australian outback humour, tall yarns and bulldust*, HarperCollins, Pymble, NSW, 2001; and Ron Edwards (ed.), *The Australian yarn: The definitive collection*, University of Queensland Press, St Lucia, 1977 and rev. edn 1996.

20   For example, Bill Wannan, 'Introduction' to his first collection, *The Australian: Yarns, ballads, legends, traditions*, 1954, pp. viii–ix.

21   See Davis & Crofts, 'Humor in Australia', p. 8. The identification of Strine, recognised by the *Oxford English dictionary* since 2000 as a variant subgroup of English, together with other well-known categories such as Singlish (Singapore English) and Franglais (French/English), owes much to a feature in *The Sydney Morning Herald* in 1964 by Professor Afferbeck Lauder (= 'alphabetical order' said quickly), Professor of Strine Studies, University of Sydney. Readers were invited to decode cryptic spellings such as 'stewnce' (= students), 'vistas' (= visitors) and 'emma chisit?' (= how much is it?). A book, *Let stalk strine*, Ure Smith, Sydney, 1965, followed. See also Ken Hunt, *The xenophobe's guide to the Aussie*, Ravette Books, Partridge Green, 1993, pp. 61–4. There is some evidence of contemporary decline in the use of and admiration for Strine.

22   http://en.wikipedia.org/wiki/Culture_of_Australia#Attitudes_and_beliefs, downloaded 19 September 2007.

23 Davies, 'The progress of Australian humour in Britain', pp. 21–5; and Davies, *The mirth of nations*, pp. 100–101.

24 Bob Hudson, *The first Australian dictionary of vulgarities & obscenities*, illus. Larry Pickering, David & Charles, Newton Abbot & London, 1987; Bill Wannan (ed.), *Great Aussie insults*, Viking O'Neil, South Yarra, 1982; Lenie Midge Johansen, *Penguin book of Australian slang: A dinkum guide to Oz English*, rev. edn, Penguin, Ringwood, 1996 (first published 1988); and John Blackman (ed.), *Don't come the raw prawn: The Aussie phrase book*, Sun Books, Chippendale, 1991. Other valuable sources are Ken Hunt, *The xenophobe's guide to the Aussie*, and *The Australian dictionary of insults and vulgarities*, Peter Antill-Rose, Castle Hill, 1988, edited by football legend Dennis Miller. Reflecting the earlier impact of censorship laws on Australian publishing, Wannan's earlier collection, *With malice aforethought: Australian insults, invective, ridicule and abuse*, Lansdowne, Melbourne, 1973, is more restrained in its selections than his 1982 *Great Aussie insults*. Confusingly, both books, like many of his collections, were reprinted several times with changes in publisher and/or title.

25 K Willey, *You might as well laugh, mate: Australian humour in hard times*; G Turcotte 'The alternative traditions: an introduction to Australian humour', pp. 3–4; Brian Matthews, 'Humour', *The Oxford companion to Australian history*, rev. edn, in G Davison, J Hirst & S Macintyre (eds), Oxford University Press, South Melbourne, 2001, pp. 334–6, 35; Dorothy Jones & Barry Andrews, 'Australian humour', in Laurie Hergenhan (ed.), *The Penguin new literary history of Australia*, Penguin, Ringwood, 1988, pp. 60–76, 74.

26 Dorothy Jones, 'Setting limits: Humour and Australian national identity', Gerard Matte & Jessica Milner Davis (eds), *Readings from international conference on humour: Australian Journal of Comedy* 3.1, 1997, pp. 33–42, 34.

27 For example, John Blackman (ed.), *Aussie gags*, Pan Macmillan, Sydney, 1998, p. 31, and Peter Cagney (ed.), *The official Aussie joke book*, Futura, London, 1979, pp. 71, 75.

28 See, for example, *Clangers, bloomers and blunders Australian style*, Macmillan, South Melbourne, 1984, the survival humour collection issued by the Spastic

Centre of South Australia; Slim De Grey, *Changi: The funny side*, Writers
World Books, Bundall, Qld, 1991; and Sophie York's interviews in her *Angels
of Aceh*, Allen & Unwin, Sydney, 2005, recording how the Australian surgical
team working in Aceh province, Indonesia, in the first weeks after the 2005
tsunami depended on in-group humour-relief.

29 Carmen C Moran, 'Humor as a moderator of compassion fatigue', C Figley
(ed.), *Treating compassion fatigue*, Routledge, New York, 2002, pp. 139–54;
and 'Humour and meaning after trauma', *Psychology, psychiatry, and mental
health monographs: Trauma: responses across the lifespan*, NSWIOP, Parramatta,
November 2005 (2), pp. 113–24.

30 Jones & Andrews, 'Australian humour', p. 60.

31 Don Watson, 'The joke after God', *Meanjin* 46.2, 1986, pp. 228–35, 230.
Such examples include many in the Bush Wisdom Contest conducted by
Brian Dibble and Jim Evans, and reported in their volume *Marking the land:
A collection of Australian bush wisdom and humour*, University of Western
Australia Press, Crawley, 2005, including an entry from F Noll of 'Karinya',
Condobolin, NSW, at p. 77: 'We might get some rain today – there are no
clouds to stop it'.

32 Ruby Langford [Ginibi], *Don't take your love to town*, Penguin Books
Australia, Ringwood, 1988, p. 201.

33 Inga Clendinnen, *Dancing with strangers*, Text Publishing, Melbourne,
2003. Quoted excerpts are from pages 203 and 288 respectively. Although,
as is traditional in Australia, I am calling this practice 'taking the mickey',
authorities on British and Australian slang agree that this is a euphemism for
an older term which has itself recently re-entered public discourse – 'taking
the piss'. For an etymological account of the two terms, see Jessica Milner
Davis, ' "Taking the mickey": a brave Australian tradition', *The fine print*
4, August 2007, pp. 20–27, at http://www.emendediting.com/html/
ezine/index.html. Bob Hudson's *First Australian dictionary of vulgarities
& obscenities* defines 'taking the mickey' as: '[t]o mock, imitate, satirise or
deflate' (unpaginated). See also note 62 below.

34 See Davis & Crofts, 'Humor in Australia'; and Terry Abraham, *From*

'*Babbler*' *to Jimmy Ah Foo: The Chinese in Australian humor*', a paper presented at the international conference on Quong Tart and his times, Powerhouse Museum, Sydney, 4 July 2004, at http://www.uidaho.edu/special-collections/papers/babbler.htm.

35 See Gerard Matte, 'Cultural war and the fate of multicultural comedy', *Australian Journal of Comedy* 1, 1995, pp. 55–88.

36 Phillip Adams & Patrice Newell (eds), *The Penguin book of more Australian jokes*, Penguin Books Australia, Ringwood, 1996, p. 8.

37 Although printed jokes in the Penguin collections use mostly 'blackfella' and 'Abo', the truly offensive terms 'nigger' and 'boong' have certainly not vanished from popular discourse, as evidenced by Hung Le's report on his tour with *Wogs out of work* (quoted later in this chapter).

38 Today 'wog' chiefly designates a member of a Mediterranean racial group (reflecting postwar patterns of heavy immigration from Greece and Italy). However, it can extend to Lebanon, Egypt and Arabia (its earlier, World War I Australian meaning) and elsewhere. At a stretch, it can be applied to almost any non-Anglo person. (Compare the use of the derogatory 'ching-chong' or 'chink' for Chinese, dating from the days of Southern Chinese immigration in the Gold Rush but now extending to anyone from anywhere in South-East Asia. Early 'humorous' use of these terms is documented in Abraham's study of the remarkable Australian pioneer Quong Tart, *From 'Babbler' to Jimmy Ah Foo: The Chinese in Australian humor*.)

39 Roberta B Sykes, 'Do caged kookaburras still laugh? Humour in Aboriginal writing', *Thalia: Studies in literary humour* 10.2, 1989, p. 46.

40 Sigmund Freud, *Jokes and their relation to the unconscious (Der Witz und seine Beziehung zum Unbewussten*, F Deuticke, Wien, 1905), trans. James Strachey, Routledge & Kegan Paul, London, 1960.

41 Personal communication received May 2006 from a man who was one of the rowdy Italian 'wog' students. For discussion of the term as used among professional Australian comics, see 'Ethnic comedy', by Lou Pardi, 9 December 2006, at www.thegroggysquirrel.com/articles/ 2006/12/09/ethnic-comedy/.

42 Hosted by the Japan Society for Laughter and Humor Studies at Kansai

University, Osaka, July 2000. An early version of a part of this present paper appeared in the conference proceedings: Hiroshi Inoue (ed.), *International humor symposium: Western humor and eastern laughter: Proceedings of the 2000 international humor conference* (bi-lingual text), IHS Organizational Committee, Faculty of Informatics, Kansai University, Osaka, 2001, pp. 22–6 (Japanese) and pp. 74–83 (English).

43 See Jessica Milner Davis, 'Introduction', J Milner Davis (ed.), *Understanding humor in Japan*, pp. 1–14, especially pp. 1–3.

44 Ken Hunt, *The xenophobe's guide to the Aussie*, 1993, p. 42.

45 Peter Ryan, 'Taking the mickey', *Quadrant*, May 2000, pp. 88–9.

46 ibid., p. 88.

47 ABC TV 2007–08. The team's own history of itself says in part: '*The Chaser* was founded in 1999 as a fortnightly satirical newspaper produced out of a spare bedroom by initial editors Charles Firth, Craig Reucassel, Julian Morrow, Dominic Knight, who were later joined by the far more talented Andrew Hansen, Chas Licciardello and Chris Taylor. Since those humble beginnings, *the Chaser* team has lost its humility and has produced Classic™ [*sic*] comedy in all media, including print, online, radio, television and Christmas crackers'. At: www.chaser.com.au/content/view/15/52/.

48 'For all its deflationary, irreverent quality, Australian humour is usually an acknowledgement of the status quo.' Jones & Andrews, 'Australian humour', p. 74.

49 Keith Cameron (ed.), *National identity*, Intellect Press, Exeter, 1999, pp. 3–4.

50 *The Chasers' war on everything* faced a court case (subsequently dropped) over its hoax in breaching security at the APEC Leaders' meeting in Sydney on 11 September 2007 (which was greeted with horror by some commentators, but largely supported by public opinion: see *The Sydney Morning Herald*, 11 September 2007, article by Matthew Ricketson at: smh.com.auhttp://www.smh.com.au/news/tv--radio/response-to-chaser-mixed/2007/09/11/1189276668319.html).

51 Robert D Putnam, *Bowling alone: The collapse and revival of American community*, Touchstone, New York, 2001; Robert D Putnam, Lewis Feldstein

& Donald Cohen, *Better together: Restoring the American community*,
Simon & Schuster, New York & London, 2004. Putnam's concept of social
capital builds on the ideas of David Hume about corn harvest outcomes
in eighteenth-century Scotland and on later work by James S Coleman
(see his *Foundations of social theory*, Harvard University Press, Cambridge,
Mass, 1990). The term is defined as 'features of social organisation, such
as trust, norms, and networks, that can improve the efficiency of society
by facilitating coordinated actions'. Robert C Putnam, Robert Leonardi &
Raffaella Y Nanetti, *Making democracy work: Civic traditions in modern Italy*,
Princeton University Press, Princeton, NJ, 1993, p. 167.

52   Reported in *Financial Times*, 8 October 2006; and as 'The Saguaro Seminar:
Civic engagement in America', at www.ksg.harvard.edu/saguaro/.

53   Reported by Prof. Alistair Ulph, *Financial Times*, Letters, 11 October 2006
(lecture text forthcoming in *Scandinavian Political Studies*).

54   John McCallum, 'Cringe and strut: Comedy and national identity in postwar Australia', in S Wagg (ed.), *Because I tell a joke or two: Comedy, politics
and social difference*, Routledge, London, 1998, pp. 202–20.

55   An annual festival (20th in 2006), now drawing talent internationally, which
has spawned several lesser festivals in other states (such as the Armidale
Women's Comedy Festival, begun in 2000).

56   McCallum, 'Cringe and strut: Comedy and national identity in post-war
Australia', pp. 213–15; Murray Bramwell & D Matthews (eds), *Wanted for
questioning*, Allen & Unwin, Sydney, 1992, pp. 205–15.

57   There were no 'wog' families on Australian TV in the 1960s and 1970s.

58   *Acropolis now!*, created by Nick Giannopoulos, George Kapiniaris and
Simon Palomares, ran on Channel 7 from 1989 to 1992. *The Wog boy* was
scripted by Nick and Chris Anastassiades, directed by Aleksi Vellis, starring
Giannopoulos, Geraldine Turner, Lucy Bell, Hung Le, John Barresi and
others. It took $1.5 million at previews, and $10 million by the sixth week
of release. See 'The commercial success of *The Wog Boy* has brought renewed
hope to the local film industry', *Australian*, 10 March 2000, p. 13.

59   The 2005 Channel 7 comedy series *Get nicked*.

60 See the duo's banner on their web-page, 'We don't make fun of minorities, we make fun of everybody!' The quotation is from *The pun*, at www. simonandgeorge.com home-page, accessed 25 October 2006.

61 Hung Le, *The yellow peril from sin city*, Penguin Books, Ringwood, 1997, p. ii.

62 'Taking the mickey' and 'taking the piss' are both now common in Australia (almost interchangeable, although the second perhaps indicates a somewhat more aggressive form of joking). The later term is a euphemism for the former, based on Cockney rhyming slang (for more detail, see Davis, '"Taking the mickey": a brave Australian tradition', pp. 20–27).

63 Quoted excerpts are from *The yellow peril*, p. 146, 145–6 and 147 respectively.

64 Barbara Joseph, 'Comic refuge[e]: the comic persona of Hung Le', Helen Gilbert, Tseen Khoo & Jacqueline Lo (eds), *Diaspora: Negotiating Asian-Australia, Journal of Australian Studies* 65, 2000, and *ACH: The Journal of the History of Culture in Australia* 19, 2000, pp. 145–9.

65 *Pizza* ran in 2000, followed by *Fat pizza* in 2003 and *World record pizza* in 2006. *Fat pizza: The movie* was directed by Paul Fenech and released in 2003 by Village Roadshow Pictures.

66 By the International Criminal Tribunal for the Former Yugoslavia (ICTY), established by the United Nations. This was not the Tribunal's first process but it was certainly its most visible and long-drawn-out one. It ended abruptly in March 2006 with the former Yugoslav leader's death from natural causes while still in custody.

67 Unpublished review of *Habib on parole*, 30 August 2002. Other cast members included Hung Le and two Lebanese-Australians, George Nassour and Rob Shehadie.

68 Bilgiç, for example, has *Show us your roots* available as DVD, and appeared as himself in 2006 in *Thank god you're here*, a reality TV show on Network 10. For websites, see the pages on individual comedians on www. thegroggysquirrel.com/ and links to personal websites.

69 Running from 1988 to 1990, *The comedy company* was created and produced

by Ian McFadyen and Media Arts for Network Ten Australia. Voices on a recent blog have called for the reinstatement of Con's contribution to ethnic comedy – see Ana on 2 March 2006 11.49 pm at http://forums.greekcity.com.au/index.php?.

70　A phenomenon also applying to travel and tourism experiences.

71　Dingo was quoted in John Van Tiggelen, 'Call this funny?', *Sydney Morning Herald, Good Weekend*, 6 October 2001, p. 33. Other up-and-coming Indigenous stand-ups include Sean 'Jilkamu' Choolburra from Townsville, already established as a dancer with Ngaru Company and the Bangarra Dance Company, and also a didgeridoo player, singer, actor and comedian, who in 2002 won the 'Raw Comedy' competition NSW state finals.

72　One can only speculate on why Bilgiç, a Turkish-Australian, can 'get away with' his Lebanese-based character of Habib the despicable drug-dealer. Lack of Australian familiarity with regional variations in the Middle East may be one explanation. Another may be that he stands close to but outside the cultural divisions that plague Lebanon, and is thus acceptable as a pseudo-Lebanese comic villain.

73　Australian humour has had few defamation or vilification complaints made against it, according to my research. However, an AUSTLII search reveals several such cases in New Zealand (where they have ultimately been unsuccessful).

74　Kristen Murray, 'The business hoaxes of Rodney Marks', *Australian Journal of Comedy* 4.1/4.2, 1998, pp. 83–8, documents some of the hoax-addresses performed by Rodney Marks, who adopts various personae as a plausible but over-the-top visiting expert, unmasking himself at the conclusion of his act if not found out before. His value to corporations is indicated by their willingness to rehire him year after year in different personae. In 2007 he was appointed by the University of New South Wales, Sydney, as a Visiting Professor-at-Large, to enlighten students with hoax lectures. Reportedly, Engineering students were the most appreciative.

'This is serious'

The author acknowledges Vane Lindesay's generous assistance in the preparation of this essay.

For copyright reasons it is not possible to reproduce the Stan Cross cartoons that are discussed. The originals are held in the National Library of Australia, and reproductions can be found in Vane Lindesay, *The Inked-in Image*, Heinemann, Melbourne, 1970, p. 184, and *Stop Laughing: this is serious: The life and work of Stan Cross*, MUP, Carlton South, 2001, pp 49 and 53.

1   AD Hope, 'Steele Rudd and Henry Lawson', *Meanjin* 15.1, 1956, 24–32, reprinted in *Native companions*, Angus & Robertson, Sydney, 1974, p. 273.

2   Frank Muir, 'Introduction', *The Oxford book of humorous prose*, Oxford University Press, Oxford and New York, 1990, p. xxxi.

3   '"The Loaded Dog": a celebration', *Australian Literary Studies* 11.1,

4   1983, pp. 152–61. See Stewart's essay in this volume, pp. 3–15.

5   See Brian Matthews, 'Louisa and Henry and Gertie and the drover's wife', *Australian Literary Studies* 9.3, 1980, pp. 286–97; EJ Zinkham, 'Louisa Lawson's "The drover's wife"', *Australian Literary Studies* 10.4, 1982, pp. 495–99, with Louisa Lawson's original essay 'The Australian bushwoman' in 'Notes and documents', pp. 500–503 of the same issue.

6   Henry Lawson, *Short stories and sketches 1888–1922: Collected prose, 1*, memorial edition, Colin Roderick (ed.), Angus & Robertson, Sydney, 1972, pp. xxii, 930. The text of the story is quoted from the same source, pp. 332–36.

7   'A colonial friend pays me a visit', *Punch* (or the *London Charivari*), vol. 98, 15 March 1890, p. 129. Published 'at the office', 85 Fleet Street, London.

8   Vane Lindesay, *Stop laughing, this is serious: The life and work of Stan Cross, 1888–1977*, Melbourne University Press, Melbourne, 2001, pp.10–11, records that during a trip to England Stan Cross published an early joke-drawing in the London *Punch*, 30 September 1914.

9   Richard White, *Inventing Australia*, Allen & Unwin, Sydney, 1981.

10   Leigh Astbury, *City bushmen: The Heidelberg School and the rural mythology*,
     Oxford University Press, Melbourne, 1985, pp. 62–79, 80–86, 136–45, and
     passim.

11   Vane Lindesay, *Stop laughing, this is serious*, p. 94.

12   Frederic Manning, *Her privates, we*, Peter Davies, London, 1964, p. 6.

13   Lindesay, *Stop laughing, this is serious*, p. 184.

14   The cited examples are drawn from editions of the *Bulletin* for July 1933,
     and from Vane Lindesay, *The inked-in image: A survey of Australian comic art*,
     Heinemann, Melbourne, 1970, pp. 179–80.

15   The examples are drawn from *Smith's Weekly*, 1930 and 1933. The Roland
     James story appeared on 1 March 1930, Slessor's skit on 25 March 1931, the
     Joynton Smith comment on 25 March 1933. Vane Lindesay, *The inked-in
     image*, pp.183–222, gives an excellent selection from *Smith's* between
     1933 and 1935, including digger humour from Frank Dunne. Cross's
     'Stop laughing . . .' appears on p. 184. The cartoon and its sequel are also
     published in Lindesay, *Stop laughing this is serious*, pp. 49 and 53.

16   Lindesay, *Stop laughing, this is serious*, p. 50.

17   John Marsden, 'The joke's on us', 'Insight', *Age*, 7 May 2005, p. 7.

18   Prime Minister Malcolm Fraser, who held office from 1975 to 1983 and
     was notoriously patrician in manner, was found befuddled and trouserless in
     the lobby of the Admiral Benbow Inn in Memphis, on 14 October 1986. A
     woman he had met in the bar had drugged and robbed him.

19   Lindesay, *Stop laughing, this is serious*, pp. 50–51, 53, 54.

Of the names of horses

1   Peter Pierce, *From go to whoa: A compendium of the Australian turf*, Crossbow
     Publications, Melbourne, 1994.

Risus sardonicus

1   The symptoms of 'dry' cholera differed from normal cholera in that the
     victim did not lose body fluid through continuous purging and vomiting;
     rather, he just shrivelled up and died and at the same time manifested a

grimace that resembled the involuntary rictus or facial spasm of tetanus patients, known as the sardonic smile. Rowley Richards, *The survival factor*, Kangaroo Press, Kenthurst, 1989, p. 146.

2   ibid., p. 140.

3   HW Fowler, *Fowler's modern English usage* (2nd edn, rev. Sir Ernest Gowers), Oxford University Press, Oxford, 1965, p. 253.

4   Dorothy Jones & Barry Andrews, 'Australian humour', in Laurie Hergenhan (ed.), *The Penguin new literary history of Australia*, Penguin, Ringwood, 1988, p. 60.

5   ibid., p. 61.

6   *The Oxford companion to Australian military history*, P Dennis, J Grey, E Morris, R Prior, with J O'Connor (eds), Oxford University Press, Melbourne 1995, pp. 299–302, acknowledges that 'Australian military humour is very diverse'. At the same time, however, it also recognises that many jokes 'highlighted the Australian soldier's stereotypically laconic and insouciant nature'.

7   The concentration in this essay on published captivity texts by males is unavoidable, given that there was a tiny minority of Australian women held by the Japanese in comparison to the 22,000 Australian men. An argument may nevertheless be made that *White coolies* (Angus & Robertson, Sydney, 1954), by captured nurse Betty Jeffrey, more so than *While history passed* (William Heinemann, Melbourne, 1954), by her colleague Jessie Simons, manifests glimpses of sardonic humour based on a sense of the ridiculous disparity between prison camp life and civilised domesticity. The *language* of the humour in books by the captured nurses is middle-class, polite and well-mannered, ironically sanitising, for example, the 'aroma' arising from the stinking drains as '4711' (*White coolies*, p. 110). An 'afternoon tea' menu consisting solely of boiled rice flavoured with scrounged additives included sardonically labelled fare such as 'Parachute drop-scones', 'Ack-ack puffs', 'Palembang pastries', 'Post-Singapore sandwiches' and 'Pre-freedom sandwiches' (ibid., p. 40). The women's light entertainments also feature this characteristic form of polite

irony. The sketches and charades that became a regular feature on Saturday
nights in the early days of captivity at Muntok (Sumatra) included
a 'Ration Parade' featuring 'Palembang Paula Salon with frocks *à la
concentration camp*' (ibid., p. 45). Feminine self-censorship, however, leads
to linguistic propriety, whereas many of the male writers freely employ
profanity and sexual and scatological references.

8   Jones & Andrews, 'Australian humour', quoting Vane Lindesay, p. 65.
9   The English captivity texts I have read to date do not usually manifest the
sardonic tone. One notable exception is Lt Col. Mordaunt Elrington's 'With
2nd Loyals in captivity', *Lancashire lad*, March 1950, pp. 32–4; June 1950,
pp. 68–70; December 1950, pp. 150–3; March 1951, pp. 186–7; June 1951,
pp. 213–4; March 1952, pp. 25–6. Hank Nelson, however, notes that the
American survivors of the sinking of the *Houston* who toiled on the Burma–
Thai Railway shared the Australian sense of humour. *POW: Prisoners of war,
Australians under Nippon*, Australian Broadcasting Corporation, Sydney,
1985, p. 64.
10   Kenneth Harrison, *The road to Hiroshima*, (rev. edn), Rigby, Adelaide, 1983,
p. 123.
11   EE Dunlop, *The war diaries of Edward 'Weary' Dunlop: Java and the
Burma–Thailand Railway 1942–1945*, Penguin, Ringwood, 1990, p. 52 (my
emphasis) and p. 310.
12   Ray Parkin, *Ray Parkin's wartime trilogy: Out of the smoke* [1960]; *Into the
smother* [1963]; *The sword and the blossom* [1968], Melbourne University
Press, Carlton South, 1999, p. 487 (my emphasis).
13   Intriguingly, though, it is absent from Richards' sole-authored memoir,
A doctor's war, Harper Collins, Pymble, 2005. A recent study of cartoons
contributed by Australian *combat* soldiers to the Australian War Memorial
Christmas books notes the relative *absence* of 'gallows humour'. See Carmen
Moran and Margaret Massam, 'A "trace of history": Cartoons from the
Australian War Memorial Christmas books of the Second World War',
Journal of the Australian War Memorial 39, October 2003. The significance
of this lack of black humour (in contrast to the sardonic POW humour) is

partly attributable to the context of publication. The Christmas books aimed to foster a positive view of involvement in the Pacific War.

14 Hugh V Clarke, *Twilight liberation: Australian prisoners of war between Hiroshima and home*, Allen & Unwin, Sydney, 1985, p. 47.

15 *The survival factor*, p. 192.

16 *POW: Prisoners of war, Australians under Nippon*, p. 64.

17 *The war diaries of Edward 'Weary' Dunlop*, pp. 77–8, 395.

18 *Ray Parkin's wartime trilogy*, p. 501.

19 Donald Stuart, *I think I'll live*, Georgian House, Melbourne, 1981, pp. 273, 258, 272, 245 respectively.

20 *The war diaries of Edward 'Weary' Dunlop*, p. 395 (my emphasis).

21 *The survival factor*, pp. 134–46.

22 *The war diaries of Edward 'Weary' Dunlop*, p. 188.

23 ibid., p. 209.

24 ibid., p. 408.

25 Douglas McLaggan, *The will to survive: A private's view as a POW*, Kangaroo Press, Kenthurst, NSW, 1995, pp. 105, 106, 104 respectively. 'Winning the yak lottery' refers to the POW's luck in finding a couple of fragments of yak meat in his meal when the camp ration was one yak per 900 men.

26 I have argued here that the derogatory nicknaming of guards by POWs exemplifies the sardonic mode. At first glance, it may seem to belong to Fowler's category of irony, which requires an 'audience' designated as 'an inner circle' who can appreciate the gap between the 'statement of fact' and the device of 'mystification'. Irony's motive of 'exclusiveness', however, does not adequately account for the overriding need among POWs for 'self-relief' within the context (or 'province') of 'adversity'. 'Invective', which according to Fowler aims to 'discredit' and takes 'misconduct' (rather than 'adversity') as its province, also seems relevant to the practice of nicknaming. Again, however, when the motive (self-relief) and the circumstances (adversity) in which the nicknaming is practised are taken into consideration, the category of the sardonic offers the best fit. See *Fowler's modern English usage*, p. 253.

27 The nicknames are drawn respectively from the following sources: Hugh V

Clarke, *When the balloon went up: Short stories from a war*, Allen & Unwin, Sydney, 1990, p. 76; Herbert James McNamara, 'Nor all thy tears', *Frontline: The Official Journal of the 1st Nineteenth & the 2nd Nineteenth Battalion* 5.3, 2006, p. 31; *The war diaries of Edward 'Weary' Dunlop*, pp. 74, 398; FWG Power, *Kurrah! An Australian POW in Changi, Thailand & Japan, 1942–1945*, RJ & SP Austin McCrae, Brunswick, 1991, p. 46; *Ray Parkin's wartime trilogy*, p. 496; Keith Wilson, *You'll never get off the island*, Susan Haynes/Allen & Unwin, North Sydney, 1989, pp. 75, 69, 77.

28 Roy Whitecross, *Slaves of the son of heaven*, Dymocks, Sydney, 1951, p. 58. See also *Ray Parkin's wartime trilogy*, p. 856, for the cathartic shouting by Australian POWs of 'vile insults' that were 'safely lost' in the general bedlam of 'various hauling cries' led by the Japanese guards during obligatory physical training at evening roll call.

29 *Slaves of the son of heaven*, pp. 114 (my emphasis), 114, 163 respectively.

30 *Ray Parkin's wartime trilogy*, pp. 598–9.

31 *The survival factor*, pp. 191–2.

32 Joseph Conrad, *The nigger of the Narcissus; Typhoon and The shadow line*, Dent/Everyman Library, London, 1973, p. 64.

33 *Slaves of the son of heaven*, pp. 9, 235 respectively.

34 See the 'avoidance' mechanisms in cases of post-traumatic stress disorder listed on http://www. anxietyaustralia.com.au/anxiety_disorders / post_traumatic.shtml. Dunlop pinpoints his lack of affect in *The war diaries of Edward 'Weary' Dunlop*, p. 391.

35 Colin Turnbull, *The mountain people*, Picador, London, 1974, p. 188.

36 Manfred Pfister, 'Beckett's tonic laughter', *Samuel Beckett Today/Aujourd'hui* 11.1, March 2002, pp. 48–50.

Aboriginal humour

1 Tom King, cited in Dave Jenkinson, review of *Redskins, tricksters and puppy stew*, *CM Magazine* 8, 2001, www.umanitoba.ca/cm/vol8/no7/redskins.html.

2 Henry D. Spalding, *Encyclopedia of Jewish humor – from Biblical Times to the Modern Age*, Jonathon David Publishers, New York, 1969, p. xiii.

3   Edward de Bono, *I am right, you are wrong. From this to the new renaissance: From rock logic to water logic*, Penguin, London, 1991.

4   Victoria Laurie, 'Contributors', *Weekend Australian* magazine, 20–21 October 2001, p. 7.

'We are but dust, add water and we are mud'

1   Cyril Pearl, 'Introduction', *The best of Lennie Lower*, Cyril Pearl and Wep [WE Pigeon] (eds), 1963, Angus & Robertson, London, 1977, p. x.

2   *Here's luck* is currently published by Prion Books in the United Kingdom.

3   Barry Dickins, 'Lower me down', *Meanjin* 46.2, 1986, p. 207. Temple Bar was a brand of roll-your-own tobacco.

4   Lennie Lower, *Here's luck*, 1930, Angus & Robertson, Pymble, 1993, p. 87.

5   ibid., p. 5.

6   On the concept of heteroglossia, see MM Bakhtin, 'Discourse in the novel', *The dialogic imagination: Four essays*, Michael Holquist (ed.), trans. Caryl Emerson and Michael Holquist, University of Texas, Austin, 1981.

7   Ronald, McCuaig, '"Here's Luck" and Lower', *Bulletin*, 29 June 1955, p. 2.

8   In narratological terms, the distinction is between *fabula* or *histoire* and *sjuzhet* or *discours*, depending on whether you follow Russian formalist or French structuralist terminology.

9   Cited in Bill Hornage, *Lennie Lower: He made a nation laugh*, Angus & Robertson, Pymble, 1993, p. 85.

10   Keith Willey, *You might as well laugh, mate: Australian humour in hard times*, Macmillan, South Melbourne, 1984, p. 58.

11   Alexander Macdonald, 'Epilogue: The melancholy of Lennie Lower', *The best of Lennie Lower*, p. 209. Also see Dickins: 'Cruelty is the true Australian joke' (p. 207).

12   Review of 'Here's luck', *Publishers Weekly*, 29 October 2001, cited on Amazon. com, http://www.amazon.com/gp/product/product-description/1853754285/ ref=dp_proddesc_0?ie=UTF8&n=283155&s=books.

13   Len [Lennie] Lower, *Here's another*, Frank C Johnson, Sydney, 1932, pp. 153–4. This style of writing bears comparison with that of the

contemporary American humorist SJ Perelman, who wrote for the *New Yorker*. Perelman's style was more self-consciously literary and rococo than Lower's but, like his, derived much of its wit from juxtaposing and jumping between different discourses. As well, Steven H Gale notes the use of clichés, allusions and puns as key elements: see *S.J. Perelman: A critical study*, Greenwood, New York, Westport and London, 1987, pp. 183–4.

14 *Here's luck*, p. 141.

15 Bakhtin, p. 301.

16 *Here's luck*, pp. 99, 19, 208. Contrast this with Shakespearian references in a contemporary such as PG Wodehouse, where humour derives not from the character's knowledge of and ability to adapt the words of the Bard but on his blissful ignorance of them. In 'Jeeves and the unbidden guest' from *Carry on, Jeeves* (1925), Bertie Wooster typically fumbles a potentially grand opening: 'I'm not absolutely certain of my facts, but I rather fancy it's Shakespeare – or, if not, it's some equally brainy bird – who says that it's always just when a fellow is feeling particularly braced with things in general that Fate sneaks up behind him with a bit of lead piping' (Penguin, Harmondsworth, 1957, p. 51). In Wodehouse, the reader is complicit with the author; in Lower, with the character.

17 Bakhtin, pp. 301–2.

18 *Here's luck*, p. 57.

19 ibid., pp. 152–3.

20 ibid., p. 70.

21 ibid., p. 158.

22 ibid., p. 167.

23 Peter Edwards, 'Cranky Jacks: Men without women in Steele Rudd's *On our selection* and Lennie Lower's *Here's luck*', in Margaret Harris and Elizabeth Webby (eds), *Reconnoitres: Essays in Australian literature in honour of G.A. Wilkes*, Oxford University Press and Sydney University Press, South Melbourne, 1992, p. 89.

24 Edwards compares Jack's situation with that of Dad Rudd in *On our selection*: 'Like Jack, Dad is particularly tormented by the aspects of his own

larrikinism that he has reproduced in his male offspring, notably Dan and Joe. Dan, the prodigal son, beloved of his father but always clashing with him and being driven away, is a loafer and sharper, a charming layabout with no scruples about duping even his own family, and with a facility for weaving myths around his exploits away from home; in all these aspects Stanley Gudgeon takes after him' (p. 86).

25 *Here's luck*, p. 156.

26 ibid., p. 9.

27 ibid., pp. 214, 222.

28 Cited in McCuaig, p. 2.

29 Macdonald, p. 207.

Why men leave home

1 Nikos Kazantzakis, *Zorba the Greek*, trans. Carl Wildman, Bruno Cassirer, Oxford, 1967, p. 19.

2 See Patricia Barton, 'Ada Cambridge: Writing for her life', in Debra Adelaide (ed.), *A bright and fiery troop: Australian women writers of the nineteenth century*, Penguin, Ringwood, 1988, pp. 133–50.

3 Tasma [Jessie Couvreur], *Uncle Piper of Piper's Hill*, 1889, Pandora, London, 1987, p. 80.

4 Louis Becke, 'Challis the doubter: The white lady and the brown woman', *By reef and palm*, T Fisher & Unwin, London, 1894, p. 33.

5 George Gordon, Lord Byron, *Don Juan*, canto III, stanza IX, in *Byron: Poetical works*, Oxford University Press, London, 1945, p. 686.

6 Kodak [Ernest O'Ferrall], 'Balloons and sausages', *Stories by Kodak*, Endeavour Press, Sydney, 1933, pp. 91–9.

7 Kodak, 'The escaped hero', *Stories*, pp. 214–19.

8 Kodak, 'The lost bishop', *Stories*, pp. 81–90.

9 Kodak, 'All at sea', *Stories*, pp. 137–49.

10 Norman Lindsay, *Halfway to anywhere*, 1947, Angus & Robertson, Sydney, 1970, p. 73.

11 ibid., p. 185.

12 ibid., pp. 203–4.

13 Lindsay, *My mask: For what little I know of the man behind it: An autobiography*, 1970, Angus & Robertson, Sydney, 1976, pp. 45–46.

14 Lennie Lower, *Here's luck*, 1930, Angus & Robertson, Pymble, 1993, p. 7.

15 WS Howard also wrote *You're telling me*, NSW Bookstall, Sydney, 1933; New Century Press, Sydney, 1938.

16 WS Howard, *Uncle Aethelred: A novel*, NSW Bookstall, Sydney, 1944, p. 185.

17 Howard (as Stewart Howard), *Forty-six*, Endeavour Press, Sydney 1934, p. 152.

18 The category of exclusive male adventure stories is explored by Richard White in 'The importance of being man', in Peter Spearritt and David Walker (eds), *Australian popular culture*, Allen & Unwin, Sydney, 1979, pp. 145–68.

19 In her 1954 novel *Cockatoos: A story of youth and exodists*, Miles Franklin [Brent of Bin Bin] describes Ignez Milford's yearning for escape from the repression she experiences at remote inland Oswald Ridges, and her successive 'virtual' escape in writing and then actual departure to America – a succession that mirrors Franklin's early career.

Seriously funny

1 Miles Franklin, *Laughter, not for a cage*, Angus & Robertson, Sydney, 1956, p. 227.

2 Ken Stewart, *Investigations in Australian literature*, Sydney Studies in Society and Culture, Sydney, 2000, pp. 111–24. Quoted passages are from pp. 113, 115 and 123 respectively.

3 Miles Franklin, *Laughter, not for a cage*, pp. 116–17.

4 Ken Stewart, review of Richard Fotheringham, *In search of Steele Rudd*, *Australian Literary Studies* 17, 3, May 1996, pp. 289–92.

5 AD Hope, 'Sancho Panza, author: Steele Rudd and Henry Lawson', *Native companions: Essays and comments on Australian literature 1936–1966*, Angus & Robertson, Sydney, 1974, pp. 265–6.

6   Bob White, 'Grim humour in short stories of the 1890s', Alan Brissenden
     (ed.), *Aspects of Australian fiction*, University of Western Australia Press,
     Nedlands, 1992, pp. 17–39.

7   *A Steele Rudd selection*, chosen by Frank Moorhouse, University of
     Queensland Press, St Lucia, 1986, p. xv.

8   Frank Moorhouse, 'Going into the heartlands with the wrong person at
     Christmas', *Meanjin* 40, 2, 1981, pp. 152–60. Reprinted as 'From a bush log
     book', in *Forty-seventeen*, Viking/Penguin, Ringwood, 1988.

9   Phillip Adams & Patrice Newell (eds), *The Penguin book of Australian jokes*,
     Penguin, Ringwood, 1994, p. 34.

10   *The yarns of Billy Borker*, Angus & Robertson, Sydney, 1977, p. 6.

11   *The yarns of Billy Borker*, p. 6 and 94 respectively; 'A shaggy billiard table
     story' is on pp. 91–4.

12   Fiona Giles, *From the verandah: stories of love and landscape by nineteenth
     century Australian women*, McPhee Gribble/Penguin, Ringwood, 1987. Rosa
     Praed's story 'Old Shilling's bush wedding' occupies pp. 71–6. The quoted
     passage is on p. 75.

13   Ellen August Chads' story 'The ghost of Wanganilla: Founded on fact' is in
     From the verandah, pp. 36–43.

14   Ken Gelder (ed.), *The Oxford book of Australian ghost stories*, Oxford
     University Press, Melbourne, 1994, p. ix.

15   Elizabeth Jolley, *Five acre virgin and other stories*, Fremantle Arts Centre
     Press, Fremantle, 1976, pp. 37–8.

16   Elizabeth Jolley, *Mr Scobie's riddle*, Fremantle Arts Centre Press, Fremantle,
     1983, p. 2.

17   Foe example in 'The curate breaker', *Hunting the wild pineapple*, Penguin,
     Ringwood, 1981, pp. 37–59.

18   ibid. Quoted passages are from pp. 65, 20 and 20–21 respectively.

19   Lily Brett, *Collected stories*, University of Queensland Press, St Lucia, 1999,
     pp. 160 and 182 respectively.

20   ibid., p. 170.

21   ibid., p. 194.

22   ibid., p. 199.

23   Herb Wharton, *Where ya' been mate?*, University of Queensland Press,
      St Lucia, 1996, pp. 102–3.

24   ibid., p. 103.

25   ibid., p. 106.

26   ibid., pp. 20–6.

27   ibid., p. 22; 'Dreamtime future: Bungo the money god', pp. 20–6.

28   ibid., p. 23.

29   ibid., p. 26.

'To write or not to write'

1   Joan Kerr, *Artists and cartoonists in black and white*, National Trust, Sydney,
      1999, pp. 27–8.

2   Edward Geoghegan, *The currency lass* (ed. Roger Covell), Currency Press,
      Sydney, 1976, pp. 41–42.

3   Marcus Clarke, *His natural life* (ed. Stephen Murray-Smith), Penguin Books,
      Harmondsworth, 1970, pp. 31–6.

4   Elizabeth Webby, 'Pipes and odes: Literature and music', in James Broadbent
      & Joy Hughes (eds), *The age of Macquarie*, Melbourne University Press,
      Melbourne, 1992, pp. 93–4.

5   Elizabeth Perkins, *The poetical works of Charles Harpur*, Angus & Robertson,
      Sydney, 1984, p. 63.

6   Phillip Butterss & Elizabeth Webby (eds), *The Penguin book of Australian
      ballads*, Penguin Books, Melbourne, 1993, pp. 102–4.

'Our serious frolic'

1   Harold Stewart, cited in Max Harris (ed.), *Ern Malley's poems*, rev. edn,
      Reed and Harris, Melbourne, 1961, p. 17. In 1944 two traditionalist
      Australian poets, James McAuley and Harold Stewart, decided to perpetrate
      a literary prank aimed at the budding avant-garde movement in Australian
      poetry. Together they concocted parodic modernist poems by one 'Ern
      Malley' – a fictitious poet whose life story they also invented, and sent them

as a package to Max Harris, young and ambitious editor of the magazine *Angry Penguins*. The hoax was spectacularly successful. For the full story see: Michael Heyward, *The Ern Malley affair*, University of Queensland Press, St Lucia, 1993.

2   Heyward, p. 93.

3   Malley, 'Sonnets for the Novachord', *Ern Malley's poems*, p. 26.

4   André Comte-Sponville, *A short treatise on the great virtues: The uses of philosophy in everyday life*, trans. Catherine Temerson, Random House, London, 2003, pp. 213–14.

5   'Sonnets for the Novachord', p. 26.

6   Heyward, p. 125.

7   Herbert Read, cited in *Ern Malley's poems*, p. 14.

8   John Wain, editorial, *Mandrake* 1.1, 1945, n.p.

9   I have checked the Dutton papers held in the National Library of Australia for any reference to the *Mandrake* publication, but to no avail. However, in his 1994 autobiography, Dutton recalled that he was initially completely taken in by Ern Malley, and had always admired the poems since. See *Out in the open: An autobiography*, University of Queensland Press, St Lucia, 1994, p. 116. Dutton also mentions Arthur Boyars, editor of the relevant issue of *Mandrake*, in these terms: 'I liked . . . Boyars, who was a stirrer and full of ideas and ambitions for new magazines' (p. 150). If Dutton was the conduit for the Malley poems, he does not say.

10 My grateful thanks go to Dr Jane Potter who very kindly located and sent me photocopies of the relevant issues.

11 'Notes on contributors to the Australian section', *Mandrake* 1.6, 1949, p. 13.

12 'Baroque Exterior', *Ern Malley's poems*, p. 34.

Writing humour

1   Cited in Bob Monkhouse obituary, *The Weekly Telegraph* (Australian edition), no. 650, 7–13 January 2004, p. 35.

2   Bruce Clunies Ross, 'Stories of things happening', in David Brooks and Brian Kiernan (eds), *Running wild: Essays, fictions and memoirs presented to*

Michael Wilding, Sydney Association for Studies in Society and Culture, and Manohar Publishers, Sydney and New Delhi, 2004, pp. 233–46.

3   In Michael Wilding, *The West Midland Underground*, University of Queensland Press, St Lucia, 1975.

4   Brian Kiernan, 'Tichborne redivivus: Re-viewing Michael Wilding's fiction', in *Running wild*, p. 202.

5   Michael Wilding, '"Weird Melancholy": Inner and outer landscapes in Marcus Clarke's stories', *Studies in classic Australian fiction*, Sydney Association for Studies in Society and Culture, Sydney, 1997, pp. 24–31. Laurie Hergenhan's exploration of some of the interrelationships between my writing and Marcus Clarke in 'Literary New Chums: Michael Wilding and Marcus Clarke' (*Running wild*, pp. 223–32) chose not to deal with cannabis, which, as Ken Stewart remarked to me, is probably for the best.

6   In Wilding, *Under Saturn*, Black Swan, Sydney, 1988.

7   Wilding, 'Henry Lawson's socialist vision', *Studies in classic Australian fiction*, pp. 69–70.

8   In an editorial in *Quadrant* 43.9, September 1999, p. 3, Paddy McGuinness wrote of: 'Michael Wilding's recent autobiographical novel, which contains some witty and very funny send-ups of the kind of paranoid beliefs about the CIA, international capital, the security services and so on common to the left. Some reviewers have clearly taken Wilding as being perfectly serious in this, no doubt reflecting their own secret prejudices'. Send-ups? Well, up to a point, cobber.

9   In Wilding, *The phallic forest*, Wild & Woolley, Sydney, 1978.

10 In Wilding, *Reading the signs*, Hale & Iremonger, Sydney, 1984.

11 All these stories in Wilding, *This is for you*, Angus & Robertson, Pymble, 1994.

12 Richard Crabtree, review of *Academia nuts*, *Southerly* 63.2, 2003, pp. 199–201.

13 Laurie Taylor, 'Laugh? I nearly signed up for early retirement', *Times Higher Education Supplement*, 13 February 2004, p. 27.

14 Wilding, *Academia nuts*, 2nd edn, Wild & Woolley, Glebe, 2003, pp. 201–2.

15   Don Graham, review of *Academia nuts*, *JAS Review of Books*,
      no. 20, 2003, www.api-network.com/cgi-bin/reviews/jrbview.
      cgi?n=0909331944&issue=20.s.

16   Wilding, *National treasure*, Central Queensland University Press,
      Rockhampton, 2007, p. 30.

'The rude rudiments of satire'

1   In *Dickens as satirist*, (Yale University Press, New Haven, 1971), Sylvia
      Manning identifies Coketown and the London waterfront as paradigmatic
      places in Dickens' satire.

2   *Age*, 19 February 1983, p. 3.

3   Keith Dunstan, *No brains at all*, Penguin, Ringwood, 1990, p. 253.

4   Barry Humphries, *My life as me*, Penguin, Ringwood, 2002, p. 130.

5   Peter Coleman, *The real Barry Humphries*, Robson Books, London, 1990,
      p. 31; Barry Humphries, *My life as me*, p. 127.

6   Peter O'Shaughnessy, 'How Edna Everage took to the stage', *Age*, 26 January
      1985, p. 9.

7   With the introduction of Sumner's UTRC there was a permanent repertory
      year-round theatre operating with a professional company. Geoffrey Milne,
      Theatre Australia (un)limited, Rodopi, Amsterdam, 2004, p. 83.

8   Conversation with John Sumner, August 2006.

9   John Sumner, *Recollections at play*, Melbourne University Press, Melbourne,
      1993, p. 38, and conversation with Sumner.

10   *The wonderful world of Barry McKenzie*, Macdonald & Co, London, 1968,
      was banned on the grounds that it relied on indecency for its humour.

11   For a full discussion of the genesis and reception of the Barry McKenzie
      films, see Anne Pender's essay 'The mythical Australian: Barry Humphries,
      Gough Whitlam and "new nationalism"', *Australian Journal of Politics and
      History* 51, 2005, pp. 67–78.

12   Conversation with John Sumner, August 2006.

13   Conversation with John Sumner and *Recollections*, p. 38.

14   Barry Humphries, *More please*, p. 133.

15 Peter O'Shaughnessy, 'How Edna Everage took to the stage', p. 9.

16 O'Shaughnessy, 'How Edna Everage took to the stage', p. 9.

17 Conversations with Peter O'Shaughnessy and John Sumner, August 2006.

18 Sumner, *Recollections*, p. 38.

19 Barry Humphries, *More please*, p. 142.

20 Conversation with Ray Lawler, February 2007.

21 Conversation with Fred Parslow, February 2007.

22 Humphries, *More please*, p. 143.

23 Conversation with Ray Lawler.

24 The hall has since been demolished.

25 John West, *Theatre in Australia*, Cassell, Stanmore, NSW, 1978, p. 205.

26 Conversation with Wendy Blacklock, 2006.

27 See Charles Osborne's book *Max Oldaker: last of the matinee idols*, O'Mara, London, 1988.

28 Barry Humphries, foreword to Charles Osborne's book, *Max Oldaker*, p. x.

29 Barry Humphries foreword to *Max Oldaker*, p. xi; Reg Livermore, *Chapters and chances*, Hardie Grant Books, Prahran, 2003, p. 17.

30 Charles Osborne, *Max Oldaker*, p. 187.

31 Barry Humphries, foreword to *Max Oldaker*, p. xi.

32 Charles Osborne, *Max Oldaker*, p. 189.

33 Opera House sketch script.

34 Peter O'Shaughnessy, 'How Edna Everage took to the stage', p. 9.

35 Conversation with Barry Humphries, August 2007.

36 Peter O'Shaughnessy, *Weekend Australian review*, 1–2 October 2005, p. 2.

37 Bruce Grant, *Age*, 31 December 1957, p. 3.

Comedy and constraint

1 Will Kaufman, *The comedian as confidence man: Studies in irony fatigue*, Wayne State University Press, Detroit, 1997, p. 111.

2 See Jack Hirschman (ed.), *Antonin Artaud anthology*, City Lights, San Francisco, 1965, pp. 135–63.

3 These and many other routines are printed in John Cohen (ed.), *The essential*

Lenny Bruce, Panther, St Albans, 1975. A video of Bruce in performance is *The Lenny Bruce performance film* (Rhino RNVD 2014, 1992).

4   For a vivid account of Bruce's personal habits, see Albert Goldman, with Lawrence Schiller, *Ladies and gentleman, Lenny Bruce!!*, WH Allen, London, 1975.

5   Eric Bogosian, Introduction, *How to talk dirty and influence people*, by Lenny Bruce, 1966, Simon & Schuster, New York, 1992, p. ix.

6   See 'An interview with Studs Terkel', in Kitty Bruce (ed.), *The (almost) unpublished Lenny Bruce: From the private collection of Kitty Bruce*, Running Press, Philadelphia, 1984, pp. 15–21.

7   Lenny Bruce, *How to talk dirty and influence people*, pp. 98–99.

8   ibid., pp. 97–103.

9   Cohen, *The essential Lenny Bruce*, p. 84.

10   Cited in Kaufman, p. 107.

11   The following account draws on material presented by CS Ainsworth in a paper 'Banning Manning vs whitewashing racism' at the 1997 conference of the International Society for Humor Studies in Oklahoma City, United States. A compilation video of Manning at work in the Embassy Club and elsewhere, with interview clips, is *Bernard Manning on the job*, produced and directed by Alastair Pirrie for Polygram Video.

12   See Stephen Dixon's obituary in the *Guardian*, 18 June 2007, for a neat summary of his career and contradictions.

13   Howard Jacobson, *Seriously funny: From the ridiculous to the sublime*, Viking, London, 1997, pp. 31–32.

14   See Margo Kingston, 'Court shirtfronts Back door man', *Sydney Morning Herald*, 29 September 1998, p. 10; Helen McCabe, 'Hanson cries, then wins', *Daily Telegraph*, 29 September 1998, p. 8; Leisa Scott and Christopher Niesche, 'Court pulls Pantsdown send-up off air', *Australian*, 29 September 1998, p. 6. The case, and the entire campaign battle between Pantsdown and Hanson, was widely reported in the national and international media.

15   Lawrence M Bogad, 'Electoral guerilla theatre in Australia: Pauline Hanson vs Pauline Pantsdown', *The Drama Review* 45.2, 2001, p. 76.

16   The CD was produced by TWA records (TWAS478).

17   For a detailed account of the campaign, and Hunt/Pantsdown's activism and impact, see Bogad; also see Simon Hunt, 'Inside the Pantsdown phenomenon', *Sydney Star Observer*, 8 October 1998, p. 8.

18   The lyrics, and other links, can be found on the unauthorised Pauline Pantsdown Fan Club website at www.pantsdown.wild.net.au/pantsdown4. htm.

19   Richard Ackland, 'Decision for Hanson has disturbing effect', *Sydney Morning Herald*, 2 October 1998, p. 23.

20   Philip Auslander, 'Comedy about the failure of comedy: Stand-up comedy and postmodernism', in Janelle G Reinelt and Joseph R Roach (eds), *Critical theory and performance*, University of Michigan Press, Ann Arbor, 1992, pp. 196–207.

21   Lisa Murray, 'Now *The Chaser* is being chased', *Sydney Morning Herald*, 28–29 April 2007, p. 2.

22   Cited in Kaufman, p. 113. Kaufman documents the censorship of Hicks in chapter 4, pp. 113–46.

23   *Bill Hicks live*, RYKO (RDVD10691).

24   Cited in Kaufman, p. 129.

25   Kaufman, p. 129.

26   Cited in Kaufman, p. 145.

'Lookatmoiye! Lookatmoiye!'

1   Albert Moran, *Moran's guide to Australian TV series*, AFTRS/Allen & Unwin, St Leonards, 1993, p. 173.

2   Deborah Klika, 'Between those of us who laugh and those of us who don't . . . A look at the sitcom genre from an Australian perspective', Research paper, Theatre and Film Studies, UNSW, 1990, p. 32.

3   Alan McKee, *Australian television: A genealogy of great moments*, Oxford University Press, Melbourne, 2001, p. 21.

4   Jason Daniel, 'Garry plays it straight in new ABC series', *Adelaide Advertiser*, 18 July 1983.

5 Shmith, Michael, 'Christmas with mother and son', *Age*, 19 December 1985.

6 Bob Weis, 'Did you hear the one about . . .', *Meanjin* 46.2, 1986, p. 268.

7 Ross Warneke, '*CrashBurn* too good to rate', *Age*, 21 August 2003, http://www.theage.com.au/articles/2003/08/21/1061434973573.html.

8 Geoffrey Atherden, Katherine Thomson & Michael Brindley, *Grass roots: series 1*, Currency Press, Sydney, 2002, pp. ix–xii.

9 Susan Lever, '*Grass roots*: series one' (review), *Australasian Drama Studies* 41, 2002, pp. 142–4.

BIBLIOGRAPHY

Abraham, Terry, *From 'Babbler' to Jimmy Ah Foo: The Chinese in Australian humour*, paper presented at the International Conference on Quong Tart and his Times, Powerhouse Museum, Sydney, 4 July 2004. At: http://www.uidaho.edu/special-collections /papers/babbler.htm.

Adams, Phillip & Newell, Patrice (eds), *The Penguin book of Australian jokes*, Penguin, Ringwood, 1994.

——, *The Penguin book of more Australian jokes*, Penguin, Ringwood, 1996.

——, *The giant Penguin book of Australian jokes*, Penguin, Ringwood, 1999.

——, *The Penguin book of all-new Australian jokes*, Penguin, Ringwood, 2000.

——, *The Penguin bumper book of Australian jokes*, Penguin, Ringwood, 2001.

Anderson, Benedict, *Imagined communities: Reflections on the origin and spread of nationalism*, Verso, London, 1983.

Astbury, Leigh, *City bushmen: The Heidelberg School and the rural mythology*, Oxford University Press, Melbourne, 1985.

Auslander, Philip, 'Comedy about the failure of comedy: Stand-up comedy and postmodernism', in Janelle G Reinelt & Joseph R Roach (eds), *Critical theory and performance*, University of Michigan Press, Ann Arbor, 1992.

Bakhtin, M[ikhail] M[ikhailovich], 'Discourse in the novel', *The dialogic imagination: Four essays*, trans. Caryl Emerson and Michael Holquist, ed. Michael Holquist, University of Texas, Austin, 1981.

Berger, Phil, *The last laugh: The world of stand-up comics*, Cooper Square, New York, 2000.

Bertrand, Ina, '*The Sentimental Bloke*: Narrative and social consensus', in Ken

Berryman (ed.), *Screening the past: Aspects of early Australian film*, National Film & Sound Archive, Canberra, 1995.

——, '*The Sentimental Bloke*: Realism and romance', in Bert Hogenkamp (ed.), *Film and the First World War*, Amsterdam University Press, Amsterdam, 1995.

Blackman, John, *Don't come the raw prawn: The Aussie phrase book*, Sun Books, Chippendale, 1991.

——, *Aussie gags*, Pan Macmillan, Sydney, 1998.

Bogad, Lawrence M, 'Electoral guerilla theatre in Australia: Pauline Hanson vs Pauline Pantsdown', *The Drama Review* 45.2, 2001, pp. 70–93.

Bramwell, Murray & Matthews D (eds), *Wanted for questioning*, Allen & Unwin, Sydney, 1992.

Brooks, David & Kiernan, Brian (eds), *Running wild: Essays, fictions and memoirs presented to Michael Wilding*, Sydney Association for Studies in Society and Culture, and Manohar Publishers, Sydney and New Delhi, 2004.

Bruce, Kitty (ed.), *The (almost) unpublished Lenny Bruce: From the private collection of Kitty Bruce*, Running Press, Philadelphia, 1984.

Bruce, Lenny, *How to talk dirty and influence people*, 1966, Simon & Schuster, New York, 1992.

Butterss, Phillip & Webby, Elizabeth (eds), *The Penguin book of Australian ballads*, Penguin Books, Melbourne, 1993.

Buzo, Alex, *Kiwese: A guide, a ductionary, a shearing of unsights*, Mandarin, Port Melbourne, 1994.

Cagney, Peter (ed.), *The official Aussie joke book*, Futura, London, 1979.

Cameron, Keith (ed.), *National identity*, Intellect Press, Exeter, 1999.

Chisholm, AH, *The making of a Sentimental Bloke: A sketch of the remarkable career of C.J. Dennis*, Georgian House, Melbourne, 1946.

Clangers, bloomers and blunders Australian style, Macmillan Australia, with Spastic Centres of South Australia, South Melbourne, 1984.

Cohen, John (ed.), *The essential Lenny Bruce*, Panther, St Albans, 1975.

Coleman, Peter, *The real Barry Humphries*, Robson Books, London, 1990.

Coleman, James S, *Foundations of social theory*, Harvard University Press, Cambridge, Mass., 1990.

Comte-Sponville, André, *A short treatise on the great virtues: The uses of philosophy in everyday life*, trans. Catherine Temerson, William Heinemann, London, 2002.

Cornwell, Allan, *The unofficial Australian office humour book: Including the office astrologer*, illus. Dennis Miller, Peter Antill-Rose and Associates, Castle Hill, NSW, 1989.

Davies, Christie, 'Ethnic jokes, moral values and social boundaries', *British Journal of Sociology* 33, 1982, pp. 383–403.

——, *Ethnic humour around the world: A comparative analysis*, Indiana University Press, Bloomington, 1990.

——, 'The progress of Australian humour in Britain', in Gerard Matte & Jessica Milner Davis (eds), *Readings from international conference on humour: Australian Journal of Comedy* 3.1, 1997, Sydney, University of New South Wales Press, pp. 15–32.

——, *Jokes and their relation to society*, Mouton de Gruyter, Berlin & New York, 1998.

——, *The mirth of nations*, Transaction, New Brunswick, 2002.

Davis, Hyram & Crofts, Peter, 'Humor in Australia', in Avner Ziv (ed.), *National styles of humor*, Greenwood, New York, 1988, pp. 1–30.

Davis, Jessica Milner (ed.), *Understanding humor in Japan*, Wayne State University Press, Detroit, 2006.

——, ' "Taking the mickey": A brave Australian tradition', *The Fine Print* 4, August 2007, pp. 20–27. At: http://www.emendediting.com/html/ezine/index.html.

De Grey, Slim, *Changi: The funny side*, Writers World Books, Bundall, 1991.

Dennis, C[larence] J[ames], *The songs of a Sentimental Bloke*, Angus & Robertson, Sydney, 1915.

Dennis, Peter, Grey, Jeffery, Morris, Ewan, Prior, Robin, with Connor, John (eds), *The Oxford companion to Australian military history*, Oxford University Press, Melbourne 1995.

Dibble, Brian & Evans, Jim (eds), *Marking the land: A collection of Australian bush wisdom and humour*, University of Western Australia Press, Crawley, 2005.

Dickins, Barry, 'Lower me down', *Meanjin* 46.2, 1986, pp. 207–11.

Dunstan, Keith, *No brains at all*, Penguin, Ringwood, 1990.

Eastwood, Jo (ed.), *100% Australian*, illus. Tony Husband, Penguin, Melbourne, 1990.

Edwards, Peter, 'Cranky Jacks: Men without women in Steele Rudd's *On our selection* and Lennie Lower's *Here's luck*', in Margaret Harris and Elizabeth Webby (eds), *Reconnoitres: Essays in Australian literature in honour of G.A. Wilkes*, Oxford University Press and Sydney University Press, South Melbourne, 1992.

Edwards, Ron (ed.), *The Australian yarn: The definitive collection*, rev. edn, University of Queensland Press, St Lucia, 1996.

Fahey, Warren (ed.), *Classic bush yarns: Australian outback humour, tall yarns and bulldust*, HarperCollins, Pymble, NSW, 2001.

Fair, Roger (ed.), *A treasury of Anzac humour*, Jacaranda Press, Brisbane, 1965.

Fotheringham, Richard, *In search of Steele Rudd*, University of Queensland Press, St Lucia, 1995.

Fowler, HW, *Fowler's modern English usage* (1926), 2nd edn, rev. Sir Ernest Gowers, Oxford University Press, Oxford, 1965.

Franklin, Miles, *Laughter, not for a cage*, Angus & Robertson, Sydney, 1956.

Freud, Sigmund, *Jokes and their relation to the unconscious* (*Der Witz und seine Beziehung zum Unbewussten*, F Deuticke, Wien, 1905), trans. James Strachey, Routledge & Kegan Paul, London, 1960.

Gelder, Ken (ed.), *The Oxford book of Australian ghost stories*, Oxford University Press, Melbourne, 1994.

Goldman, Albert, with Lawrence Schiller, *Ladies and Gentleman, Lenny Bruce!!*, WH Allen, London, 1975.

Green, H[enry] M[ackenzie], *A history of Australian literature: Pure and applied*, 2 vols, rev. edn, Angus & Robertson, London and Sydney, 1984–85.

Harris, Max, 'Morals and manners', in Peter Coleman (ed.), *Australian civilization: A symposium*, FW Cheshire, Melbourne, 1962, pp. 47–68.

Harrison, Kenneth, *The road to Hiroshima*, rev. edn, Rigby, Adelaide, 1983.

Hayllar, Tom & Sadler, Rex (eds), *Aussie humour: Classic Australian humour – from Henry Lawson to Dame Edna Everage*, Macmillan Australia, Sydney, 1988.

Heyward, Michael, *The Ern Malley affair*, University of Queensland Press, St Lucia, 1993.

Hope, AD, 'Sancho Panza, author: Steele Rudd and Henry Lawson', *Native companions*, Angus & Robertson, Sydney, 1974, pp. 262–76.

Hornage, Bill, *Lennie Lower: He made a nation laugh*, Angus & Robertson, Pymble, 1993.

Hudson, Bob, *The first Australian dictionary of vulgarities & obscenities*, illus. Larry Pickering, David & Charles, Newton Abbot & London, 1987.

Humphries, Barry, *The wonderful world of Barry McKenzie*, Macdonald & Co, London, 1968.

——, *More please*, Penguin, Ringwood, 1992.

——, *My life as me*, Penguin, Ringwood, 2002.

Hunt, Ken, *The xenophobe's guide to the Aussie*, Ravette Books, Partridge Green, 1993.

Hutchinson, Garrie, 'The funny Melbourne television phenomenon', *Meanjin*, 46.2, 1986, pp. 255–65.

Inoue, Hiroshi (ed.), *International humor symposium: Western humor and eastern laughter: Proceedings of the 2000 international humor conference*, bilingual text, IHS Organizational Committee, Faculty of Informatics, Kansai University, Osaka, 2001.

Jacobson, Howard, *Seriously funny: From the ridiculous to the sublime*, Viking, London, 1997.

Johansen, Lenie Midge (ed.), *The Penguin book of Australian slang: A dinkum guide to Oz English*, rev. edn, Penguin, Ringwood, 1996.

Johnson, Rob & Smiedt, David, *Boom-Boom! A century of Australian comedy*, Hodder Headline, Sydney, 1999.

Jones, Dorothy, 'Setting limits: Humour and Australian national identity', in Gerard Matte & Jessica Milner Davis (eds), *Australian Journal of Comedy: Readings from international conference on humour* 3.1, 1997, University of New South Wales Press, Sydney, pp. 33–42.

Jones, Dorothy & Andrews, Barry, 'Australian humour', in Laurie Hergenhan (ed.), *Penguin new literary history of Australia*, *Australian literary studies* 13.4,

Penguin, Melbourne, 1988, pp. 60–76.

Joseph, Barbara, 'Comic refuge[e]: The comic persona of Hung Le', in Helen
Gilbert, Tseen Khoo & Jacqueline Lo (eds), *Diaspora: Negotiating Asian-
Australia, Journal of Australian Studies* 65, 2000, and *ACH: Journal of the
History of Culture in Australia* 19, 2000, pp. 145–9.

Kaufman, Will, *The comedian as confidence man: Studies in irony fatigue*, Wayne
State University Press, Detroit, 1997.

Kerr, Joan, *Artists and cartoonists in black and white*, National Trust, Sydney,
1999.

Kiernan, Brian, *Studies in Australian literary history*, Sydney Association for
Studies in Society and Culture, Sydney, 1997.

Klika, Deborah, 'Between those of us who laugh and those of us who don't . . . A
look at the sitcom genre from an Australian perspective', Research Paper,
Theatre and Film Studies, UNSW, 1990.

Lake, Marilyn, 'The politics of respectability: Identifying the masculinist context',
Historical Studies 22.86, 1986, pp. 116–31.

Lauder, Afferbeck [Alastair Ardoch Morrison], *Let stalk strine*, Ure Smith, Sydney,
1965.

Le, Hung [Le Trung Hung], *The yellow peril from sin city*, Penguin Books,
Ringwood, Vic., 1997.

Lever, Susan, '*Grass Roots: series one*' (review), *Australasian Drama Studies* 41,
2002, pp. 142–4.

Lindesay, Vane, *Stop laughing, this is serious: The life and work of Stan Cross,
1888–1977*, Melbourne University Press, Melbourne, 2001.

——, *The inked-in image: A survey of Australian comic art*, Heinemann,
Melbourne, 1970.

Livermore, Reg, *Chapters and chances*, Hardie Grant Books, Prahran, 2003.

Manning, Sylvia, *Dickens as satirist*, Yale University Press, New Haven, 1971.

Marc, David, *Comic visions: Television comedy and American culture*, Unwin
Hyman, Boston, 1989.

Matte, Gerard, 'Cultural war and the fate of multicultural comedy', *Australian
Journal of Comedy* 1, 1995, pp. 55–88.

Matthews, Brian, 'Louisa and Henry and Gertie and the drover's wife', *Australian Literary Studies*, 19.3, 1980, pp. 286–97.

——, 'Humour', G Davison, J Hirst & S Macintyre (eds), *The Oxford companion to Australian history*, rev. edn, Oxford University Press, South Melbourne, 2001, pp. 334–6.

McCallum, John, 'Cringe and strut: Comedy and national identity in post-war Australia', in Stephen Wagg (ed.), *Because I tell a joke or two: Comedy, politics and social difference*, Routledge, London, 1998, pp. 202–20.

McKee, Alan, *Australian television: A genealogy of great moments*, Oxford University Press, Melbourne, 2001.

McLaren, Ian, *C.J. Dennis: A comprehensive bibliography based on the collection of the compiler*, Libraries Board of South Australia, Adelaide, 1979.

——, *Talking about C.J. Dennis*, English Department, Monash University, Melbourne, 1982.

Miller, Dennis (ed.), *The Australian dictionary of insults and vulgarities*, Peter Antill-Rose, Castle Hill, 1988.

Milne, Geoffrey, *Theatre Australia (un)limited*, Rodopi, Amsterdam, 2004.

Moran, Albert, *Moran's guide to Australian TV series*, AFTRS/Allen & Unwin, St Leonards, 1993.

Moran, Carmen, 'Humor as a moderator of compassion fatigue', in Charles R Figley (ed.), *Treating compassion fatigue*, Routledge, New York, 2002, pp. 139–54.

——, 'Humour and meaning after trauma', *Psychology, psychiatry, and mental health monographs: Journal of the NSW Institute of Psychiatry 2: Trauma: Responses across the lifespan.* November 2005, pp. 113–24.

Moran, Carmen & Massam, Margaret, 'A "trace of history": Cartoons from the Australian War Memorial Christmas books of the Second World War', *Journal of the Australian War Memorial* 39, 2003.

Muir, Frank (ed.), *The Oxford book of humorous prose*, Oxford University Press, Oxford and New York, 1990.

Murray, Kristen, 'The business hoaxes of Rodney Marks', *Australian Journal of Comedy* 4.1/4.2, 1998, pp. 83–8.

Murray, Les, *Blocks and tackles: Articles and Essays 1982–1990*, Angus & Robertson, North Ryde, 1990.

Nelson, Hank, *P.O.W. prisoners of war: Australians under Nippon*, Australian Broadcasting Corporation, Sydney, 1985.

Osborne, Charles, *Max Oldaker: Last of the matinee idols*, O'Mara, London, 1988.

O'Shaughnessy, Peter, 'How Edna Everage took to the stage', *Age*, 26 January 1985, pp. 9–10.

Pearl, Cyril and Wep [WE Pigeon] (eds), *The best of Lennie Lower* (1963), Angus & Robertson, London, 1977.

Pender, Anne, *Christina Stead: Satirist*, Common Ground Publishing, Melbourne, 2002.

——, ' "The mythical Australian": Barry Humphries, Gough Whitlam and "new nationalism" ', *Australian Journal of Politics and History*, 51.1, 2005, pp. 67–78.

Pfister, Manfred, 'Beckett's tonic laughter', *Samuel Beckett today/Aujourd'hui* 11.1, 2002, pp. 48–53.

Pierce, Peter, *From go to whoa: A compendium of the Australian turf*, Crossbow Publications, Melbourne, 1994.

Putnam, Robert D, *Bowling alone: The collapse and revival of American Community*, Touchstone, New York, 2001.

Putnam, Robert D, Feldstein, Lewis & Cohen, Donald, *Better together: Restoring the American community*, Simon & Schuster, New York & London, 2004.

Putterman, Barry, *On television and comedy: Essays on style, theme, performer and writer*, McFarland, Jefferson, North Carolina & London, 1995.

Richards, Rowley & Walsh, Marcia, *The survival factor*, Kangaroo Press, Kenthurst, 1989.

Routt, William D, 'Me cobber, Ginger Mick: Stephano's story and resistance to Empire in early Australian film', in Deb Verhoeven (ed.), *Twin peeks: Australian and New Zealand feature films*, Damned, Melbourne, 1999, pp. 15–37.

Ryan, Peter, 'Taking the mickey', *Quadrant*, May 2000, pp. 88–9.

Spalding, Henry D, *Encyclopedia of Jewish humor – From Biblical Times to the Modern Age*, Jonathan David Publishers, New York, 1969.

Stewart, Ken, *Investigations in Australian literature*, Sydney Studies in Society and Culture, Sydney, 2000.

Stuart, Donald, *I think I'll live*, Georgian House, Melbourne, 1981.

Sumner, John, *Recollections at play*, Melbourne University Press, Melbourne, 1993.

Sykes, Roberta B, 'Do caged kookaburras still laugh? Humour in Aboriginal writing', *Thalia: Studies in literary humour* 10.2, 1989, pp. 45–8.

Turcotte, Gerry, 'The alternative traditions: An introduction to Australian humour', *Thalia: Studies in literary humour* 10.2, 1989, pp. 3–6.

Turnbull, Colin, *The mountain people*, Picador, London, 1974.

Van Tiggelen, John, 'Call this funny?', *Sydney Morning Herald (Good Weekend)*, 6 October 2001, pp. 31–4.

Wannan, Bill (ed.), *Bill Wannan's treasury of Australian humour 1796–1950* (1960), Currey O'Neil, Melbourne, 1981.

——, *Bill Wannan's classics of Australian humour*, Currey O'Neil, Melbourne, 1982.

——, *Dictionary of humorous Australian quotations and anecdotes*, Macmillan, South Melbourne, 1974.

——, *Great Aussie insults* (1982), Penguin, Ringwood, 1995.

——, *Modern Australian humour*, Lansdowne, Melbourne, 1962.

——, *The Australian: Yarns, ballads, legends, traditions of the Australian tradition*, Viking O'Neil, Ringwood, 1988.

——, *With malice aforethought: Australian insults, invective, ridicule and abuse*, (1973) Sun Books, South Melbourne, 1978.

Watson, Don, 'The joke after God', *Meanjin* 46.2, 1986, pp. 228–35.

Webby, Elizabeth, 'Pipes and odes: literature and music', in James Broadbent & Joy Hughes (eds), *The age of Macquarie*, Melbourne University Press, Melbourne, 1992, pp. 88–100.

——, *Early Australian poetry*, Hale & Iremonger, Sydney 1982.

Weis, Bob, 'Did you hear the one about . . .', *Meanjin* 46.2, 1986, pp. 267–9.

West, John, *Theatre in Australia*, Cassell, Stanmore, NSW, 1978.

White, Richard, 'The importance of being man', in Peter Spearritt & David Walker (eds), *Australian popular culture*, Allen & Unwin, Sydney, 1979, pp. 145–68.

——, *Inventing Australia*, Allen & Unwin, Sydney, 1981.

Wilding, Michael, *Studies in classic Australian fiction*, Sydney Association for Studies in Society and Culture, Sydney, 1997.

Willey, Keith, *You might as well laugh, mate: Australian humour in hard times*, Sun Books, South Melbourne, 1984.

Zinkham, EJ, 'Louisa Lawson's "The Drover's Wife"', *Australian Literary Studies* 10. 4, 1982, pp. 495–9.

Index

IN THE VERNACULAR
A Generation of Australian Culture and Controversy

Stuart Cunningham

In the Vernacular brings together important writing over a twenty year period from one of Australia's leading scholars of media, culture and policy.

With a foreword by cultural studies expert Meaghan Morris, this insightful book tracks across Australia's still-neglected film heritage, and reflects on the achievements of Australian television in the 1980s and 1990s, and exemplifies the benefits of close attention to both history and industry context and the attractions of popular aesthetics.

In the Vernacular engages with the global debate on multi-ethnic societies by focusing on extraordinary, yet barely visible, creativity 'at the margins'. It argues that industrial and social trends in media, communications and culture are outstripping the academic frameworks that were erected to deal with them, and provides a way forward that connects the discipline to the career outlooks and prospects of students – the future of the field.

ISBN 978 0 7022 3670 9

UQP